Subjects of 1

Manchester University Press

THEORY FOR A GLOBAL AGE

Series Editor: Gurminder K. Bhambra

Globalization is widely viewed as a current condition of the world, but there is little engagement with how this changes the way we understand it. The *Theory for a Global Age* series addresses the impact of globalization on the social sciences and humanities. Each title will focus on a particular theoretical issue or topic of empirical controversy and debate, addressing theory in a more global and interconnected manner. With contributions from scholars across the globe, the series will explore different perspectives to examine globalization from a global viewpoint. True to its global character, the *Theory for a Global Age* series will be available for online access worldwide via Creative Commons licensing, aiming to stimulate wide debate within academia and beyond.

Previously published by Bloomsbury:
Connected Sociologies
Gurminder K. Bhambra

Eurafrica: The Untold History of European Integration and Colonialism
Peo Hansen and Stefan Jonsson

On Sovereignty and Other Political Delusions
Joan Cocks

Postcolonial Piracy: Media Distribution and Cultural Production in the Global South
Edited by Lars Eckstein and Anja Schwarz

The Black Pacific: Anti-Colonial Struggles and Oceanic Connections
Robbie Shilliam

Democracy and Revolutionary Politics
Neera Chandhoke

Published by Manchester University Press:
Debt as Power
Tim Di Muzio and Richard H. Robbins

John Dewey: The Global Public and Its Problems
John Narayan

Subjects of modernity

Time-space, disciplines, margins

Saurabh Dube

Manchester University Press

Copyright © Saurabh Dube 2017

The right of Saurabh Dube to be identified as the author of this work has been asserted by him in accordance with the Copyright, Designs and Patents Act 1988.

Published by Manchester University Press
Altrincham Street, Manchester M1 7JA, UK
www.manchesteruniversitypress.co.uk

British Library Cataloguing-in-Publication Data is available

This work is published subject to a Creative Commons Attribution Non-commercial No Derivatives Licence. You may share this work for non- commercial purposes only, provided you give attribution to the copyright holder and the publisher. For permission to publish commercial versions please contact Manchester University Press.

ISBN 978 1 5261 0511 0 *hardback*
ISBN 978 1 5261 0513 4 *open access*
ISBN 978 1 5261 4027 2 *paperback*

First published by Manchester University Press in hardback 2017

This edition first published 2019

The publisher has no responsibility for the persistence or accuracy of URLs for any external or third-party internet websites referred to in this book, and does not guarantee that any content on such websites is, or will remain, accurate or appropriate.

For Anna
a book of her own

Contents

List of figures	*page* ix
Series editor's foreword	xi
Preface	xiii
1 Subjects of modernity: an introduction	1
2 Intimations of modernity: time and space	29
3 Maps of modernity: antinomies and enticements	63
4 Disciplines of modernity: entanglements and ambiguities	105
5 Margins of modernity: identities and incitements	143
6 Modern subjects: an epilogue	171
Bibliography	189
Index	217

Figures

1. Savindra Sawarkar, "Untouchable, Peshwa in Pune," etching, 35 x 29 cm (reproduced with kind permission of the artist) — *page* 99
2. Savindra Sawarkar, "Untouchable with Dead Cow," dry-point, 26 x 19 cm (reproduced with kind permission of the artist) — 100
3. Savindra Sawarkar, "Untitled 0.9," dry-point, 36 x 28 cm (reproduced with kind permission of the artist) — 101
4. Savindra Sawarkar, "Devadasi with pig voice," drawing on paper, 20 x 26 cm (reproduced with kind permission of the artist) — 102
5. Savindra Sawarkar, "Introspecting Buddha," line drawing, 23 x 30 cm (reproduced with kind permission of the artist) — 103
6. Savindra Sawarkar, "Pregnant Devadasi with upside-down Brahman," mixed media on paper, 18 x 18 cm (reproduced with kind permission of the artist) — 104

Series editor's foreword

Contestations of modernity cover the historical and cultural origins of the phenomenon while questioning understandings of "the modern condition" itself. This erudite and beautifully argued book encompasses both elements in its carefully crafted prose and analysis. *Subjects of Modernity* takes modernity as its subject and also enables those subject to modernity to be heard. This should not come as a surprise, however, as the author, Saurabh Dube, is himself located at the intersections of critical historical scholarship and an engaged anthropological tradition sensitive to the voices in need of amplification.

Subjects of Modernity takes on the disciplinary mappings of this key concept through a fresh consideration of the times and spaces of modernity, as well as examining the marginalized intimacies that inhabit its various forms. Drawing on the traditions of postcolonial thought, subaltern studies, and historical anthropology – and the artistic reflections of Savindra Sawarkar – Dube develops a nuanced deliberation of the academic and aesthetic trajectories of modernity. At the same time, he opens up new considerations of identities formed by and through such movements.

The broader empirical terrain covered by the book extends the scope for the reinvigoration and renewal of the associated concepts, categories, and paradigms of modernity. This is a renewal that enables us to rethink what we understand of, and with, modernity and ideas of the modern (subject). In this way, the book clearly illuminates one of the key concerns of the Theory for a Global Age series, that is, the call for the concurrent engagement of deep analysis with theoretical reconstruction. Dube not only presents a lucid account of the "subjects of modernity," but accounts for those subjects in diverse and innovative ways. It is powerful, politically engaged scholarship at its best.

Gurminder K. Bhambra
University of Warwick

Preface

Subjects of Modernity was conceived in maculate ways.

Stellenbosch is a beautiful town, held as though in a glass bubble. It is caught in an uncanny warp, a vortex even, of snarled space and twisted time, which turn upon each other. Stellenbosch is set amid the hills of the Cape Winelands, a mere fifty kilometers or so from the haunting (and haunted) Cape Town. The stunningly gorgeous region, which produces some of the finest wines in the world, has been home to slavery, indenture (formal and informal), apartheid, and what followed. It was in these terrains – which embody the contradictions of modernity, articulate the contentions of modernity, and express the contingencies of modernity – that this book was born.

Late in the Antipodean winter of 2013, I was a fellow for three months at the spectacular Stellenbosch Institute for Advanced Study, commonly known as STIAS, aka the "Stellenbosch Institute for Advanced Salads," something of a measure of the local envy for the place. My principal project there had begun as a history and anthropology of my high-school class in New Delhi, only to expand into something wider, a curious account of contemporary India. The critical archives for the project were the digital recordings of conversations with my cohorts, collected as part of my "homework" (not mere fieldwork, for we are speaking of school here). These were contained on my laptop computer, a rather raggedy machine yet one with sufficient memory. Enthusiastic and excited about working through the recordings, I had begun to settle into the rhythms of STIAS and Stellenbosch.

But then, the laptop was gone. It had been filched from our heavily secured apartment, provided by the Institute, in central Stellenbosch. The deed was done on a weekend. We (my partner, Ishita, and I) were out for the day with friends driving around the coast of the Western Cape. On a whim we had gone to Cape Agulhas, the southernmost tip of the African continent, which is actually strangely uninspiring, at least at deepening dusk. After losing our way in the dark – and nearly colliding with an enormous porcupine – our bedraggled party of four returned home late at night to discover something amiss: an overturned vase, a flowerpot askew, the immense dining table out of place, yet little that was obviously missing, except the tiny computer.

The pilfering had been quite a production. While locking up everything carefully, we had forgotten about a loose slat on a side window blind in the living room. It was this sliver that had been forced open, a thingamajig improvised from a long broom handle and wires lying in the patio had been used to pull the humongous and heavy dining table toward the window, and the laptop lifted. There was nothing else gone. The arrival of the Falstaff-like Stellenbosch police constables at midnight, and of the smart detective from Paarl the next day, are tales within tales best reserved for another time.

For all the effort, what had the thief gained? Did not a laptop with an operating system and keyboard in Spanish – in a principally Afrikaans- and Xhosa-speaking part of the Cape – seem a little pointless, whether for sale or as an acquisition? Even assuming the innards of the machine were unknown to the pilferer, why had its power supply, plugged in next to the window and thus terribly easy to pick up, been left behind? It all seemed very peculiar, beyond strange, until the concierge of the swishy hotel in front of our apartment block told us that the theft was not business as usual: no, not at all.

Rather, the laptop had been taken on a weekend that was ritually significant. It was at that time of the year, in those days, that Cape Coloured young women aged fourteen to sixteen were initiated into girl gangs, after a spectacular derring-do. The child, if I may, had pulled off the incredible, considering the weight of the table, the modus operandi, and the security/surveillance all around her. The theft of a computer with research materials on my cohort, intimating privilege and entitlement, led to a ritual initiation into a colored cohort, inhabiting vulnerability and worse. Here was testimony to the necessarily split yet ever entangled nature of modernity.

Now I was at a loose end, at least by way of a research and writing project at STIAS. Yet I was also footloose and fancy-free. Through long rambles in pretty Stellenbosch, disparate bits that had been delivered as parts of talks and published as segments of essays, which had inchoately indicated a book ahead, now began to fall into place. For a work that approached modernity as being constitutively contradictory, thinking it through on Stellenbosch Mountain proved particularly productive. Here was a sentinel that gazed out toward the vineyards and valleys of God's own country, yet a spectator that stood mute testimony to the formative violence that was sown into the spirit and substance of the soil – here, there, and everywhere in sight. My endless long walks, communing with this magic mountain, have shaped *Subjects of Modernity*.

None of this should suggest a latter-day, postcolonial habitation of Walden Pond. Far from it, I was insinuated in the excitement that was STIAS, its existence of words and worlds, spirit and flesh – at long lunches, seminar sessions, wine receptions, and impromptu dinners. For all of this (and much more), I acknowledge the good denizens of the Institute, who are thanked ahead. Amid these scenes was the inimitable Athol Fugard, ethereal but immanent, floating yet grounded. He touched me with even more than his acute wit and immense wisdom. Alongside him, the anarchic aesthetic – comprising art, life, and friendship – of Aryan Kaganof made me live many lives in a handful of moments.

Actually, Stellenbosch Mountain was made incarnate for my companion fellows at STIAS – in 2013, as in spring 2014, when I visited again for a week – as we went for walks into its lap and embrace. During the first visit, as I climbed up with Walter Mignolo, one of the scholarly protagonists who is to be encountered ahead (especially in Chapter 2), he proclaimed while looking down at the green pastures and lush vineyards, "This is amazing, like Switzerland or something." To which I could not contain my retort, since it echoed the mountain: "The incredible whiteness of being, Walter, the incredible whiteness of being."

It followed, too, that my last meeting with Stellenbosch Mountain in 2014 produced twin tales. Through the long, rigorous hike, almost everyone, especially the runners, smiled or waved back at me. All the while, from the middle of a forest, a strange sound, human yet eerie, haunted my communion. It is the smiles and the strangeness (and the joy and the horror), ever together, which bid goodbye to me from Stellenbosch Mountain, that make modernity so compelling. As William Mazzarella puts it, "Only those ideas that compel our desire as well as our resistance receive and deserve our most sustained critique."

While the lineaments of the work were clear, *Subjects of Modernity* had to be substantialized, made of the world, as it were. From the earliest days through to the immediate present, senior scholars and brilliant editors, who are also friends, have supported and provoked me. In no particular order, let me thank here Sharad Chari, Michael Herzfeld, David Brent, John Comaroff, Debjani Majumdar, Ajay Skaria, Ken Wissoker, and Dipesh Chakrabarty. No less salient has been the belief and friendship of my former research assistants, Eduardo Acosta and Lucía Cirianni, who are surely on their way to becoming formidable scholars.

This book was destined to find place in the Theory for a Global Age series. Its editor, Gurminder Bhambra, has been an extraordinary presence: forceful and forthright, decisive and supportive, imaginative and sharp, quick and critical. Having read the final version of the manuscript, there was a key question that she put to me gently, concerning the absence of women authors in the text, as distinct from the notes. The question turns on the politics of gender, citation, and knowledge – taken together – and I would like to respond to it, as a tiny token, too, of the fabulous editorship and graceful friendship that Gurminder has provided me.

On the one hand, citational economies structure discipline(s) and knowledge(s), often reproducing male, racial, class, caste, ethnocentric, and hetero-normative privileges. And the struggle for the opening up of the academy, as part of wider endeavors against entitlement, has to precisely query such citational structures and practices. On the other hand, if the struggle is shifted principally to the arena of citational economies, it is that distinct "margins" and "minorities" not only simply cite each other – and maybe a few other intersecting critical ones – but can do so in ways that tend to mirror the exact hierarchies they are questioning, albeit on alternative terms. If there are resonances here of Joan Scott's "only paradoxes to offer," it is equally the case that also overlooked is the exact embedding of the academy in the wider force fields of power and privilege, which shore up, structure, and toss around the university. I hope it is clear that mine is not a clarion call for a more truly radical struggle out there, somewhere – although it would help if academics joined democratic struggles (wider and immediate) with a greater sense of modesty – and much more a suggestion toward querying carefully the hierarchy, privilege, and entitlement in which the tenured professoriate is embedded. To interrogate entitlement and privilege is to unlearn privilege and entitlement, laughing hard, especially at oneself. In relation to the vexed matter of citational economies, this can mean finding different, critical ways of writing.

Now, authors, works, and perspectives that are "minor" and "marginal" in the academy have featured prominently, if distinctly, in my previous writings – always alongside more certified critical doxas and radical traditions – most of which I draw upon as well as question. (Polemic has never been my strong point and, besides, it has little place in the sort of work that I do.) However, this book adopts a particular tack in its style of argument, writing, and citation. As I critically engage dominant delineations of subaltern, decolonial, and postcolonial studies as well as of modernity, anthropology, and history, all of which I learn from yet carefully question, especially attentive to their underenunciated and little-appreciated meanings and resonances, it is more male protagonists than women authors (although there are some) that appear in the text. At the same time, the critical doing and undoing of these understandings, disciplines, and knowledge(s) is embedded in the notes, where women and men, non-Western and Western, black and white crucially sustain the heavy lifting. On offer, indeed, is an entangled interchange between the text and the note, which allows me narrative continuity in the former (text) alongside the securing of arguments in the latter (note). Of course, this is only a tiny, provisional incision in a dense corpus of questions. But then, we must try to repay our debts.

I do not know how successful I will be in even attempting the task of repaying debts as I return to the formative site in the making of this book, STIAS, and the people who populated its magnificent environs and graceful sensibilities. Again, in no particular order, I thank Hendrik Geyer (and his wry humor); Duncan and Tracey F. Brown ("Yes, I have had my water," T and D); Christofer R. and Carina G. Edling (and Carl, Tove, and Axel); Edgar Pieterse and family (for lessons in imagination and struggle); and – considering friendship, warmth, stimulation, and care – Karin Brown, Bernard Lategan, Gudrun Schirge, Gerhard Mare, Christoff Pauw, Philippe Van Haute, Leonard (Lenny) Katsokore, Gladys Lechini, Ryland Fisher, Maria Mouton, and Maggie Pietersen.

The materials and arguments that shore up this book have been presented at talks, conferences, and seminars – in institutions too numerous to mention here – spread across Argentina, Brazil, Canada, Colombia, Costa Rica, Ecuador, Germany, India, Mexico, Singapore, Taiwan, the UK, and the US. I thank the organizers, participants, and interlocutors on those occasions. Needless to say, such prior transcripts, quite like previous publications (for all of which I hold the copyright), which intimated *Subjects of Modernity* stand transformed in their new avatar, their second coming. The editors and designers at Bloomsbury and Manchester University Press have facilitated the final version. I offer my sincere thanks.

At the end I move (closer) toward home. Miraculously, Savi Sawarkar came back into our lives as this book was being finalized. His art and warmth, friendship and persona have not only taught me how to listen to what pictures want, what images desire, but have provided me with lessons on life, history, and theory. I am grateful to him also for allowing me to reproduce the images that appear in the middle of this book.

Ishita Banerjee-Dube has been around, as always, shoring up my worlds while listening to every new paragraph as it was written, also providing me water and sustenance along the way. Needless to say, without her this book could not have been imagined and articulated a year after the death of my mother.

Prior generations pass and newer ones come around. Earlier this year, I wished happy birthday to Anurati Tandon, whom I had seen when she was quite the babe in arms, only a few months old. By way of a gift, it seemed to me, dedicating *Subjects of Modernity* to her might be in order, an apposite gesture. And so this book is dedicated to a modern subject who is also a subject of modernity, Anurati Tandon or, simply, Anna.

Kolkata/New Delhi/Mexico
March 2016

1

Subjects of modernity: an introduction

This book explores modernity, the disciplines, and their interplay by drawing in critical considerations of time, space, and their enmeshments. Based in anthropology and history, and drawing on social-political theory (as well as other, complementary, critical perspectives), it focuses on socio-spatial/disciplinary subjects and hierarchical-coeval tousled temporalities. My effort is to carefully consider the oppositions and enchantments, the contradictions and contentions, and the identities and ambivalences spawned under modernity. At the same time, rather than approach such antinomies, enticements, and ambiguities as analytical errors or historical lacks, which await their (eventual) correction or (inexorable) overcoming, *Subjects of Modernity* attempts to critically yet cautiously unfold these elements as constitutive of modern worlds. The work's affiliation with distinct borderlands and its acknowledgment of the production of time and space by subjects, social and disciplinary, play a crucial role here.

To adopt such an apparently oblique, ostensibly elliptical, perspective on modernity is not only to interrupt the long-standing, straightforward storylines of the phenomenon, it is also to query routine portrayals of homogeneous time (that are yet founded on inaugural, spatial ruptures) and antinomian blueprints of social space (which nonetheless entail a singular temporal hierarchy), each one binding the other. Needless to say, such projections undergird the frequently formalist and often a priori representations of modernity which abound in our present. Together at stake in this book are efforts to explore modernity as a contradictory and checkered historical-cultural entity and category as well as a contingent and contended process and condition. That is to say, on offer is an understanding of modernity as acutely construed by social-spatial/ disciplinary subjects *and* as crucially defined by heterogeneous-coeval hierarchically ordered temporalities. As we shall see, all of this shores up, as well, what the work might contribute to discussions of modernity after so much has been said and written about the subject.

Primary matters

It warrants emphasis that the conditions of possibility for this work lie in a series of critical questions concerning modernity, history, and the West/Europe, which have been raised by distinct perspectives in recent decades.[1] I indicate three such sets of queries here.[2] The first set concerns vigorous challenges to univocal conceptions of universal history under the terms of modernity. Imaginatively exploring distinct pasts that were forged within wider intermeshed matrices of power, such emphases have questioned pervasive imperatives of historical progress and the very nature of the historical archive, both intimately linked to aggrandizing representations of a reified (yet palpable) Europe/West.[3]

Second, for some time now, critical scholarship has contested the enduring oppositions – for example, binaries between tradition and modernity, ritual and rationality, myth and history, and East and West – that have shaped influential understandings of the past, key conceptions of culture(s). On the one hand, such theoretical interventions have derived support from critiques of a subject-centered reason and a meaning-legislating rationality, critiques that have thought through the dualisms of Western thought and post-Enlightenment traditions. On the other, critical discussions of cultures and pasts have equally challenged the analytical antinomies of modern disciplines, interrogating essentialized representations of otherness and querying abiding projections of progress, which are variously tied to the totalizing templates of universal history and ideological images of Western modernity.[4]

Third, close to our times, dominant designs of a singular modernity have been increasingly interrogated by contending intimations of heterogeneous moderns. Such explorations have critically considered

Subjects of modernity: an introduction 3

the divergent articulations and discrete representations of the modern and modernity, which have structured and sutured empire, nation, and globalization. As a result, modernity/modernities have been themselves revealed as contradictory and contingent processes of culture and control, as checkered, contested histories of meaning and mastery in their sedimentation, formation, and elaboration. It follows, too, that questions of modernity today increasingly often escape the limits of sociological formalism and exceed the binds of a priori abstraction, emerging instead as matters of particular pasts and attributes of concrete histories and defined by projects of power and molded by provisos of progress.[5]

Key questions

Engaging and extending such inquiries and emphases, this book explores modernity, the disciplines, and time-space in specific ways, precisely through its location in the disciplinary borderlands of anthropology and history, articulating from their margins areal knowledge(s), including of South Asia as envisioned from Latin America. Of particular significance here is my thinking through of the place and play in influential scholarship of the face-off between portrayals of community, subaltern, tradition, and difference with projections of state, West, modernity, and power. On the one hand, these presumptions reveal linkages with enduring oppositions between "enchanted spaces" and "modern places," which themselves rest upon pervasive procedures of the temporalization of space and the spatialization of time. On the other hand, I do not cast the recent writings and protocols under discussion as distant enemies which can then be easily interrogated and banished forthwith. Rather, such scholarship is acknowledged to be lying closer to home, informing the present inquiry.

Here the crucial questions turn on the unsteady oppositions – as well as their productive ambiguities – concerning temporal/spatial distinctions of the modern and the non-modern/trans-modern that have characterized South Asian subaltern studies, Latin American scholarship on coloniality/decoloniality, and postcolonial perspectives at large. The critical concerns extend to the tangible presence yet ambivalent articulations of time/space – turning on "culture" and "tradition" – in formations of history, anthropology, and historical anthropology. On offer are intellectual articulations of hegemonic and critical representations of the temporal and the spatial; at stake also are epistemic productions, strange and familiar, of space and time. Several of these considerations will emerge through a rather personal narrative in the following chapter.

Next I explore how the developmental idea of a surpassing of the past is central to modern imaginaries, of academic and everyday natures as well as their entwined expressions. At the same time, the work highlights that such segregation of the past from the present, although assumed to be principally temporal, nonetheless embodies profoundly spatial attributes. Thus, the place-holding presumption of a homogeneous history allows an imaginary yet palpable West – its singular temporal trajectory working in tandem with its exclusive spatial location – to become the horizon for the present and posterity of other cultures, which are seen as succeeding or failing to meet their destiny. Yet historical ruptures also insinuate stubborn knots, which once again irreducibly braid the temporal and the spatial. This is to say that prior places/times, at once anachronistic yet entirely coeval, appear enmeshed with contemporary stages/spaces, thus intimating the tangles, tatters, and textures of the past and the present, the spatial and the temporal.

Taken together, these overlapping measures reveal that routine representations of historical temporal ruptures alongside their hierarchical, spatial distinctions under discussion, underlie homologous oppositions between tradition and modernity, ritual and rationality, myth and history, the magical/medieval and the modern, community and state, and East and West. This is true of the distinctions yet overlaps between modernity, modernization, and modernism. Now, such matrices require understanding as the enduring enticements of modernity. But here are exactly found narratives, oppositions, and enchantments that should not be treated as mere objects of knowledge which can then be readily discarded or easily overcome. Rather, these stories, antinomies, and seductions need to be approached as key conditions of knowing under modernity.

Further, I track the interplay between disciplines, focusing on the relationship between anthropology and history. Here, my effort is to discuss formations of modern knowledge as themselves insinuating crucial attributes of procedures of modernity, especially the antinomian articulations of time-space that shore up disciplinary subjects. On the one hand, I explore the mutual reinforcements of time (in the form of history and temporality) and space (in the guise of tradition and culture) as simultaneously separating yet holding together these knowledge formations, whose disciplinary configurations have wide implications in social worlds. On the other, I consider the terms and textures of ambiguity and ambivalence in the recent renovations of anthropology and history, including in the making of historical anthropology. Under discussion throughout are distinct contradictions and contentions of modernity: from the formidable interleaving of analytical and hermeneutic orientations – especially, their competing conceptions of the relationship between knowing/explication and place/location – as underpinning modern knowledge(s) through to the ongoing presence of "heroic histories" in explanations of disciplines and their makeovers, where such projections often overlook their own presuppositions regarding temporal location, spatial locution, and historical progress. Unsurprisingly, it is also the larger undoing, often implicit, of hierarchical mappings of space and time that have revealed the critical possibilities of historical anthropology.

As the next step, the work explores issues of identity under modernity. Here, through their essential association with particular places, bounded spaces, identities are frequently rendered as a means of negotiating or overcoming modernity, which in turn is apprehended as an unbound yet homogeneous entity, seeking to remake the world in its temporal and spatial image. Staying with and thinking through such portrayals of identities as preceding modernity and/or as antidotes to it, I focus on the simultaneity of spatial imaginings, temporal schemes, and developmental sequences in these arenas. This makes it possible to register that, across the past few decades, the increasing inflation of identities – one that is, unsurprisingly, accompanied by the constant clamor over them – forms part of the spatial segregations, developmental distinctions, and historicist hierarchies of modernity.

At the same time, these measures offer an opportunity to propose a distinct perspective on identity, one that holds up a mirror to modernity. Drawing upon historical anthropology, subaltern studies, postcolonial perspectives, and social-political theory, I make a case for the enmeshed productions of modernity and identity, formed and transformed within spatial/temporal processes. Here are to be found entangled procedures of empire and Enlightenment, race and reason, colony and nation, history and community, power and meaning, and authority and alterity, which stretch across while they equally construe continents and epochs, space and time.

Finally, the thematic fabrics and critical motifs outlined above are unraveled and sutured through interpretive threads and analytical stitches of time and space. Considering that both these concepts-entities are often apprehended as being not only amorphous but also abstract, a few clarifications are in order at the outset. Recognizing that space and time have each found varied salient expressions in the disciplines studying physical worlds, my concern in this book is with the social dimensions of these categories and processes. Intimately enmeshed, the one with the other, social space and social time are far from being merely passive contexts, readily given backdrops, and already received conduits for human action. Rather, under consideration is the incessant interplay between routine cultural understandings, dominant ideological representations, and fraught everyday productions of space and time as constitutive of – shoring up as well as shaped by – social conventions and historical practices. Put differently, time and space, elaborated in tandem by social subjects, are at once critical constituents and active outcomes, formative attributes and key consequences of meaning and power, alterity and authority, and practice and process that define our worlds and their divisions.[6] In this book, I will attend to the active interchanges between the usual understandings, the hegemonic representations, and the quotidian constructions of space and time, principally focusing on their elaborations in modern social imaginaries, especially of scholarly persuasions.

Critical concerns

A handful of common concerns joins these critical considerations together.[7] Let us begin with my notion of *subjects of modernity*, which shores up the study. Now, the category-entity refers to historical actors who have been active participants in processes of modernity: social-spatial actors who have been *subject to* (shaped by) these processes, but also *subjects of* (themselves shaping) these processes.[8] Unsurprisingly, these temporal/spatial subjects have registered within their measures and meanings the formative contradictions, contentions, and contingencies of modernity. Clearly, these propositions rescue modernity and its subjects from their ready conflations with exclusive images of the (Euro-American, often male) *modern subject*, a point that becomes especially evident in my discussion of historical identities as shaped by global processes of empire, nation, community, and modernity. At the same time, there is rather more to the picture. For, under the rubric of subjects of modernity, I equally include *subject* as implying branch of learning and area of study, topic and theme, question and matter, and issue and business. Such *subjects* appear no less formed and transformed by spatial imperatives and temporal stipulations. Taken together, my articulation of subjects of modernity can productively widen the range of address of modernity and its participants, not only in an empirical manner but, saliently, in conceptual, critical ways, including the entangled productions of time and space in these arenas.

Moreover, there is a persuasive reason for conjoining these distinct registers of *subjects* of modernity. Arguably, disciplinary formations of modern knowledge often sharply separate academic arenas from everyday worlds. Here, the unsullied arrangements of the former are assumed as readily understanding the murky manifestations of the latter. Indeed, on offer often is the privileged view from nowhere that becomes the compelling vista for everywhere. Thinking through such pervasive supposition and its formidable scholasticism, this book is acutely aware instead of the mutual constitution of the academic and the everyday (as well as of the analytical and the affective, the rational and the embodied, and the hermeneutical and the experiential), especially vigilant of how these terrains simultaneously come together yet fall apart. Here, I unravel academic knowledge(s) and disciplinary protocol(s) as insinuated in wider social worlds and their constitutive conceits, each shaping and sheltering the other, and I register how analytical and scholarly procedures split yet suture embodied and everyday arenas of affect and identity under modernity, ever attentive to the spatial/temporal imperatives in these arenas.

Further, it only follows that *Subjects of Modernity* is held together by overlapping critical dispositions. Here are to be found orientations that refuse to render the worlds of modernity and its subjects as mere objects of knowledge awaiting their ineluctable endorsement, inevitable refinement, or irrevocable exorcism at the hands of prescient knowledge(s). Instead, the work crucially acknowledges and approaches these arenas and subjects as acutely intimating *conditions of knowing*. Indeed, such prudent avowal becomes the means to explore the generative meanings and practices of spatial/temporal/disciplinary subjects of modernity as key coordinates that shore up our worlds.

Lastly, the study is premised upon the recognition that the practices and meanings under discussion demand not only *critical articulation*, but also *careful affirmation*. Such procedures of the simultaneous querying and affirmation of historical/contemporary worlds and socio-spatial/disciplinary subjects of modernity entwine hermeneutic impulses and critical considerations. This is to say that they imply protocols entailing the interplay of prudent questionings of cultural worlds and their academic apprehensions *with* close attention to the diversity and distinction of these terrains. Here, there is neither an excision of the details by their being assimilated to the endless analytics of unpicking and unmasking, principally unhinged from temporal/spatial matrices, nor is there a privileging of particulars by their being presented as innate embodiments of alterity and locality, difference and place.

Having outlined the broad lineaments of the endeavor ahead, before proceeding any further it is only appropriate that I now introduce the key tendencies that both influence my wider work and carry key implications for this Theory for a Global Age series.[9] Here are to be found bodies of writing that have been deeply contentious and that I read critically in *Subjects of Modernity*. For these reasons, it is only after presenting their emphases and attending to the protocols of their arguments – rather than assimilating them to my purposes, as is often the case with readings of these tendencies – that I filter this corpus through its own conceits, especially through the means of a personal narrative in the next chapter. (Those readers who are already very familiar with postcolonial perspectives and subaltern studies can, of course, skip the ensuing section and move to the one that follows.)

Unraveling orientations: the postcolonial and the subaltern

Around four decades ago, Edward Said's seminal study, *Orientalism*, crucially underscored the mutual entailments of European colonialism and empire with Western knowledge and power.[10] Of course, long before the appearance of this work there existed several studies of European images of non-European peoples which identified various stereotypes, especially surrounding the identities of the "self" and the "other." However, such work tended to be "documentary rather than critical or analytical," so that an intriguing array of examples of European representations was presented, but their "discursive affiliations and underlying epistemologies" were frequently underplayed.[11] Intervening in this field, *Orientalism* made a persuasive case for the discursive fabrication – at once ideological and material – of the Orient as an object and identity through the profound dynamic of knowledge and power constitutive of Western empires.

Now, it is not only that anticolonial thinking has a longer past than Said's study – a question to which I will return – but that, exactly at the time of the first publication and early receptions of *Orientalism*, there were other writings expressing related concerns.[12] At the same time, it is equally the case that Said's arguments had an unprecedented ripple effect on scholarship. On the one hand, *Orientalism* had shifted the terms of debate and discussion on metropolitan representations of non-European peoples and their historical identities. Here was a shift from uncovering the singular biases of determinate depictions to unraveling the deeper domains of discursive domination, a move that further highlighted the complicity between earlier imperial imaginings and contemporary academic renderings of the Orient. On the other hand, Said's work came to crystallize the key emphases – and critical tensions – of an emergent academic arena, one entailing explorations of colonial discourses and imperial representations.

In this terrain, the implications and weaknesses of prior critical work on colonial writing, including *Orientalism*, were elaborated, extended, and exceeded by studies bearing distinct orientations. Especially important were Homi Bhabha's explorations of the inherent "ambivalence" of colonial discourse[13] – as well as the disruptive "hybrid" identities of colonized subjects – in order to challenge singular conceptions of colonial cultural writings.[14] Such endeavors further intersected with other ongoing struggles around issues of identity and history, especially those undertaken by minorities and feminists.[15] They also acutely elaborated post-structuralist theory, expressly endorsing antihumanist perspectives.[16] Taken together, from the early 1980s, discussions and debates on Western representations of non-Western worlds, as part of the wider elaboration of critical theories of colonial discourse, led to the gradual emergence of the field (now even considered a discipline) of postcolonial studies, not solely in metropolitan academic arenas but gradually also in provincial scholarly terrains.[17]

Over the past two decades, important interventions by postcolonial critics – as well as by scholars of anthropology, history, and religion – have gone on to access yet exceed colonial discourse theory. Exploring the "idea," "invention," and "imagination" of diverse subordinate, geopolitical terrains, histories, and identities across the globe,[18] such endeavors have further seized upon the contradictory, contingent, and contested dynamics of empire and nation. These dynamics were driven by interlocking identities of class, gender, race, and sexuality. As we shall see, such writings have focused on projects of power as shaped by the acute entanglements of the dominant and the subaltern, the colonizer and the colonized, and the metropolis and the margins. They have variously questioned thereby the unchallenged efficacy accorded to authoritative agendas of empire, nation, modernity, and globalization. Indeed, such scholarship has drawn upon historical, ethnographic, and literary materials to trace the interplay between the construction and institutionalization of emergent articulations of time and space, entailing key conjunctions of racial and sexual boundaries and gender and class divisions as constitutive of colonial cultures, postcolonial locations, and Western orders.[19]

Accompanying these developments, from the end of the 1970s critical departures were afoot in the history writing of the Indian subcontinent. Reassessments of nationalism in South Asia were often central to such endeavors.[20] Here an important role was played by the formation of the subaltern studies project, based on meetings between a small set of enthusiastic younger historians of India, most of them then in England, with a distinguished senior scholar of colonial India, Ranajit Guha, who taught history at the University of Sussex. The protagonists were separated by a generation, yet shared a mutual political and ethical sensibility.[21] The purpose of their discussions in England and India was to thrash out a new agenda for the historiography of the subcontinent, an agenda that recognized the centrality of subordinate groups – rightful, but disinherited, protagonists – in the making of the past, and thereby redressed the elitist imbalance of much of the writing on the subject. Thus the subaltern studies project was born.[22]

Drawing on yet departing from wider traditions of "histories from below," especially its British variants, an opening programmatic statement defined the aim of the endeavor as an effort "to promote a systematic and informed discussion of subaltern themes in the field of South Asian Studies to rectify the elitist bias of much research and academic work."²³ Here, the category of the subaltern, derived from the writings of Italian socialist Antonio Gramsci, was used as a metaphor for the general attribute of subordination in South Asia, whether such subordination was expressed in terms of class, caste, age, gender, race, or office.

It follows that the earlier exercises within the endeavor reconstructed the varied trajectories and the modes of consciousness of the movements of subordinate groups in India, in order to emphasize the autonomy and agency of these communities.²⁴ Such articulations of historical action within subaltern studies had a dual dimension: for one part, the notion of subaltern could acquire the attributes of a singular and homogeneous entity; at the same time, expressed as a critical category, the subaltern held possibilities of sustaining analyses that elaborated the articulation of distinct identities, of community and class, caste and race, and gender and nation.

Not surprisingly, as part of the extended development of the subaltern studies project, the articulations of the subaltern – as a category and an entity – have found ever varied and ever wider manifestations. On the one hand, more recent writings within the project have discussed the multiple mediations and diverse modalities – social and epistemic in nature, cultural and discursive in character – that shore up the production of subaltern subjects and their mutating identities. Here especially significant are the ways in which the notion of the subaltern has served to interrogate dominant knowledge(s) of empire and nation, state and modernity.²⁵ On the other hand, with the original impulse of subaltern studies finding varied appropriations and extensions across different continents from at least the 1990s, there have arisen debates and discussions that have been animated by broader considerations of colonial knowledge and postcolonial difference, multicultural politics and cultural identities.²⁶ Especially influential in these arenas are the writings of Gayatri Spivak, for instance, that harness "deconstructionist" readings and "strategic" sensibilities to fashion against-the-grain readings of subaltern subjects.²⁷ All of this has further underscored the question of the convergences between subaltern and postcolonial studies.

Now it warrants emphasis that postcolonial and subaltern approaches are often elided. Yet, as the discussion so far has indicated, the two should not be simply collapsed together. Thus, while postcolonial orientations emerged under the sign of the colony, the subaltern studies project was born under the mark of the nation. This is to say that, whereas postcolonial understandings privileged colonialism as a historical departure in the making of the modern world, subaltern studies project took as its starting point the requirements of examining "the failure of the nation to come into its own."[28]

It is also the case, however, that from the beginning critical engagements both with colony and nation have characterized these two approaches, at the very least implicitly. This should not be surprising. To start with, the ideological antecedents not only of postcolonial perspectives but also of subaltern studies lay in long and critical traditions of anticolonial thought and decolonizing practice. Here, the writings and politics of Frantz Fanon, Amílcar Cabral, and Aimé Césaire could acutely influence the very formations of postcolonial scholarship. At the same time, the terms and textures of subaltern studies – in a manner convergent with postcolonial perspectives – emerged equally informed by wider anti-imperial sensibilities. Such sensibilities extended from the diverse politics of counter-colonialism and decolonization that began in the 1940s through to the events of the 1960s entailing critiques of imperialism and racism – embodied, for example, in the dramatic moment of 1968 – and the continuation of these struggles into the 1970s across different parts of the world.

Together, postcolonial and subaltern studies were preceded and shaped by these wider developments and the extension of their spirit into academic arenas, especially the emergent critiques of reigning paradigms within the disciplines as well as formations of new perspectives on the Left, including combative social sciences, "world systems" theory, radical peasant studies, and critical revisions of Marxism.[29] Indeed, having registered the limitations of readily collapsing subaltern and postcolonial perspectives, it is worth noting the key intersections between these inquiries, which have also influenced the terms and textures of historical anthropology, another important tendency undergirding this book.

Historical anthropology

This book is located on the cusp of anthropology and history. Now, if the association between these two disciplines has been checkered and contradictory, the alliance between them has also been passionate and productive.[30] Displaying limited comprehension and lingering mistrust of each other, history and anthropology have often talked past one another.[31] Conversely, at different times and in distinct locations, important practitioners of these bodies of knowledge have underscored their key convergences, highlighting the necessity of crossing borders and straddling the boundaries that separate them. However, over the last four decades, the interchanges between these inquiries have acquired fresh purposes in theoretical and empirical studies. The conjunctions have been accompanied by key considerations of the history of anthropology and the anthropology of history. At stake has been a serious rethinking of the status of the two disciplines.[32]

How are we to understand historical anthropology? Is it a form of knowledge principally entailing archival research *and* fieldwork, themselves framed as prefigured and already known procedures that subsequently find productive combination in this interdisciplinary terrain? Is historical anthropology, then, only an inquiry that conjoins the methodologies and techniques of two taken-for-granted disciplines? As Brian Axel has argued: "In all the bustle to try and figure out how history and anthropology can use each other's techniques (and thus, supposedly, constitute a historical anthropology), what most often goes without comment is the presumption that history and anthropology are whole and complete in themselves. Here, we regard such a presumption as a problem – one leading to the very common way of speaking about historical anthropology as exemplifying the dialogue between history and anthropology."[33]

My own attempts involve approaching historical anthropology in a manner that rethinks its constituent disciplines and their wider interplay. To do this is to look beyond merely tracing the "dialogue" between anthropology and history, in order to attend instead to their critical makeovers and mutual renovations, which signal convergent dispositions yet divergent articulations.[34] This is also to say that the shared entailments of history and anthropology are grounded in common assumptions and mutual denials, disciplinary genealogies that have deep provenance and wide implications in social worlds. Examining such reciprocal principles, turning on space and time, which prop up history and anthropology, I seek to probe the business-as-usual of anthropology and history as well as to present the consequences at large of the meeting and mating of these inquiries.[35]

In more recent years, as anthropologists and historians have rethought theory, method, and perspective, archival materials have been read through anthropological filters and fieldwork has been harnessed to the historical imagination. All this has significantly opened up questions of the nature of the "archive" and the "field" as well as of time and space, albeit often implicitly. Anthropological agendas have been yoked to historical accounts of the interleaving of meaning and practice. Historical sensibilities have informed ethnographic explorations of the interplay between culture and power. Such blending has produced hybrid narratives, rendering the strange as familiar and accessing the familiar as strange, the better to unsettle our notions of strangeness and familiarity regarding historical worlds and contemporary ones. While such developments have not been all of a piece, the critical possibilities they suggest intimately inform the account ahead.

Pathways

Rather more than a conventional monograph, *Subjects of Modernity* is better understood as an extended essay in the sense of an argument in six parts. It draws together the past and the present as well as theory and narrative by sowing the empirical, the historical, the ethnographic, and the methodological deep into its critical procedures. Thus the work straddles the standard splits between the contemporary and the historical as well as the theoretical and the empirical: indeed, their conjunctions spell the spirit and substance of the study from this introductory endeavor, through its distinct chapters, and on to an eventual epilogue.

Chapter 2 is cast as something of a personal narrative. It recounts how I arrived at inklings and intimations of space and time – in tandem with understandings of disciplines and subjects, modernity and identity – beginning with my pre-apprentice days in Delhi through to my apprenticeship at Cambridge, moving on to my journeyman sojourns in Mexico and to my artisanal concerns in the present. At stake especially are encounters and entanglements with time and space as folded within the creases of subaltern studies, decolonial understandings, and postcolonial perspectives. On the one hand, I explore how these shifting orientations have drawn upon hegemonic representations as well as non-certified imaginations of time and space, to now press familiar associations and unravel unusual enunciations of these concepts and processes. On the other, I track the active construal, the exact production, of space and time *within* the epistemic practice of these critical perspectives.

Chapter 3 draws on social theory, political philosophy, and other scholarship in the critical humanities in order to make its claims concerning the mutual binds between everyday oppositions, routine enchantments, temporal ruptures, and spatial hierarchies of a modern provenance. My reference is to productions of space and time, antinomies and enticements, as hegemonic representation and quotidian presumption. Laboring together, these have split, sutured, and shaped modernity by intimately informing the meanings and practices of its socio-spatial disciplinary subjects. The spatial/temporal templates under discussion not only clarify the distinctions and overlaps between modernity, modernization, and modernism, but also reveal how modern enticements and antinomies, far from being analytical abstractions, intimate instead ontological attributes and experiential dimensions of the worlds in which we live, and the spaces and times that we inhabit and articulate.

Chapter 4 charts its course through a large, varied corpus of anthropologies and histories, produced principally in the twentieth century. On the one hand, I elaborate the incessant interplay of temporality and tradition, spatiality and history, and place and culture by tracking the formidable presence and acute articulations of hegemonic representations of time and space, of the modern and the non-modern, in these disciplines. On the other, I register that these arenas are equally shot through with an unstable entwining of hermeneutical and analytical assumption. Now, the focus on the braiding of the analytical and the hermeneutical, each entailing a distinct relationship between knowledge and place, knowing and location, has critical consequences. It helps to unravel the unstable production of space and time precisely as part of disciplinary practice, which now instated and now interrogated dominant blueprints. Such measures, in turn, serve to think through temporal ruptures and to scrabble spatial hierarchies, revealing wider antipodal modalities at the core of different critical traditions.

My deliberations include the work on time-reckoning and historical dynamics – implicitly insinuating *particular places* and *abstract spaces* respectively – in the writings of "masters" such as Franz Boas, E. E. Evans-Pritchard, and Pierre Bourdieu. They extend to mid-twentieth-century social-scientific considerations, located on the cusp of colony and nation, alongside older and more recent writings in history and anthropology across different parts of the world. Here are to be found tacit assumptions concerning space, time, and progress that hold a mirror up to the ambiguities and ambivalences of modernity and its disciplines. Yet also encountered are possibilities of other imaginings and critical expressions of socio-spatial and hetero-temporal disciplinary subjects and cultural terrains, past and present.

Chapter 5 turns to issues of identity and modernity. Based on rather particular readings of an array of historical and anthropological writings, it critically conjoins these with salient emphases of subaltern studies, postcolonial scholarship, and social theory, which are also configured in newer ways. Specifically, I render these understandings, including against their own assumptions, as bearing distinctive expressions of space and time. Thus, I approach identities as referring to broad-ranging temporal-spatial processes of formations of subjects, intimating at once particular personhoods and collective groupings. Here, identities comprise a crucial means through which such processes are perceived, experienced, and articulated. Indeed, defined within cultural-temporal and socio-spatial relationships of production and reproduction, appropriation and approbation, and power and difference, cultural identities (and their mutations) appear as essential elements in the quotidian constitution (and routine transformations) of social worlds. Following these propositions, historical anthropologies, postcolonial perspectives, and subaltern studies – when unraveled along *and* against the grain of their claims and conceits – have a broad purchase. They untangle cultural/historical identities, grounded in space/time, as constitutive of colony and empire, history and community, and nation and modernity across the continents. Such critical and processual, theoretical and empirical, understandings not only militate against the attribution of an inescapable a priori particularity to identity, but they actively uncover the spatial segregations and temporal hierarchies that attend mappings of modernity.

Chapter 6, an extended epilogue, weaves together the different strands of the study by exploring the terms of modernism on the Indian subcontinent. I focus first on critical modernist moments, cutting across aesthetic forms and the twentieth century, in South Asia. Self-conscious breaks with prior artistic traditions within the subcontinental aesthetic landscape – alongside engagements with wider modernist imaginaries – have instilled these tendencies with rather specific energies, twists, and textures. Alongside, however, are claims of a surpassing of the past that appear variously inflected by empire and nation, communitarianism and nationalism, memory and history, the mythic and the primitive, a fractured independence and violent Partition, the political and the postcolonial, gender and sexuality, body and pain, and the epic and the contemporary.

Taken together, the discussion suggests the salience of tracking heterogeneous, yet overlaying, temporalities of modernisms in South

Asia, including the creation of time and space within aesthetic practices of modern subjects. Indeed, these considerations are further clarified through the formidable images and fragmentary texts of Savindra Sawarkar, an expressionist and Dalit artist. Central to his unsettling iconography and imagination are distinctive representations of history and the here and now working in tandem, which evoke and create space and time, past places and present tempos, in order to reveal their immanent frames while pointing toward other futures. Here the claims, contentions, and contradictions of a rather particular modern subject, his twisted times and places, bring to life the anxieties, ambivalences, and identities spawned by modernity and its subjects, who construe temporal-spatial matrices even as they are shaped by snarled spaces and tangled times.

Notes

1 Before proceeding any further, it requires registering that an acute irony surrounds the fact that over the past three decades abiding articulations of these critical dispositions in academic terrains, and intellectual arenas more broadly, have been accompanied by the consolidation of an entirely predatory capitalist order in the world at large.

2 These theoretical orientations have been expressed in a variety of ways, constituting an enormous corpus. Keeping this in mind, I provide in the notes below a few representative examples, especially writings that early on intimated to me each of these tendencies throughout the long 1990s. At the same time, it warrants emphasis that distinct disciplines reveal different textures of the orientations under discussion. On the one hand, critical histories, construed from methodological margins, might have acutely interrogated familiar frames for approaching the past and the present, but dominant disciplinary dispositions suggest otherwise, often persisting with the reproduction of dead certainties. On the other hand, disciplines such as sociology, at the very least in the Euro-American academe, have only rarely recently engaged with postcolonial perspectives (and decolonial departures). Upon taking such steps, they have often

intersected – critically and conceptually – with work in historical sociology that articulates colonial pasts, also putting a distinct spin on sociological writings that offer critical elaborations of Western modernity. For a sustained engagement with postcolonial (and decolonial) perspectives within sociology, see Gurminder Bhambra, *Rethinking Modernity: Postcolonialism and the Sociological Imagination* (New York: Palgrave Macmillan, 2007) and *Connected Sociologies* (London: Bloomsbury, 2014). On a historical sociology of colonial pasts, see George Steinmetz, *The Devil's Handwriting: Precoloniality and the German Colonial State in Qingdao, Samoa, and Southwest Africa* (Chicago, IL: University of Chicago Press, 2007). See also George Steinmetz (ed.), *Sociology and Empire: The Imperial Entanglements of a Discipline* (Durham, NC: Duke University Press, 2013); Edgardo Lander (ed.), *La colonialidad del saber: eurocentrismo y ciencias sociales. Perspectivas latinoamericanas* (Buenos Aires: UNESCO/CLACSO, 2000).

3   Johannes Fabian, *Out of Our Minds: Reason and Madness in the Exploration of Central Africa* (Berkeley: University of California Press, 2000); Nancy Florida, *Writing the Past, Inscribing the Future: History as Prophecy in Colonial Java* (Durham, NC: Duke University Press, 1995); Saidiya H. Hartman, *Scenes of Subjection: Terror, Slavery, and Self-Making in Nineteenth-Century America* (New York: Oxford University Press, 1997); Kerwin Lee Klein, *Frontiers of Historical Imagination: Narrating the European Conquest of Native America, 1890–1990* (Berkeley: University of California Press, 1999); Walter Mignolo, *The Darker Side of the Renaissance: Literacy, Territoriality, and Colonization* (Ann Arbor: University of Michigan Press, 1995); Richard Price, *Alabi's World* (Baltimore, MD: Johns Hopkins University Press, 1990); Joanne Rappaport, *Cumbe Reborn: An Andean Ethnography of History* (Chicago, IL: University of Chicago Press, 1994); Shahid Amin, *Event, Metaphor, Memory: Chauri Chaura 1922–1992* (Berkeley: University of California Press, 1995); Ishita Banerjee-Dube, "Taming traditions: legalities and histories in eastern India," in Gautam Bhadra et al. (eds.), *Subaltern Studies X: Writings on South Asian History and Society* (New Delhi: Oxford University Press, 1999), pp. 98–125; Dipesh Chakrabarty, *Provincializing Europe: Postcolonial Thought and Historical Difference* (Princeton, NJ: Princeton University Press, 2000); Saurabh Dube, *Untouchable*

Pasts: Religion, Identity, and Power among a Central Indian Community, 1780–1950 (Albany, NY: State University of New York Press, 1998); and Ajay Skaria, *Hybrid Histories: Forests, Frontiers, and Wildness in Western India* (New Delhi: Oxford University Press, 1999). See also Brian K. Axel, *The Nation's Tortured Body: Violence, Representation, and the Formation of a Sikh "Diaspora"* (Durham, NC: Duke University Press, 2001); Uday Singh Mehta, *Liberalism and Empire: A Study in Nineteenth Century British Liberal Thought* (Chicago, IL: University of Chicago Press, 1999); and Michel-Rolph Trouillot, *Silencing the Past: Power and the Production of History* (Boston, MA: Beacon Press, 1995).

4   Talal Asad, *Genealogies of Religion: Discipline and Reasons of Power in Christianity and Islam* (Baltimore, MD: Johns Hopkins University Press, 1993); Zygmunt Bauman, *Intimations of Postmodernity* (London: Routledge, 1992); John Comaroff and Jean Comaroff (eds.), *Modernity and its Malcontents: Ritual and Power in Postcolonial Africa* (Chicago, IL: University of Chicago Press, 1993); Shelly Errington, *The Death of Authentic Primitive Art and Other Tales of Progress* (Berkeley: University of California Press, 1998); Walter Mignolo, *Local Histories/Global Designs: Coloniality, Subaltern Knowledges and Border Thinking* (Princeton, NJ: Princeton University Press, 2000); Edward W. Said, *Orientalism* (New York: Pantheon, 1978); Richard Rorty, *Contingency, Irony, and Solidarity* (New York: Cambridge University Press, 1989); Laurie J. Sears, *Shadows of Empire: Colonial Discourse and Javanese Tales* (Durham, NC: Duke University Press, 1996); Michael Taussig, *The Magic of the State* (New York and London: Routledge, 1997). See also Lisa Lowe and David Lloyd (eds.), *The Politics of Culture in the Shadow of Capital* (Durham, NC: Duke University Press, 1997); and David Scott, *Refashioning Futures: Criticism after Postcoloniality* (Princeton, NJ: Princeton University Press, 1999).

5   Partha Chatterjee, *The Nation and its Fragments: Colonial and Postcolonial Histories* (Princeton, NJ: Princeton University Press, 1993); Frederick Cooper and Ann Stoler (eds.), *Tensions of Empire: Colonial Cultures in a Bourgeois World* (Berkeley: University of California Press, 1997); John Comaroff and Jean Comaroff, *Of Revelation and Revolution: The Dialectics of Modernity on the South African Frontier*, vol. 2 (Chicago, IL: University of Chicago Press, 1997); Fernando Coronil, *The Magical State: Nature,*

Money, and Modernity in Venezuela (Chicago, IL: University of Chicago Press, 1997); Saurabh Dube, *Stitches on Time: Colonial Textures and Postcolonial Tangles* (Durham, NC, and London: Duke University Press, 2004); James Ferguson, *Expectations of Modernity: Myths and Meanings of Urban Life on the Zambian Copperbelt* (Berkeley: University of California Press, 1999); Paul Gilroy, *The Black Atlantic: Modernity and Double Consciousness* (Cambridge, MA: Harvard University Press, 1993); Akhil Gupta, *Postcolonial Developments: Agriculture in the Making of Modern India* (Durham, NC: Duke University Press, 1998); Thomas Blom Hansen, *The Saffron Wave: Democracy and Hindu Nationalism in Modern India* (Princeton, NJ: Princeton University Press, 1999); Gyan Prakash, *Another Reason: Science and the Imagination of Modern India* (Princeton, NJ: Princeton University Press, 1999); Richard Price, *The Convict and the Colonel: A Story of Colonialism and Resistance in the Caribbean* (Boston, MA: Beacon Press, 1998); and Michael Taussig, *Shamanism, Colonialism, and the Wild Man: A Study in Terror and Healing* (Chicago, IL: University of Chicago Press, 1987). See also Arjun Appadurai, *Modernity at Large: Cultural Dimensions of Globalization* (Minneapolis: University of Minnesota Press, 1996); Arturo Escobar, *Encountering Development: The Making and Unmaking of the Third World* (Princeton, NJ: Princeton University Press, 1993); Harry Harootunian, *Overcome by Modernity: History, Culture, and Community in Interwar Japan* (Princeton, NJ: Princeton University Press, 2000); Charles Piot, *Remotely Global: Village Modernity in West Africa* (Chicago, IL: University of Chicago Press, 1999); and Lisa Rofel, *Other Modernities: Gendered Yearnings in China after Socialism* (Berkeley: University of California Press, 1999).

6   These understandings of time and space – and their elaboration across *Subjects of Modernity* – draw upon and bring together the key emphases of a range of critical scholarship, which unravel the production of space, especially under capitalism, critiques of disciplinary uses of time, and everyday articulations of space and time across cultures, societies, and histories. I provide very few indicative references here, registering that a discussion of the ways these analyses differ from one another – and the ways in which I set their emphases to work in my arguments – would well require another chapter, maybe even a book. Henri Lefebvre, *The*

Production of Space, trans. Donald Nicholson-Smith (Oxford: Blackwell, 1991); Edward Soja, *Postmodern Geographies: The Reassertion of Space in Critical Social Theory* (London: Verso, 1989); Johannes Fabian, *Time and the Other: How Anthropology Makes its Object* (New York: Columbia University Press, 1983); Chakrabarty, *Provincializing Europe*; Nancy Munn, "The cultural anthropology of time: a critical essay," *Annual Review of Anthropology*, 21 (1992): 93–123; Nancy Munn, *The Fame of Gawa: A Symbolic Study of Value Transformation in a Massim (Papua New Guinea) Society* (Durham, NC: Duke University Press, 1992). See also Pierre Bourdieu, Outline of a Theory of Practice, trans. Richard Nice (Cambridge: Cambridge University Press, 1977); Michel de Certeau, *The Practice of Everyday Life*, trans. Steven F. Rendall (Berkeley: University of California Press, 1984); Reinhart Koselleck, *The Practice of Conceptual History: Timing History, Spacing Concepts*, trans. Todd Samuel Presner (Stanford, CA: Stanford University Press, 2002); and Nicholas Thomas, *Out of Time: History and Evolution in Anthropological Discourse* (Cambridge: Cambridge University Press, 1989).

7   The concerns and considerations being discussed have been developed, in conversation with the relevant scholarly literature, in my work over the last decade. Rather than recall and rehearse that theoretical apparatus, allow me only to point to some of those writings: Dube, *Stitches on Time*; Saurabh Dube, *After Conversion: Cultural Histories of Modern India* (New Delhi: Yoda Press, 2010); and Saurabh Dube, *Modernidad e historia*, trans. Adrían Muñoz (Mexico City: El Colegio de México, 2011).

8   Over the past few centuries, the subjects of modernity (and globalization) have included, to take just a few instances, peasants, artisans, and workers in South Asia that have diversely articulated processes of colony and post-colony; indigenous communities in the Americas under colonial and national rule; peoples of African descent not only on that continent but in different diasporas across the world; and, indeed, subaltern, marginal, and elite women and men in non-Western and Western theaters. For a wider discussion, see Dube, *Stitches on Time*.

9   This is clarified, for instance, by recent work in critical sociology that engages postcolonial perspectives and subaltern studies, two of the orientations discussed below. See, for instance, Bhambra, *Rethinking Modernity* and *Connected Sociologies*.

10 Said, *Orientalism*.
11 Nicholas Thomas, *Colonialism's Culture: Anthropology, Travel and Government* (Princeton, NJ: Princeton University Press, 1994).
12 Alain Grosrichard, *The Sultan's Court: European Fantasies of the East*, trans. Liz Heron (London: Verso, 1998); Fabian, *Time and the Other*; Ashis Nandy, *The Intimate Enemy: Loss and Recovery of the Self under Colonialism* (Delhi: Oxford University Press, 1982); Anouar Abdel-Malek, "Orientalism in crisis," *Diogenes*, 44 (1963): 104–12; Abdul R. JanMohamed, *Manichean Aesthetics: The Politics of Literature in Colonial Africa* (Amherst: University of Massachusetts Press, 1983).
13 Homi K. Bhabha, *Location of Culture* (London and New York: Routledge, 1994).
14 Other critical assessments of Said's text within cultural literary studies include Bart Moore-Gilbert, *Postcolonial Theory: Contexts, Practices, Politics* (London: Verso, 1997), pp. 34–73; Robert Young, *White Mythologies: Writing History and the West* (London: Routledge, 1990), pp. 119–40. See also Meyda Yegenoglu, *Colonial Fantasies: Towards a Feminist Reading of Orientalism* (Cambridge: Cambridge University Press, 1998). Constructive critical engagements with *Orientalism* within anthropology and history include James Clifford, "On *Orientalism*," in James Clifford, *The Predicament of Culture: Twentieth-Century Ethnography, Literature, and Art* (Cambridge, MA: Harvard University Press, 1988); Thomas, *Colonialism's Culture*, pp. 5–7, 21–7. See also Carol Breckenridge and Peter van der Veer (eds.), *Orientalism and the Postcolonial Predicament: Perspectives on South Asia* (Philadelphia: University of Pennsylvania Press, 1993).
15 For example, Abdul R. JanMohamed and David Lloyd (eds.), *The Nature and Context of Minority Discourse* (New York and Oxford: Oxford University Press, 1990); Gayatri Chakravorty Spivak, "Subaltern studies: deconstructing historiography," in Ranajit Guha (ed.), *Subaltern Studies IV: Writings on South Asian History and Society* (Delhi: Oxford University Press, 1985), pp. 330–63.
16 See Gayatri Chakravorty Spivak, "Can the subaltern speak?," in Cary Nelson and Lawrence Grossberg (eds.), *Marxism and the Interpretation of Culture* (Urbana/Chicago: University of Illinois Press, 1988), pp. 271–313; and Bhabha, *Location of Culture*.

17 Writings introducing postcolonial theory are an academic industry. Here I refer the interested reader to the following texts: Robert Young, *Postcolonialism: An Historical Introduction* (Cambridge, MA: Wiley-Blackwell, 2001); Robert Young, *Postcolonialism: A Very Short Introduction* (Oxford: Oxford University Press, 2003); and also Young, *White Mythologies*; John McLeod, *Beginning Postcolonialism* (Manchester: Manchester University Press, 2000); Leela Gandhi, *Postcolonial Theory: A Critical Introduction* (New York: Columbia University Press, 1998); Ania Loomba, *Colonialism/Postcolonialism* (London and New York: Routledge, 1998); Moore-Gilbert, *Postcolonial Theory*; Padmini Mongia (ed.), *Contemporary Postcolonial Theory: A Reader* (London: Hodder Arnold, 1996); and Neil Lazarus (ed.), *The Cambridge Companion to Postcolonial Literary Studies* (New York: Cambridge University Press, 2004).

18 Valentin Yves Mudimbe, *The Invention of Africa: Gnosis, Philosophy, and the Order of Knowledge* (Bloomington: Indiana University Press, 1988); Valentin Yves Mudimbe, *The Idea of Africa* (Bloomington and London: Indiana University Press, 1994); Ronald B. Inden, *Imagining India* (Cambridge, MA: Basil Blackwell, 1990); José Rabasa, *Inventing America: Spanish Historiography and the Formation of Eurocentrism* (Oklahoma: University of Oklahoma Press, 1993).

19 For wider discussions, see Dube, *Stitches on Time*; Saurabh Dube, "Terms that bind: colony, nation, modernity," in Saurabh Dube (ed.), *Postcolonial Passages: Contemporary History-Writing on India* (New Delhi: Oxford University Press, 2004), pp. 1–37; Saurabh Dube, "Anthropology, history, historical anthropology: an introduction," in Saurabh Dube (ed.), *Historical Anthropology: Oxford in India Readings in Sociology and Social Anthropology* (New Delhi: Oxford University Press, 2007), pp. 1–73; Saurabh Dube, *Historias esparcidas,* trans. Gabriela Uranga Grijalva (Mexico City: El Colegio de México, 2007).

20 Sumit Sarkar, *Modern India: 1885–1947* (New Delhi: Macmillan, 1983); Dipesh Chakrabarty, *Habitations of Modernity: Essays in the Wake of Subaltern Studies* (Chicago, IL: University of Chicago Press, 2002).

21 Gyan Prakash, "Subaltern studies as postcolonial criticism," *American Historical Review*, 99 (1994): 1475–90.

22 For details, see Dube, *Stitches on Time*.

23 Ranajit Guha, "Preface," in Ranajit Guha (ed.), *Subaltern Studies I: Writings on South Asian History and Society* (Delhi: Oxford University Press, 1982), p. viii.

24 Ranajit Guha (ed.), *Subaltern Studies I–VI: Writings on South Asian History and Society* (Delhi: Oxford University Press, 1982–89).

25 Amin, *Event, Metaphor, Memory*; Chatterjee, *The Nation and its Fragments*; Partha Chatterjee, *The Politics of the Governed: Reflections on Popular Politics in Most of the World* (New York: Columbia University Press, 2004); Chakrabarty, *Provincializing Europe*; Chakrabarty, *Habitations of Modernity*; Gyanendra Pandey, *Remembering Partition: Violence, Nationalism and History in India* (Cambridge: Cambridge University Press, 2001); Gyanendra Pandey, *Routine Violence: Nations, Fragments, Histories* (Stanford, CA: Stanford University Press, 2006); Prakash, *Another Reason*.

26 A single example should suffice, concerning the impact of the (South Asian) subaltern studies project on writings on Latin America. Not only was there the formation of a wide-ranging Latin American subaltern studies project in the US, but the work of the South Asian collective has equally found wide discussion in Latin America itself. For the former tendency, see José Rabasa et al. (eds.), *Subaltern Studies in the Americas*, special issue of *dispositio/n: American Journal of Cultural Histories and Theories*, 46 (1994 [published 1996]); Ileana Rodríguez (ed.), *A Latin American Subaltern Studies Reader* (Durham, NC: Duke University Press, 2001); John Beverley, *Subalternity and Representation: Arguments in Cultural Theory* (Durham, NC: Duke University Press, 1999). On the latter initiatives, see Silvia Rivera Cusicanqui and Rossana Barragan (eds.), *Debates post coloniales: una introducción a los estudios de la subalternidad* (La Paz: Sierpe, 1997); John Kraniauskas and Guillermo Zermeño (eds.), "Historia y subalternidad," special issue of *Historia y Grafía*, 12 (1999): 7–176; Saurabh Dube (ed.), *Pasados poscoloniales: colección de ensayos sobre la nueva historia y etnografía de la India*, trans. Germán Franco (Mexico City: El Colegio de México, 1999). Consider also Florencia E. Mallon, "The promise and dilemma of subaltern studies: perspectives from Latin American histories," *American Historical Review*, 99 (1994): 1491–515; and my own authored quintet in historical anthropology in the

Spanish language comprising: *Sujetos subalternos: capítulos de una historia antropológica*, trans. Germán Franco and Ari Bartra (Mexico City: El Colegio de México, 2001); *Genealogías del presente: conversión, colonialismo, cultura*, trans. Ari Bartra and Gilberto Conde (Mexico City: El Colegio de México, 2003); *Historias esparcidas; Modernidad e historia*; and *Formaciones de lo contemporáneo*, trans. Lucía Cirianni (Mexico City: El Colegio de México, forthcoming 2017).

27 Gayatri Chakravorty Spivak, *In Other Worlds: Essays in Cultural Politics* (London: Methuen, 1987); Gayatri Chakravorty Spivak, *A Critique of Postcolonial Reason: Toward a History of the Vanishing Present* (Cambridge, MA: Harvard University Press, 1999); Ranajit Guha and Gayatri Chakravorty Spivak (eds.), *Selected Subaltern Studies* (New York: Oxford University Press, 1988).

28 Guha, "Preface," p. ix.

29 Talal Asad (ed.), *Anthropology and the Colonial Encounter* (London: Ithaca Press, 1973); Joan Vincent, *Anthropology and Politics: Visions, Traditions, and Trends* (Tuscon: University of Arizona Press, 1990), pp. 225–9, 308–14; Patrick Wolfe, "History and imperialism: a century of theory, from Marx to postcolonialism," *American Historical Review*, 102 (1997): 380–420.

30 I use the term "anthropology" to refer to social and cultural anthropology in their widest sense, also including those writings in sociology that are shored up by ethnographic sensibilities. "Ethnography" is used as shorthand for practices constituting social and cultural anthropology.

31 This is especially reflected in the manner in which certain stark statements concerning history and anthropology become leitmotifs for discussing one's own and the other discipline. Such statements include Maitland's comment that "by and by anthropology will have the choice of becoming history or nothing"; Radcliffe-Brown's assertion that, for the most part, history "does not explain anything at all"; and Trevor-Roper's dismissal of the history of Africa, except for the European presence there, and of pre-Columbian America as "largely darkness" that never could be "a subject of history." For the difficulties of conducting discussions by invoking such statements, usually quoted out of context, see Shepard Krech III, "The state of ethnohistory," *Annual Review of Anthropology*, 20 (1991): 345–6.

32 This includes the cautious questioning of contemporary celebrations of interdisciplinary departures – of the "anthropological turn" in history and of the "historical turn" in anthropology – as being insufficiently conceptualized.
33 Brian K. Axel, "Introduction: historical anthropology and its vicissitudes," in Brian K. Axel (ed.), *From the Margins: Historical Anthropology and its Futures* (Durham, NC: Duke University Press, 2002), p. 13.
34 This means that my efforts engage yet extend the emphases of several influential discussions of the interplay between anthropology and history. Axel, "Introduction: historical anthropology"; Saloni Mathur, "History and anthropology in South Asia: rethinking the archive," *Annual Review of Anthropology*, 29 (2000): 89–106; John Kelly and Martha Kaplan, "History, structure, and ritual," *Annual Review of Anthropology*, 19 (1990): 119–50; Peter Pels, "The anthropology of colonialism: culture, history, and the emergence of Western governmentality," *Annual Review of Anthropology*, 26 (1997): 163–83; Ann Laura Stoler and Frederick Cooper, "Between metropole and colony: rethinking a research agenda," in Cooper and Stoler, *Tensions of Empire*, pp. 1–56; James D. Faubion, "History in anthropology," *Annual Review of Anthropology*, 22 (1993): 35–54; Krech, "The state of ethnohistory"; and John Comaroff and Jean Comaroff, *Ethnography and the Historical Imagination* (Boulder, CO: Westview, 1992).
35 In terms of the organization of disciplines concerning South Asia, what I am calling "historical anthropology," arguably my main "area" of study, remains only an uncertainly demarcated form of scholarly inquiry, especially in the subcontinent. This fact itself has its genealogies, turning on disciplinary specializations and unsteady articulations of space-time, issues to which I will return.

2

Intimations of modernity: time and space

This chapter is cast as a personal narrative. It unravels how I arrived at inklings and understandings of space and time – alongside those of disciplines and subjects, modernity and identity – that were explored in the Introduction and which lie at the core of this book. At stake are intimations that are at once familiar and strange. For, born to anthropologist parents, I grew up in Sagar (central India), Delhi (old and new), and Shimla (northern India). My formative years were imbued with a lingering sense of how terrains (or times/spaces) of the "vernacular" and the "cosmopolitan" ever overlapped yet only met each other in curious, quirky, and contradictory ways. A little later, seeking my vocation in research and teaching, I was trained in history but drawn toward anthropology, especially as I cut my pre-apprentice scholar's teeth on the subaltern studies endeavor. (Indeed, I initiate here an artisanal coming-of-age metaphor that shores up the narrative.)

Early encounters

As was noted in this book's introduction, from the latter half of the 1970s, critical departures were afoot in the history of the subcontinent. If reassessments of the pasts of Indian nationalism were often central to such endeavors, on offer equally were other convergences of significance. Especially important were imaginative readings of historical materials: from conventional archival records, including reports of colonial administrators, to earlier ethnographies as sources of history; and from previously maligned vernacular registers of history to diverse subaltern expressions of the past. Such readings could problematize the very nature of the historical archive as well as initiate conversations with other orientations, including those of structural linguistics and critical theory.[1] No less salient were incipient acknowledgments of the innately political character of history writing.

In this wider scenario, attending the history (honors) undergraduate program in St. Stephen's College, several of my cohorts and I were insinuated in the intellectual excitement that surrounded the emergence of subaltern studies. Soon, pursuing a (taught) master's in (modern) history, also at Delhi University, the debates and ferment of those times led to wider critical engagements with historiographical and theoretical currents then underway across the world. Here, even as subaltern studies powerfully pointed in newer historical directions, the endeavor also appeared as privileging the spectacular moments of the subalterns' overt rebellions over these people's more routine, everyday negotiations of power. This suggested, in turn, inadequate, abbreviated articulations of culture and consciousness, of religion and caste, within the project.

Unsurprisingly, seeking a research theme for the MPhil in history, also at Delhi University, I was interested in studying the conduct of resistance in a religious idiom. Specifically, I wished to rescue such negotiations and contestations of authority from their being subordinated – as insubstantial, even epiphenomenal – to the underlying determinations of endlessly economic imperatives and/or principally progressive politics, which abounded in the heroic histories of the time. Rather, at stake was the manner in which the institutions and imaginings of caste, the practices and processes of religion (in this case, Hinduism dominant and popular) could critically structure and shape the actions and expressions of subordinate communities. For a subject of study, I chanced upon a heretical and "untouchable" caste-sect, the Satnamis of Chhattisgarh. The auspices of my parents proved important here, both having conducted, ages ago, at the time of Indian independence and soon thereafter, their doctoral research in this large linguistic and cultural region in central India.

Working toward a social history of the Satnamis for my MPhil dissertation, in unsteady yet insistent ways, the potentialities and problems of subaltern studies concerning temporalities came to the fore.

On the one hand, the analyses within the endeavor located the actions and apprehensions of these groups as entirely contemporaneous, formatively coeval, with the time-space of the British colony and the Indian nation. Thus, in his writings about the peasant insurgent in nineteenth-century India, especially through his criticism of the notion of the "pre-political," Guha rendered this historical subject as completely coeval with and a co-constituent of processes of politics under colonialism.[2] On the other hand, the sensibilities of a recuperative paternalism – alongside the procedures of a somewhat salvage scholarly style – meant that within the project the meanings and motivations of these peoples appeared filtered through the master distinction between community and state. The subalterns equally inhabited a distinct prior/a priori time, turning on an implicitly unchanging tradition, marked by a passive space, shaped by the dead hand of ruling culture. Thus, it was only when these subordinate groups claimed the "essence" of their initiatives in the shape of insurgency, an autonomous and truly emancipatory expressive moment involving a "prescriptive reversal" aimed at the complete subversion and erasure of the insignia of subalternity, that they emerged as being within, actually at the cutting edge of, the temporal stage of modern politics.[3]

Of course, I did not experience or express matters in quite this manner, but the intimations of uncertainty haunted as something of a shadowy presence. Indeed, far from being disabling, the ambiguity was productive. A sign of the times, the tension was fruitful. Now, alongside other theoretical tendencies, I critically engaged subaltern studies in order to build on their former sensibilities, which placed dispossessed protagonists as being formatively within history, while querying their later emphases that presented these subjects as, uncertainly, out of time.

Thus, seeking to understand Satnami articulations of the past, centered on their gurus/preceptors, I found in the group's myths a modality of historical consciousness which elaborated distinct conventions. Here were to be found renderings and procedures that accessed and exceeded, in their own way, Brahman kingly and popular devotional configurations, but also imperial and nationalist representations. Quite simply, Satnami conceptions of the past were entirely coeval with modern historiography, even holding a mirror up to its conceits, rather than signaling yet another exotic exception, as dictated by the imperatives of a hierarchical but singular temporality.[4] Similarly, focusing on colonial justice and village disputes in the Chhattisgarh region, what came to the fore were the contentious conversations, mutual imbrications, and formative face-offs between modern law/order and popular legalities/illegalities. That is to say, far from the indolent opposition between folk-disputing processes and Western adjudicatory rules, which temporally and spatially segregate these terrains, at stake were incessant entanglements between everyday norms, familiar desires, and alien pathologies.[5]

In hindsight, I was exploring processes that braided time, space, and their enmeshments. However, at the time the concerns centered, for instance, on the absolute, even arithmetic, antinomy between the elite and the subaltern. Now, read through the filters of patricians and plebs in eighteenth-century England or the contours of consciousness of African-American slave subjects in the US South,[6] this opposition within subaltern studies bracketed or short-circuited the making of subalterns and elites – indeed, of class, community, and gender – as relational processes. Further, there seemed to be a vacillation here between, on the one hand, a privileging of elementary codes, or underlying structures, governing subaltern action/insurgency and, on the other, a somewhat naive celebration of their ungoverned agency/autonomy. Filtered through debates on the relationship between agency and structure, especially as expressed in the work of Philip Abram, Pierre Bourdieu, and Anthony Giddens, such fluctuation appeared as analytically inadequate, profoundly problematic, and often unproductive.[7] Yet my point is that these easy oppositions and ambivalent analytics carried even wider implications. Although barely expressed in this manner, it was hard not to feel a lingering, latent disquiet toward uneasy determinations of singular hierarchical time – that indicated antinomian social spaces – within subaltern studies.[8]

Clearly, my research project – and wider academic interests – turned on the interplay between history and anthropology. It followed that I read enthusiastically in the emerging field of historical anthropology, particularly works exploring historicity and temporality, practice and process, meaning and power, in Africa and Oceania, Europe and the Americas. Now, it became clear that even as Indian anthropology, particularly its specialization from the 1950s onwards, was shored up by distinct disciplinary demarcations with history, exactly in this scenario, there were discrete efforts by some anthropologists to engage historical issues. At the same time, it was also evident that such efforts were less concerned with rethinking anthropology and history by blurring disciplinary boundaries and more with expressing conventional anthropological considerations by drawing on historical materials and understandings, many of which remained suspect to the professional historians of the time. Also, well into the 1960s, these efforts were often influenced by wider formulations of interactions between "great" and "little" traditions, between processes of "universalization" and "parochialization."[9] Held up by quasi-evolutionist schemas, these projections of an overarching Indian civilization unsteadily de-historicized the past and the present, principally rendering vacuous various grounded articulations of time and space, which all too readily turned upon one another.[10]

At the same time, I realized that the institutionalization and unraveling of professional history writing of the subcontinent had also proceeded at a distance from anthropological inquiry across most of the twentieth century.[11] Concerning the historiography of modern India, earlier studies of British administrators and administration were honed further yet also supplanted by fiercely contending scholarship on nationalism (and communalism), accounts that drew on the steadily increased availability from the early 1960s of previously classified materials.[12] This decade and the one following were further marked by impressive achievements in the writing of economic history, which had its corollaries for understandings of societal patterns.

From the middle of the 1960s, influenced by divergent strains of Marxism in the context of radical upheavals across the world, the social sciences witnessed a wider concern with the place of the peasantry in economic development, historical change, and revolutionary transformation.[13] These concerns had their effect on historical writing on peasant society, usually entailing questions of economic history yet also concerned with issues of culture and power. The impact extended to social-political histories on counter-colonial movements and popular nationalisms of peasant groupings, working classes, and adivasi (indigenous) communities.[14] As we saw, all of this set the stage for critical debates within history from the late 1970s onward that recast the discipline, including by raising new questions and initiating possible conversations, including with critical theory, sociological understandings, and ethnographic inquiry, thereby augmenting the study of South Asia.[15] However, two points stand out. On the one hand, prior to these transformations, productive engagements with anthropology were very rare in historical scholarship on modern India conducted on the subcontinent. On the other, as was noted, the articulations of time and space in the newer tendencies came with their twists and tendentiousness.

At the same time, from the beginning of the 1960s at any rate, the entanglements between these disciplines found varied articulations in the work of at least one scholar of South Asia. My reference is to the wide-ranging scholarship (and critical inspiration) of Bernard S. Cohn, who over time straddled and subverted the boundaries between anthropology and history.[16] Belonging to the first generation of postwar US anthropology that was trained to conduct sustained fieldwork in Indian villages, Cohn nonetheless resisted the lure of a purely synchronic study. For example, his doctoral work on the Chamars of the village of Senapur in North India, conducted in the 1950s, attended to processes of social change among these subalterns.[17] Within a matter of a few years, Cohn extended his inquiries into diverse questions of history and anthropology, based on varied crossovers between these disciplines.[18] Across the 1960s, these studies entailed explorations set in northern India concerning, for instance, the relationship between revenue policies and structural change, the levels of political integration in precolonial regimes, and the shaping of local life and legal practice by systems of colonial law. Most of this work rested on archival materials yet it was also influenced by Cohn's earlier fieldwork in the region.[19]

Such emphases were followed by other departures as Cohn shifted his attention more and more to "the historical anthropology of colonial society itself."[20] Here, Cohn's prior concern with investigating the historical bases of social relations in South Asia was not simply forgotten. Rather, it found newer configurations. For example, during the 1970s Cohn's work on the development and deployment of colonial knowledge of India engaged with the "ethnosociology" of his colleagues McKim Marriott and Ronald Inden.[21] Such dialogue is evident in Cohn's seminal essay on the Imperial Assemblage of 1877, held to proclaim Queen Victoria the Empress of India, where he explores the logics and forms of Indian society precisely as he elaborates the cultural constitution and historical transformation of rituals and symbols of colonial authority and imperial power.[22] Yet, it is also the case that Cohn came to increasingly recognize colonial cultures of rule as fundamentally restructuring Indian society. Together, in essays written after the 1980s on themes as diverse as colonial usages of language, the law, and clothing, Cohn focused on wide-ranging dynamics between knowledge and power and the colonizer and the colonized.[23] Cohn wrote two playful and provocative programmatic pieces charting the relationship between history and anthropology, which saw him at home in both these disciplines.[24] These garnered wide circulation, much as Evans-Pritchard's reflections on the theme had found a generation earlier. At the same time, it is in the entire body of Cohn's work that we find the several signposts and emergent formations of historical anthropology.

This is all the more true since Cohn's studies were frequently followed and sometimes accompanied by the work of other scholars on related questions, especially his students. Of course, such inquiries were often also influenced by other scholarly tendencies.[25] Nonetheless, they can all be seen as articulating a wider set of issues that had been brought to the fore by Cohn's writing, teaching, and supervision.[26] Here is to be found scholarship explicitly yet variously based on conjunctions between anthropology and history: from the study of patterns of social and economic transformation across the nineteenth and twentieth centuries in a single village in the Punjab through to explorations of the historical structure of local-level political groupings and their interactions with state governmental machinery in parts of northern India;[27] and from discussions of worlds of temples across time through to an "ethnohistory" of a "little kingdom," each of these works rethinking caste and kingship by focusing on royal and godly honors, favors, and services, including processes of their redistribution, which were constitutive of differential groups, ranks, and identities.[28] These departures were accompanied by other studies that also combined anthropology and history as part of distinct scholarly traditions. Such scholarship elaborated questions of sect, caste, and their transformations,[29] configurations of kinship and kingship in South India,[30] and the ideological nature of official and ethnographic (colonial) representations of India.[31]

Apprentice engagements

Unsurprisingly, for my PhD at the University of Cambridge and the book based on it, I sought out a dialogue between subaltern studies, historical anthropology, and the "everyday" as a critical perspective as I continued to research the Satnamis.[32] Now, various critical encounters and contingent entanglements – in the archive, the field, the library, and elsewhere – pointed me to the immense power encoded in the signs and symbols, metaphors and mappings, and practices and persuasions of the government and the state. Such authority crucially structured imaginings and endeavors of subaltern and community. These emphases ran counter to the central problematic that variously ran through subaltern studies. Two quick important illustrative examples should suffice.

Dipesh Chakrabarty's salient study of jute mill workers in eastern India issued an invitation for a critical understanding of the everyday experience of hierarchical relations in order to attend to forms of culture and consciousness, which were "the 'unthought' of Indian Marxism." This was the central question for the writing of working-class history in South Asian society where the assumptions of a hegemonic bourgeois culture did not apply. Nonetheless, Chakrabarty ended up exploring the culture and consciousness of Calcutta jute mill workers through innately a priori attributes entailing "strong primordial loyalties of community, language, religion, caste, and kinship," principally homeostatic features of a precapitalist society.[33] Similarly, Gyanendra Pandey's sustained critique of the construction of the colonial sociology of "communalism" seized upon community – defined quite simply as "Indian society beyond the confines of the state" – as the sign of alterity and difference, a sign that served to interrogate dominant knowledge(s) of colony, nation, state, and history.[34] Here, precisely by holding the two apart, the presence of difference/community was read as opposing formations of power/state. This served to uncertainly upbraid and uphold an exclusive historical temporality, exactly through acute expressions of segregated spaces of community/difference and state/power, with the former taking epistemological and ethical priority over the latter.

Against the grain of such influential emphases, my work tracked the entanglements between community/subaltern/difference and state/dominance/power in at least four overlapping ways.[35] First, the very making of the Satnami caste-sect endeavor was shaped by these enmeshed dynamics of meaning and power, which articulated and interrogated the interweaving of divine, ritual, social, and governmental hierarchies, as well as their attendant temporal and spatial matrices. Second, at stake were the ways in which the patterns of power within arrangements of caste involved the formative braiding of pervasive protocols of authority, at once substantive and symbolic, turning on ritual purity and pollution, cultural kingship and dominant castes, and colonial governance and law. Third, the historical conceptions of the Satnamis – embodied in their mythic and other representations – arrived at distinct spaces of sect/caste and novel temporalities of order/legality by negotiating and querying figures of dominance, which orchestrated the necessarily enmeshed "cosmic" and "social" worlds. Fourth and finally, these orientations toward authority and alterity found different but overlapping expressions as part of Satnami organizational endeavors within Indian nationalism, especially as I sieved middle-class presumptions through subaltern imaginaries in these arenas, thereby revealing alternative glimmers of legality and legitimacy, politics and nation(s).[36]

At the core of my research, then, lay the incessant interpenetration between constitutive aspects of state/governmental power and quotidian forms of subaltern/community life. These enmeshments straddled and scrambled a singular hierarchical temporality and its attendant antinomian spaces. It is exactly such entanglements that were frequently kept at a distance in the anthropology and history of South Asia, as witnessed in important work on the subcontinent. At issue were pervasive procedures of the spatialization of time and the temporalization of space, which served to split apart subaltern and state, community and history, tradition and modernity, and emotion and reason as embodying separate spaces through the assumption of an exclusive temporality. At the same time, it is once more the case that none of this appeared to me as a blazing revelation. Rather, these intimations unfolded little by little, bit by bit.

Here, a crucial role has been played by a project on evangelical entanglements in imperial India, which had found its first intimations at the time of my PhD – when I conducted archival work in missionary archives in the US (and Britain) – and which became my first postdoctoral research endeavor, a month after I had submitted my doctoral dissertation. This is a study of American evangelical missionaries and their Indian Christian converts in colonial and independent India. Combining archival and field research, ethnographic and historical perspectives – that are further conjoined with considerations of social theory – the aim of the endeavor is at least threefold. First, it discusses the interleaving of evangelical activities and converts' practices with formations of caste-sect and the dynamics of village life. The contentious enmeshments shaped the mission project and a vernacular Christianity. Second, the endeavor considers the conjunctions and contradictions between the mission project and imperial power, evangelical initiatives and "home" congregations, and a vernacular Christianity and colonial cultures. Such fraught linkages underlay critical articulations of modernity, evangelism, and empire. Third and finally, the study explores wide-ranging expressions of community and nation in the wake of conversion. These underscore controversial issues of the "majority" and the "minority," politics and religion, and the citizen and the convert, especially in independent India. These processes each appear molded by distinctions of gender and caste, race and community.[37]

If this is how the study has developed over the last two decades, it is also the case that from its very beginnings my concerns stood at odds with much scholarship on South Asia, including especially the uneasy demarcations of time and space in subaltern studies. Consider now my emphases concerning the acute entanglements between missionary and convert, colonizer and colonized, the dominant and the subaltern, colonial cultures and vernacular Christianity, empire and modernity, and power and difference, shored up by overlapping yet heterogeneous articulations of time and space. Away from the mutual constitution of these critical copulas by their constitutive elements as well as each other, the work of subaltern studies principally rested on keeping the segments apart, bringing into play temporal-spatial demarcations, as the following examples illustrate.

To begin with, we have noted that Ranajit Guha (and subaltern studies at large) presented the nineteenth-century subaltern insurgent as temporally coeval with British colonialism on the subcontinent. Although at once undercut by uncertain temporal-spatial demarcations of the South Asian peasant, the analytical measure principally intimated the possibilities of approaching the subaltern in imperial (and independent) India as a subject of modernity, and consequently of understanding modernity itself in newer ways. But this did not come to pass. Only a few years later, Guha made a case for "dominance without hegemony" in colonial India, positing an archetype of bourgeois hegemony where persuasion outweighs coercion in the composition of its dominance.[38] On offer was the classic prototype of the hegemonic liberal state representing a revolutionary bourgeoisie and democratic politics in metropolitan Britain, against which stood the hapless instance of dominance without hegemony in colonial India.

Shaped by immaculate assumptions of a vigorous democratic culture and a vital liberal politics of the modern West, Guha's analytics rendered the central historical narrative of power on the subcontinent under colonial rule as one of failure and lack.[39] Evacuated of their own particularity, the meaning of these pasts of dominance inhered innately in their ever lagging behind the time and space of Europe. In these teleological projections of colonial pasts and metropolitan histories, the incomplete transitions of the former appeared routinely measured against the fulsome trajectories of the latter, so that each shored up the other. At stake here are articulations of an exclusive hierarchical temporality that spatially segregates Britain and India, the empire and its outpost, the West and the Rest.[40] Put simply, all of this was quite contrary to my attempts to explore the common constitution and reciprocal labor of modernity and colonialism in the metropolis and the margins, as well as the orientations to the temporal, the spatial, and their enmeshments intimated by these emphases.

This brings me to the second example. Partha Chatterjee's influential book, *The Nation and its Fragments*, critically locates forms of community within regimes of modernity, rather than reifying these as "pre-modern remnants that an absent-minded Enlightenment forgot to erase."[41] (This is a fact often overlooked in careless readings of the work.) The move makes it possible for Chatterjee to construe forceful readings that think through the categories of the state and civil society, while equally allowing him to suggest other imaginings of community, nation(s), and modernity. At the same time, it is also the case that such possibilities in Chatterjee's work are at once upheld *and* undercut by two measures: first, the sharp separation that he sets up between state and community, which totally brackets any interchange between symbols of state and contours of community; second, his remarkable assertion that "by its very nature, the idea of community marks a limit to the realm of disciplinary power."[42] Taken together, in *The Nation and its Fragments* the precise glimmers of newer orientations to modernity and community cannot be separated from the work's postulations regarding the potential of modernity as being realized through the virtue of community, which insinuates a pure difference, an unsullied alterity.

To learn from both the possibilities and the problems of the work requires at least two measures. On the one hand, it is imperative to attend to Chatterjee's implicit interrogation of an exclusive modernity, centered on state and capital, as exhausting all modern imaginaries and actions. This is a critique conducted in the name of community, but one that has rather wider implications. On the other, it is crucial to register that the work's assertion of a single historical time of community and state is principally a narrative ruse, a temporal placeholder for political modernity that is then filled with two competing storylines. Here, saliently, community/difference is premised upon an epistemological and ethical *priority and precedence* over capital/power: at their core, these contending categories insinuate sharply separate essences, distinct spatial-temporal loci.

Journeyman entanglements

Actually, several of these concerns were gradually clarified on my joining the faculty of the Center of Asian and African Studies at El Colegio de México and moving to live in Mexico City from the mid-1990s. Here, an overlapping yet distinct set of concerns now equally came to the fore. I soon realized that in Latin American worlds, Asia and Africa were filtered through rather particular, somewhat peculiar, optics of space and time. This was true of everyday arenas and scholarly spaces. With (mestizo) Latin America uncertainly yet readily poised in the likeness of a reified modern West, Africa's and Asia's cultural/spatial difference and temporal/social otherness, working in tandem, signified a mark of enchantment, *algo bello* (something beautiful); but their political-economic backwardness, entailing a time lag, also embodied a historical holdup, a lack of modernity, a temporal social-spatial inferiority, *algo feo* (something ugly). Thinking through these simultaneous spatial/temporal distinctions, I engaged scholarship on the coloniality/decoloniality of power as well as a range of other vital writing on/from the south of the Rio Grande. Indeed, as I worked toward juxtaposing and connecting critical understandings of Latin America and South Asia, especially in teaching, it was modernity and its multiple linkages with the Enlightenment and empire, reason and race, and colonies (settler and non-settler) and nations that emerged as apposite arenas of conversation.

Questions of colonialism have been apprehended in Latin America as occupying a dim and distant past. After two centuries of formal freedom, modernity is ever understood as an attribute of the independent nation, unconnected with empire, which is a far-off time, a strange space, an all-but-forgotten episode and entity, except among specialist scholars. At the same time, it soon became equally evident that, following a Baroque aesthetic, the pasts of the colonial quotidian are also often presented in these terrains in celebratory ways, such that markers of space represent the triumph of history, conjoining it with the here and now. Thus Coyoacán, the sixteenth-century *colonia* (neighborhood) where we live, has frequently been joyously described to us by delighted well-wishers as being, well, "muy colonial [very colonial]."

Against these dominant dispositions, an important body of critical thought on Latin America has focused on the subterranean schemes, the pervasive presumptions, and the overwrought apparitions of the modern and the colonial.[43] This corpus takes as its starting point the first modernity of Southern Europe – as held together by the Renaissance, the conquest of the "New World," and the empires of Spain and Portugal – in the margins and the metropolis. It thereby critically considers the place and presence of colonial stipulations of power within modern provisions of knowledge. The writings no less work their way through the second modernity of the Global North, constituted by empires of the Enlightenment and thereafter, holding up a mirror to modernity as a deeply ideological project and a primary apparatus of domination, in the past, present, and posterity. Here, the recursive possibility of secular-messianic redemption often appears as an exclusive future horizon.[44]

Now, these emphases have formidably foregrounded the Eurocentric propensities and epistemic violence of modernity that is already/always colonial, further underscoring the importance of other forms of gnosis and knowing that reveal horizons other than those of the dominant Western modern.[45] On the other hand, the unraveling by these writings of the "coloniality of power" and "decoloniality of knowledge" is founded on presumptions of the innately dystopian nature of the former and the ethically utopian possibilities of the latter.[46] These carry profoundly temporal and spatial implications. I shall base my discussion around the arguments and implications of the Argentine philosopher,

Enrique Dussel, in order to unravel the emphases of the coloniality/decoloniality perspective, turning on space and time.

Crucial for Dussel are the writings of Emmanuel Levinas concerning ethics, alterity, and exteriority.[47] For Levinas, as is generally known, the "other" is a constitutive haunting presence which relationally reveals the limits and horizons of "self," such that "ethics [was] the first philosophy" rather than epistemology or, say, the Heideggerian ontology of "Being."[48] Now, Dussel transforms these innately emergent, necessarily nonempirical attributes of the ethical "encounter between the Same and what forever remains exterior to it" into split and substantialized spaces with concrete geopolitical, factual referents, namely, Europe and Latin America.[49] In this scenario, it is not only that Latin America is ever temporally contemporaneous with Europe/Euro-America, revealing the dark side of the latter. It is also that Latin America, a unitary space that readily subsumes as well the self of the philosopher, is already/always ethically ahead of Europe, which is a space of unethical hegemony, articulating the colonial dimensions of modern power.

All of this has wide implications. To start with, Dussel's singular split between Europe and Latin America – alongside the exclusive emphasis on the "coloniality of power" – was too pat, too ready, too tendentious. Unsurprisingly, it came to be supplanted soon by the geopolitical, spatial-moral contrast between Europe/Euro-American hegemony and the "other [or subaltern] side of colonial difference," variously named as "trans-modernity," "border knowledge," and "de-colonial perspectives."[50] At the same time, these ethically segregated entities continue to enact, within a shared historical stage, a principled drama, an endless clash between good and bad, virtue and evil, morality and immorality.

Moreover, while Dussel's original claims concerned a supersession of phenomenology by an ethically oriented politics (recall Levinas's proclamation of "ethics as first philosophy"), under the decolonial turn the primacy of ethics and politics means that they appear elided, implicitly and a priori, with epistemology and ontology, reading/writing and being/becoming, as ways of knowing and acting, an antidote to authority before the dystopia of power. Put differently, the "subaltern side of colonial difference" has principled precedence (and always triumphs) over the "coloniality of power." Here, decolonial scholars not only take the side of but are *already the same as* critical bearers of subjugated knowledge(s), all inhabitants of geopolitical margins.

Finally, the logics of such segregated spaces in these understandings orchestrate time and temporality in distinct ways. On the one hand, the temporal appears here as something of a chronological placeholder, defining the innate coevality of modernity/coloniality and its others. Saliently, such simultaneity signals discrete verities. While forms of colonialism, modernity, and nation evince juridical-political shifts and transformations, coloniality of power has innately unchanging attributes. Alongside this, the other/subaltern side of coloniality, including decolonial perspectives, might have heterogeneous manifestations, but their core logic inheres in unceasing interrogations of modernity/coloniality and heroic articulations of pluriversality/diversality. This is because decolonizing perspectives have innate, a priori *precedence* – in terms of ethics and politics, knowing and being – over modern power.[51] On the other hand, time can be cast in this corpus as a category of reckoning and not of experience, attributed to "culture" and not to "nature". Time is explicitly articulated as a central concept of the imaginary of the colonial/modern world system, entirely interwoven with the coloniality of power and the production of colonial difference.[52] However, this querying of time as colonization, as reckoning and representation, while opening critical possibilities, nonetheless remains circumscribed through the positing of the ethical/epistemic/ontological incommensurables that were explored above. It seeks to find entirely *other* expressions of space/time rather than staying with, thinking through, their formative heterogeneity as practice and production in social worlds at large.

Put simply, I was excited by the problems proffered, but uncertain about the answers offered, by this formidable corpus.[53] The conjoint impulses had wider consequences. Grappling with the issues and arguments outlined above – a process of implicit unease rather than ready resolution – I realized the importance of approaching postcolonial perspectives and subaltern studies in a critical yet cautious way. From their beginnings, these understandings have been characterized by intellectual silences and theoretical tensions which circulate amid their formative plurality.[54] Reading these writings alongside critical work on Latin America crucially brought home to me that to understand these scholarly tendencies as shaped by key contentions is far from a disparaging move. Rather, it is to actually acknowledge the conditions of possibility of subaltern studies and postcolonial perspectives. It has followed, too, that such bids to simultaneously think through their limitations and potentialities, the one braided with the other, require that these knowledge formations be considered in the manner of critical rubrics, rather than readily hypostatized as privileged perspectives and exclusive inquiries. To take these simultaneous steps has been to discover heterogeneous interpretive dispositions that bear productive articulation with other theoretical orientations, especially those offering critical considerations of time, space, disciplines, and modernity.

On the one hand, the persistent contentions of the postcolonial and the subaltern as categories and perspectives register unproductive ambiguity. Actually, this unhelpful obscurity is intimately linked to the simultaneous exclusive claims made on behalf of these knowledge formations. Apparent certainty and actual ambivalence regarding demarcations of time and space both have an important role here. Thus, as has been repeatedly emphasized by prominent postcolonial critics among others, the concept of the postcolonial has rested upon the divide between the colonial and the postcolonial.[55] Here, an entirely exclusive temporal trajectory and formidably split social spaces mutually sustain one another, such that narrative ruses of historical time lead from one totalized terrain (the colonial) to another undifferentiated arena (the postcolonial). This serves to homogenize critical difference, instate historical hierarchy, elide unequal social spaces, and sanitize postcolonial politics.

Yet there is more at stake. For, at the very moment postcolonial understandings cast the colonizer and colonized as inhabiting a common history, undoing temporal hierarchies among them, they implicitly sharply segregate the habitations of Europe, its proper space-time, from that of the colony, which is accorded an exclusive epistemic revelatory priority. And so is it also worth asking whether the charges against subaltern studies of empirical imprecision, analytical aggrandizement, and epistemological obfuscation are not, actually, closely linked to presumptions that the perspectives constitute unified, fully finished understandings? Rather than rely on such easy assumption, is it not important to stay with and think through the constitutive limits and formative possibilities that shore up the heterogeneity, the contention, and the curious elision and expression of space and time within subaltern (and postcolonial) studies?

On the other hand, across different scholarly disciplines and diverse academic contexts, various endeavors engaging and articulating postcolonial and subaltern perspectives, broadly understood, can be cautiously read and understood as having undertaken salient tasks. To begin with, such efforts have variously rethought empire. Especially important here have been pointers to the prior and persistent play of colonial schemes in contemporary worlds. These emphases have highlighted the immense import and ongoing influence of the enmeshments between Enlightenment and empire, race and reason, the metropolis and the margins, and religion and politics. Moreover, as noted earlier, writings in this terrain have severally questioned the place of an imaginary yet palpable West as history, modernity, and destiny for each culture and every people. This has suggested newer understandings of community, history, and modernity which have challenged prior modular conceptions of these categories-entities. Finally, endeavors elaborating subaltern and postcolonial perspectives have unraveled the terms and limits of state, nation, and citizen in Western and non-Western worlds, prudently underscoring the significance of critical difference in such distinct yet entangled terrain.[56]

Indeed, in taking up the tasks outlined above, the most prescient efforts have pointed to the critical place and presence not only of elite and heroic protagonists, but of marginal and subaltern subjects – simultaneously shaped by the crisscrossing matrices of gender and race, caste and class, age and office, community and sexuality – in the making of colony and modernity, empire and nation, religion and politics, and state and citizen. To register such critical developments is to cast postcolonial propositions and subaltern studies – in constant conversation with historical anthropology and social theory – as participant interlocutors in wider ongoing debates rethinking the nation-state and the West, the colony and the post-colony, and history and modernity, including especially their socio-spatial-temporal attributes.[57]

Some of what I have been saying about reading for possibilities and limitations of critical understandings – including decolonial, postcolonial, and subaltern perspectives – can be clarified by considering the work of Dipesh Chakrabarty which offers salient reflections on history and modernity, articulating questions of space and time. To begin with, he has imaginatively raised key questions concerning the presence of Europe in the writing of history. Carefully constructing his arguments against the backdrop of Heidegger's interrogation of the artifice of a meaning-legislating reason, Chakrabarty has focused on "history" as a discourse that is produced at the institutional sites of academe, making a compelling case for the ways in which Europe remains the sovereign theoretical subject of all histories. Admitting that "Europe" and "India" are "hyper-real" terms that refer to certain figures of the imagination, Chakrabarty critically points toward how – in the "phenomenal world" of everyday relationships of power – Europe stands reified and celebrated as the site and scene of the birth of the modern, working as a silent referent that dominates the discourse of history. Unraveling the consequences of this routine privileging of Europe as the universal centerpiece of modernity and history, Chakrabarty reveals how the past and present of India or Mexico – indeed, of all that is not quite an imaginary yet tangible West – come to be cast in terms of irrevocable principles of failure, lack, and absence, since they are always/already measured against apparent developments in European/Euro-American arenas.[58]

These are outcomes of developmental regimes of time, temporality, and history that Chakrabarty frames as "historicism": a pervasive mode of thinking and manner of knowing, which appears intimately implicated in social-scientific understandings and wider historical practice. Based on the principle of "secular, empty, homogeneous time," historicism has found acute articulations since the nineteenth century, when it made possible "the European domination of the world."[59] Here are to be found, then, key queries concerning a singular yet hierarchizing time that splits social words into "developed" spaces and "backward" ones. Indeed, Chakrabarty further opens up questions of historical difference, revealing glimmers of heterogeneous temporal-spatial terrains through various measures: explorations of the deferral-difference of a Bengali modernity in colonial India; discussions of the time of gods and the writing of history; and avowals of the plurality of lifeworlds against an overweening historicism.[60]

At the same time, it is worth considering the closures that accompany the opening up of these questions by Chakrabarty. Thus, he imaginatively attempts to "write difference into the history of our [Bengali/Indian] modernity in a mode that resists the assimilation of this history to the political imaginary of European-derived institutions ... which dominate our lives." Nonetheless, Chakrabarty ends up by replicating a priori attributes of the principal categories that lie at the heart of the "epistemic violence" he seeks to challenge and interrogate.[61] This is because the gendered domains of the public and the domestic, the key concepts of personhood and the civil-political, and indeed the opposed categories of state and community, seemingly derived from a master scheme of modern history, appear as always there, already in place, under every modernity. Here is a rendering of difference *against, into,* and *ahead* of discipline. Exactly this manner of reading continues into Chakrabarty's attempt to recuperate the difference of subaltern pasts (and the time of gods and spirits) in front of the discipline of minority histories (and the work of the radical historian), and in his bid to articulate the alterity of "necessarily fragmentary histories of human belonging that never constitute a one or a whole" as existing alongside yet exceeding the authority of historicism.[62]

How are these measures connected to questions of time and space? Consider now pervasive constructivism(s), ever in the air, that project totalities and universals as principally insubstantial because they are socially constructed. Against these presumptions, Chakrabarty rightly sees totalizing universals, their disciplines and logics, as actually existing.[63] Yet, it warrants asking if this acceptance overlooks the making of these universals in relation to particulars, of totalities in relation to margins, entailing processes of meaning and power, acutely producing space and time. Do these measures reading difference against, into, and ahead of discipline – bracketing their mutual fabrications and productions – result in analytically segregated spaces, whose sociopolitical attributes derive from their epistemic bases? Does Chakrabarty query the aggrandizing terms of homogeneous time yet accept the ruptures of modernity on which they are founded?

Latter-day enmeshments

As I reach the end of this personal narrative, it is time to tie together my uncertain yet insistent apprehensions of time and space, unraveled above, with issues of their usual understandings, hegemonic representations, and quotidian productions, which were broached in the last chapter. Especially important in these considerations is the production of space-time within academic practice as itself a species of everyday activity.[64] Such construal through epistemological action occurs in dialogue with routine and hegemonic apprehensions of space and time quite as it articulates underlying terms of power and difference. Here, the first formations of subaltern studies were founded on dominant singular yet hierarchizing temporal and spatial representations that located (passive) subaltern groups and their governing (feudal) cultures of rule in times and spaces that lay behind those of modern politics. However, acutely interrogating the pre-political and political divide, on offer equally were instantiations of novel temporal-spatial matrices: but only once the subalterns broke through the codes that governed their passivity, since in place now were entirely autonomous expressions that were not merely coeval with, but at the cutting edge of, modern democratic politics.

Such production of time-space as part of knowledge-making activity continued through the broader opposition between community and state within subaltern studies. This was the case whether, through principally antimodernist measures, the temporal-spatial valences of modernity were inverted to find communities (and fragments) rooted in custom as triumphing over nation-state (and history);[65] or, through recourse to Foucault's spatial-temporal distinction between prior authority and modern power, the cultures of hierarchy of Indian subalterns, grounded in custom, were shown as querying the hegemonic assumptions of historiographical discipline;[66] or, community was placed at the heart of modernity in ways in which innate virtues of community and difference became antidotes to endless aggrandizements of capital and state.[67] In each instance, the hegemonic spatial-temporal blueprints of modernity, as analytical template and chronological placeholder, were accessed yet also exceeded: community, subaltern, fragment, and difference were now accorded ethical and political priority, epistemological and interpretive precedence, over capital, state-nation, history, and power. At stake was the epistemic fabrication of space-time, insinuating an alterity ahead of authority, as part of the everyday practice of subaltern studies.

Actually, these presumptions and protocols of subaltern studies hesitantly unfolded as linked to wider dispositions to difference and power within anti- and post-foundational understandings. Quite simply, here are orientations that render power – of state, nation, empire, modernity, patriarchy, or discipline – as dystopian totality, frequently a distant enemy. Against this, on offer is the work of difference – of community, subaltern, alterity, border, and margin – as "unrecuperated particulars," ever an antidote to depredations of dystopia.[68] Much more than formal analytics, we are in the face of structures of sensibility, tissues of sentiment, which then undergird critical orthodoxies, also underlying their distinct production of time and space in the quotidian key.[69] If the antinomies of community and state within the labor of subaltern studies provide one illustration, decolonial perspectives proffer another apposite example of such elaborations.

As was explored above, in these dispositions space stands configured in mainly bounded or relatively open ways and time can be rendered as a chiefly neutral chronological framework or a highly normative colonizing device. Yet the ethical, epistemological, political, and indeed affective force of arguments for/of decoloniality derive from the manner in which they actively produce, as image and practice, the discrete moral locations of "the subaltern [or other] side of colonial difference" as unvaryingly ahead of – bearing principled precedence and a priori priority over – the dystopian spatial-temporal coordinates of "modernity/coloniality" that seek to overwhelm all in their wake. Indeed, as sentiment, sensibility, and spirit, the split between authority and alterity has formidable force. This means, too, that a scholar such as Dipesh Chakrabarty, having been formed once within such imaginaries, might not now subscribe to discipline as distant enemy and look beyond difference as essentially heroic, yet in practice must segregate the two. Here are to be found epistemic productions of space-time, of difference and discipline, which often actually coalesce but whose exact analytical separation allows the presence of the former to be read into/against the claims of the latter, such that formidable radical heterogeneity faces up to inescapable critical singularity.

These considerations foreground two sets of critical questions. On the one hand, what is at stake in critically exploring terms of power and dominant knowledge(s) without turning these into totalized terrain? Are attempts to pluralize power – for example, the forces of colonialism and capitalism, the stipulations of globalization and modernity – mere exercises in the empirical and conceptual refinement of these categories? Alternatively, do they also imply an "ontological turn," not only pointing to the problem of "what entities are presupposed" by theories and worldviews, but also carefully questioning "those 'entities' presupposed by our typical ways of seeing and doing in the modern world"?[70] What is the place of the particular, of "details" in unraveling the determinations of power and difference?[71] How are we to learn from yet reach beyond newer critical orthodoxies that render dominant categories as dystopian totalities?[72] Put briefly, what are the terms and textures of understanding power as shaped by difference, of authority as inflected by alterity?

On the other hand, what distinctions of meaning and power come to the fore through the elaboration of tradition and community, the local and the subaltern as oppositional categories? Must such contending categories inhabit the locus of "unrecuperated particulars" as a priori antidotes to authority in the mirrors of critical understandings?[73] How are we to articulate the dense sensuousness and the acute mix-ups of social life, not only to query cut-and-dried categories and modular schemes of ordering the world, but also to think through axiomatic projections of resistant difference that abound in the here and now, characterizing scholarly apprehensions and commonplace conceptions? Put simply, what is at stake in understanding the determination of difference as stamped by the productivity of power, of subaltern formations as bearing the impress of dominant designs? These questions run through *Subjects of Modernity*.

Notes

1 Ranajit Guha, "The prose of counter-insurgency," in Ranajit Guha (ed.), *Subaltern Studies II: Writings on South Asian History and Society* (Delhi: Oxford University Press, 1983), pp. 1–42; Ranajit Guha, *Elementary Aspects of Peasant Insurgency in Colonial India* (Delhi: Oxford University Press, 1983); Spivak, "Subaltern studies: deconstructing historiography"; and Rosalind O'Hanlon, "Recovering the subject: subaltern studies and histories of resistance in colonial South Asia," *Modern Asian Studies*, 22 (1988): 189–224.

2 Guha, *Elementary Aspects*. Such a reading of Guha's work on the insurgent peasant in colonial India was powerfully developed later in Chakrabarty, *Habitations of Modernity*, especially pp. 8–14. However, Chakrabarty does not stay longer with the tensions in this work as well as in Guha's other writings.

3 Guha, *Elementary Aspects*.

4 Saurabh Dube, "Social history of Satnamis of Chhattigarh," unpublished MPhil dissertation (University of Delhi, 1988); some of this work was later embodied in Saurabh Dube, "Myths, symbols, and community: Satnampanth of Chhattisgarh," in Partha Chatterjee and Gyanendra Pandey (eds.), *Subaltern Studies VII: Writings on South Asian History and Society* (Delhi: Oxford University Press, 1992), pp. 121–56.

5 Dube, "Social history"; Saurabh Dube, "Telling tales and trying truths: transgressions, entitlements and legalities in village disputes, late colonial central India," *Studies in History*, 13 (1996): 171–201.

6   E. P. Thompson, *Customs in Common: Studies in Traditional Popular Culture* (New York, The New Press, 1993); Lawrence Levine, *Black Culture and Consciousness: Afro-American Folk Thought from Slavery to Freedom* (Oxford: Oxford University Press, 1977); Eugene Genovese, *Roll, Jordan, Roll: The World the Slaves Made* (New York: Pantheon, 1974).
7   Anthony Giddens, *Central Problems in Social Theory: Action, Structure, and Contradiction in Social Analysis* (Berkeley: University of California Press, 1979); Bourdieu, *Outline of a Theory*; Philip Abrams, *Historical Sociology* (Shepton Mallet: Open Books, 1982).
8   I admit to space having been for me then a somewhat nebulous, hazy idea, except for its articulations in Bourdieu, *Outline of a Theory*.
9   Robert Redfield, *Peasant, Society, and Culture* (Chicago, IL: University of Chicago Press, 1956).
10 Here important work included the study of patterns of "local" history in North Indian bardic castes and their genealogical accounts, the social structure of a village in early nineteenth-century western India, and historical linkages between state formation, royal myths, and tribal integration. Not all such writings were (equally) influenced by the "great" and "little" traditions paradigm. See, respectively, Mckim Marriott, "Village structure and the Punjab government: a restatement," *American Anthropologist*, 55 (1953): 137–43; A. M. Shah and R. G. Shroff, "The Vahivancha Barots of Gujarat: a caste of genealogists and mythographers," in Milton Singer (ed.), *Traditional India: Structure and Change* (Philadelphia, PA: American Folklore Society, 1959), pp. 40–70; A. M. Shah, *Exploring India's Rural Past: A Gujarat Village in the Early Nineteenth Century* (New Delhi: Oxford University Press, 2002), which is based on earlier research; and Surajit Sinha, "State formation and Rajput myth in tribal central India," *Man in India*, 42 (1962): 25–80. These emphases came to be extended in the 1970s to explorations, set in precolonial middle India, of the formations of myth, legend, and kinship in royal genealogy as well as of social structure, kingship, territory, and property in these regions. See, for example, K. S. Singh (ed.), *Tribal Situation in India* (Shimla: Indian Institute of Advanced Study, 1972), and Ravindra K. Jain, *Between History and Legend: Status and Power in Bundelkhand* (Hyderabad: Orient Longman, 2002), which contains several essays written in the 1970s.

11 For a survey, see Sumit Sarkar, *Writing Social History* (Delhi: Oxford University Press, 1997), ch. 1; see also Partha Chatterjee, "Introduction: history and the present," in Partha Chatterjee and Anjan Ghosh (eds.), *History and the Present* (New Delhi: Permanent Black, 2002), pp. 1–23. In different ways, Sarkar and Chatterjee both point to the existence of social histories in vernacular idioms that have for at least a century now existed outside of the canons of professional history writing. Such issues require further examination.

12 It bears emphasis that since independence the developments in the study of ancient and medieval Indian history have been rich and revealing, including the more recent emphasis on "social formations" in this terrain, but only a few scholars in these fields have engaged the terms of anthropology. I discuss this issue in Dube, "Anthropology, history, historical anthropology."

13 Indeed, social scientists could turn toward the historical record to explicate considerations of peasant societies and movements. See, for example, Kathleen Gough, *Rural Society in Southeast India* (Cambridge: Cambridge University Press, 1981); D. N. Dhanagre, *Peasant Movements in India, 1920–1950* (Delhi: Oxford University Press, 1983); and Hetukar Jha, *Social Structures of Indian Villages: A Study of Rural Bihar* (New Delhi: Sage, 1991).

14 For example, Ravinder Kumar (ed.), *Essays on Gandhian Politics: The Rowlatt Satyagraha of 1919* (Oxford: Clarendon Press, 1971); Gyanendra Pandey, *The Ascendancy of the Congress in Uttar Pradesh, 1926–1934: A Study in Imperfect Mobilization* (Oxford: Clarendon Press, 1978); David Hardiman, *Peasant Nationalists of Gujarat: Kheda District 1917–1934* (Delhi: Oxford University Press, 1981); and Majid Siddiqi, *Agrarian Unrest in North India: The United Provinces, 1918–22* (New Delhi: Vikas, 1978).

15 Bernard Cohn, "The command of language and the language of command," in Guha (ed.), *Subaltern Studies IV*, pp. 276–329; Veena Das, "Subaltern as perspective," in Ranajit Guha (ed.), *Subaltern Studies VI: Writings on South Asian History and Society* (Delhi: Oxford University Press, 1989), pp. 310–24; Upendra Baxi, "'The state's emissary': the place of law in subaltern studies," in Chatterjee and Pandey (eds.), *Subaltern*

Studies VII, pp. 257–64. See also Sherry Ortner, "Resistance and the problem of ethnographic refusal," *Comparative Studies in Society and History*, 37 (1995): 173–93.

16 For different assessments of Cohn's work, see Nicholas Dirks, "Foreword," in Bernard Cohn, *Colonialism and its Forms of Knowledge: The British in India* (Princeton, NJ: Princeton University Press, 1996), pp. ix–xvii.; Axel, "Introduction: historical anthropology," especially pp. 7–9; and Ranajit Guha, "Introduction," in Bernard Cohn, *An Anthropologist among the Historians and Other Essays* (Delhi: Oxford University Press, 1987), pp. vii–xxvi.

17 Cohn, *Anthropologist among the Historians*, chs. 11 and 12.

18 Bernard Cohn, *India: The Social Anthropology of a Civilization* (Englewood Cliffs, NJ: Prentice-Hall, 1971).

19 Cohn, *Anthropologist among the Historians*.

20 Dirks, "Foreword," p. xii.

21 Some among Cohn's anthropologist colleagues working on South Asia at the University of Chicago also addressed questions of temporality and history in distinct ways. See, for instance, Ronald B. Inden, *Marriage and Rank in Bengali Culture: A History of Caste and Clan in Middle Period Bengal* (Berkeley: University of California Press, 1976); Milton B. Singer, *When a Great Tradition Modernizes: An Anthropological Approach to Indian Civilization* (New York: Praeger, 1972). See also Milton B. Singer and Bernard Cohn (eds.), *Structure and Change in Indian Society* (Chicago, IL: Aldine, 1968).

22 Cohn, *Anthropologist among the Historians*, ch. 23.

23 Cohn, *Colonialism and its Forms of Knowledge*.

24 Bernard Cohn, "History and anthropology: the state of play," *Comparative Studies in Society and History*, 22 (1980): 198–221, and "Anthropology and history in the 1980s: towards a rapprochement," *Journal of Interdisciplinary History*, 12 (1981): 227–52.

25 All these understandings discussed below, not unlike some of Cohn's own writings, frequently carried echoes and resonances of dominant disciplinary notations of time and mappings of space. These require a separate discussion, which I cannot offer here. The point is that work in historical anthropology should not be seen as easily, inexorably, solving problems of the temporalization of space and the spatialization of time.

26 It is important to note that the impact of Cohn's work was equally felt in the world of historiography. Such impact can be traced from the manner in which his writings – on the census, for example – could open up specific fields of research through to the ways they served to orient wider terms of historical inquiry. Cohn, *Anthropologist among the Historians*, ch. 10; Frank F. Conlon, *A Caste in the Changing World: The Chitrapur Saraswat Brahmans, 1700–1935* (Berkeley: University of California Press, 1977); David Lelyveld, *Aligarh's First Generation: Muslim Solidarity in British India* (Princeton, NJ: Princeton University Press, 1978).

27 Tom G. Kessinger, *Vilyatpur 1848–1968: Social and Economic Change in a North Indian Village* (Berkeley: University of California Press, 1974); Richard G. Fox, *Kin, Clan, Raja and Rule* (Berkeley: University of California Press, 1971). See also Richard G. Fox (ed.), *Realm and Region in Traditional India* (Durham, NC: Duke University Press, 1977).

28 Arjun Appadurai, *Worship and Conflict under Colonial Rule: A South Indian Case* (Cambridge: Cambridge University Press, 1982); Arjun Appadurai and Carol Breckenridge, "The South Indian temple: authority, honour, and redistribution," *Contributions to Indian Sociology* [n.s.], 10 (1976): 187–211; Nicholas Dirks, *The Hollow Crown: Ethnohistory of an Indian Kingdom* (Cambridge: Cambridge University Press, 1987). This is of course an indicative list. Other writings intimating distinct emphases and arenas include Paul Greenough, *Prosperity and Misery in Modern Bengal* (New York: Oxford University Press, 1982); Richard G. Fox, *Lions of the Punjab: Culture in the Making* (Berkeley: University of California Press, 1985); and Nita Kumar, *The Artisans of Banaras: Popular Culture and Identity, 1880–1986* (Princeton, NJ: Princeton University Press, 1988).

29 Richard Burghart, *The Conditions of Listening: Essays on Religion, History, and Politics in India*, ed. C. J. Fuller and Jonathan Spencer (Delhi: Oxford University Press, 1996); Peter van der Veer, *Gods on Earth: The Management of Religious Experience and Identity in a North Indian Pilgrimage Centre* (Delhi: Oxford University Press, 1988); Susan Bayly, *Saints, Goddesses and Kings: Muslims and Christians in South Indian Society 1700–1900* (Cambridge: Cambridge University Press, 1989); and D. H. A. Kolff, *Naukar, Rajput, and Sepoy: The Ethnohistory of the Military*

Labour Market of Hindustan, 1450–1850 (Cambridge: Cambridge University Press, 1990).
30 Thomas Trautmann, *Dravidian Kinship* (Cambridge: Cambridge University Press, 1982).
31 Inden, *Imagining India*.
32 Saurabh Dube, "Religion, identity and authority among the Satnamis in colonial central India," unpublished PhD dissertation (University of Cambridge, 1992); Dube, *Untouchable Pasts*.
33 Dipesh Chakrabarty, *Rethinking Working-Class History: Bengal 1890–1940* (Princeton, NJ: Princeton University Press, 1989), pp. xii, 69, and *passim*.
34 Gyanendra Pandey, *The Construction of Communalism in Colonial North India* (New Delhi: Oxford University Press, 1990), p. 109 and *passim*. From a different perspective, Sandra Freitag examines the domain of "public arenas" – a coherent and consistent realm of symbolic behavior in which "community has been expressed and redefined through collective activities in public spaces" – as being in opposition to (and by implication, in its internal constitution, sealed off from) the imperial state and its institutions. Sandra B. Freitag, *Collective Action and Community: Public Arenas and the Emergence of Communalism in North India* (Berkeley: University of California Press, 1989), p. 6 and *passim*.
35 The early 1990s were exciting times to conduct research in Cambridge, and my own work took forward some of the concerns arising from the writings of C. A. Bayly as well as profiting from conversations with Ajay Skaria on archival work and fieldwork, history and anthropology. C. A. Bayly, *Indian Society and the Making of the British Empire* (Cambridge: Cambridge University Press, 1987); Skaria's work was later published as *Hybrid Histories*.
36 Dube, "Religion, identity, and authority"; Dube, *Untouchable Pasts*.
37 For some of my work on the subject articulating these emphases, see Dube, *Stitches on Time* and *After Conversion*. The wider project is embodied in Saurabh Dube, "Formations of an evangelical modernity: Christianity, conversion, colonialism, 1860–2005," manuscript in progress; and Saurabh Dube, "Native witness: colonial writings of a vernacular Christianity," manuscript in progress.
38 Ranajit Guha, *Dominance without Hegemony: History and Power in Colonial India* (Cambridge, MA: Harvard University Press, 1997), ch. 1.

58   Subjects of modernity

39 According to Guha, the lack was assiduously articulated by the bad faith of an autocratic imperial power and the ingrained limits of an ineffectual indigenous bourgeoisie.
40 It is precisely by attending to the simultaneous discourses in different tongues in Guha's writings that it becomes possible to query the notion of an implacable breach, an innate contradiction, between a modern democratic regime at home and its endless retrograde omissions in the colony – and to question as well other common assertions regarding the entirely exceptional nature of "colonial governmentality" and "colonial modernity" – in order to track instead the mutual constitution and reciprocal labor of modernity and colonialism in the metropolis and the margins.
41 Chatterjee, *The Nation and its Fragments*.
42 *Ibid.*, pp. 237–8.
43 Unsurprisingly, not long after the move to Mexico City, I attempted to initiate a dialogue with these writings as part of critical conversations between distinct perspectives from/on the south. See, for example, Saurabh Dube, Ishita Banerjee-Dube, and Edgardo Lander (eds.), *Critical Conjunctions: Foundations of Colony and Formations of Modernity*, special issue of *Nepantla: Views from South*, 3 (2002): 193–431; Saurabh Dube, Ishita Banerjee-Dube, and Walter Mignolo (eds.), *Modernidades coloniales: otros pasados, historias presentes* (Mexico City: El Colegio de México, 2004); Saurabh Dube and Ishita Banerjee-Dube (eds.), *Unbecoming Modern: Colonialism, Modernity, Colonial Modernities* (New Delhi: Social Science Press, 2006).
44 This corpus is an immense one, known earlier under the rubric of (understandings of) "coloniality of power" and more recently grouped under (perspectives on) "decoloniality of knowledge." Having linkages with prior traditions in Latin America of "dependencia" theory and "liberation theology," in its current configurations an important presence are the works of Aníbal Quijano, Enrique Dussel, and Walter Mignolo, alongside a host of other scholars, some of whom will be cited below. While it would an error to underplay their internal distinctions by readily folding these writings together, it is also the case that work within these perspectives often attempts to express their principal commonalities, mutual unity, rather than dwell on their differences. See, for example, Ramon Grosfoguel, "Decolonizing post-colonial studies and paradigms of political economy: transmodernity, decolonial thinking, and global coloniality,"

Transmodernity: Journal of Peripheral Cultural Production of the Luso-Hispanic World, 1, 1 (2011): 1–37. Most articles on coloniality/decoloniality in this journal, *Transmodernity*, bear out my claims above.

45 Enrique Dussel, *The Invention of the Americas: Eclipse of "the Other" and the Myth of Modernity* (New York: Continuum, 1995); Enrique Dussel "Europe, eurocentrism and modernity (introduction to the Frankfurt lectures)," *Boundary 2*, 20 (1993): 65–76; Mignolo, *Darker Side of the Renaissance*; Nelson Maldonado-Torres, *Against War: Views from the Underside of Modernity* (Durham, NC: Duke University Press, 2008).

46 These are lingering implicit sensibilities, sometimes strikingly explicitly expressed, that course through most of the works cited below on colonial/decolonial perspectives.

47 Emmanuel Levinas, *Time and the Other*, trans. Richard A. Cohen (Pittsburgh, PA: Duquesne University Press, 1987); Enrique Dussel, *Etica de la liberación en la edad de la globalización y de la exclusión* (Madrid: Trotta, 1998). See also Emmanuel Levinas, *Totality and Infinity: An Essay on Exteriority*, trans. Alphonso Lingis (Pittsburgh, PA: Duquesne University Press, 1987). In considering the relationship between Levinas and Dussel, I have found especially illuminating Silvana Rabinovich, "Alterity," in Robert McKee Irwin and Mónica Szurmuk (eds.), *Dictionary of Latin American Cultural Studies* (Gainesville: University Press of Florida, 2012), pp. 17–22; and Maldonado-Torres, *Against War*. Maldonado-Torres ethically attends to the tensions and contradictions as well as problems and possibilities in the work of both Levinas and Dussel, particularly when they are read together. Having learned from his splendid work, it should be clear that the critical affirmation that I seek intersects with, yet also departs from, Maldonado-Torres's emphases.

48 Levinas, *Time and the Other*; Maldonado-Torres, *Against War*.

49 Dussel, *Etica de la liberación*; Maldonado-Torres, *Against War*, p. 176.

50 Dussel, *Invention of the Americas*; Enrique Dussel, "Transmodernity," in Dube, Banerjee-Dube and Lander (eds.), *Critical Conjunctions*, pp. 221–44; Aníbal Quijano, "Colonialidad y modernidad/racionalidad," *Perú Indígena*, 29 (1991): 11–21; Aníbal Quijano, "La colonialidad del poder y la experiencia cultural latinoamericana," in Roberto Briceño-León and Heinz R. Sonntag (eds.), *Pueblo, época y desarrollo: la sociología de América Latina* (Caracas: Nueva Sociedad, 1998), pp. 139–55; Aníbal Quijano

"Coloniality of power, ethnocentrism, and Latin America," *Nepantla*, 1 (2000): 533–80; Mignolo, *Local Histories/Global Designs*; Grosfoguel, "Decolonizing post-colonial studies"; and Walter Mignolo, *The Darker Side of Western Modernity: Global Futures, Decolonial Options* (Durham, NC: Duke University Press, 2011).

51 My concern here is with the assumptions and presumptions – frequently tacit, often underenunciated – that shore up these writings.

52 See, for instance, Walter Mignolo, "Coloniality at large," in Saurabh Dube (ed.), *Enchantments of Modernity: Empire, Nation, Globalization* (London: Routledge, 2009), pp. 67–95. See also, Walter Mignolo, "The enduring enchantment (or the epistemic privilege of modernity and where to go from here)," in Saurabh Dube (ed.), *Enduring Enchantments*, special issue of *South Atlantic Quarterly*, 101 (2002): 927–54.

53 Some of this excitement and these possibilities are revealed by my efforts at conversations with protagonists of coloniality/decoloniality noted above.

54 Dube, *Stitches on Time*; Dube, "Terms that bind."

55 Anne McClintock, *Imperial Leather: Race, Gender, and Sexuality in the Colonial Contest* (New York: Routledge, 1995); Ella Shohat, "Notes on the post-colonial," in Padmini Mongia (ed.), *Contemporary Postcolonial Theory: A Reader* (London: Arnold Publication, 1996), pp. 321–34.

56 As we shall see, particularly in Chapter 5, all of these carry acute implications for critical considerations of modernity, time, space, and the disciplines offered by this book.

57 None of this is to deny the tangible tensions that abound in historical anthropology, postcolonial perspectives, and subaltern studies. For example, in these terrains approaches according analytical primacy to processes of political economy and state formation contend with orientations attributing theoretical privilege to discursive orders and representational regimes. I return to this question in Chapter 5. See also, Dube, *Stitches on Time*.

58 Dipesh Chakrabarty, "Postcoloniality and the artifice of history: who speaks for 'Indian' pasts?," *Representations*, 37 (1992): 1–26.

59 Chakrabarty, *Provincializing Europe*.

60 Dipesh Chakrabarty, "The difference-deferral of a colonial modernity: public debates on domesticity in British Bengal," in David Arnold and

David Hardiman (eds.), *Subaltern Studies VIII: Essays in Honor of Ranajit Guha* (Delhi: Oxford University Press, 1994), pp. 50–88; Chakrabarty, *Habitations of Modernity*.

61 Chakrabarty, "The difference-deferral," p. 84.
62 Chakrabarty, *Habitations of Modernity*; Chakrabarty, *Provincializing Europe*, p. 255.
63 See Dipesh Chakrabarty and Saurabh Dube, "Presence of Europe: an interview with Dipesh Chakrabarty," in Dube (ed.), *Postcolonial Passages*, pp. 254–62.
64 Needless to say, such production of space-time as part of epistemic practice can be tracked equally in relation to the tendencies in historical anthropology discussed earlier, but I defer these issues to another time, another space.
65 Pandey, *Construction of Communalism*; Gyanendra Pandey, "In defense of the fragment: writing about Hindu–Muslim riots in India today," *Representations*, 37 (1992): 27–55. These dispositions bear affinities with the writings of Ashis Nandy that have expressed and endorsed anti- and counter-modern sensibilities (which have of course been a critical formative part of modernity for a very long time now). Nandy's work has envisioned and articulated modernity (and its associated institutions and imaginings) as signaling an overweening project, constitutive of a colonization of the mind (of the colonized and the colonizer), against which have to be pitted the labors of creative difference, psychic decolonization, and resolute recuperations of critical tradition, in the past and the present. Nandy, *The Intimate Enemy*; Ashis Nandy, *Traditions, Tyranny, and Utopias: Essays in the Politics of Awareness* (New Delhi: Oxford University Press, 1992); Ashis Nandy, *The Savage Freud and Other Essays on Possible and Retrievable Selves* (Princeton, NJ: Princeton University Press, 1995); Ashis Nandy, *An Ambiguous Journey to the City: The Village and Other Odd Remains of the Self in the Indian Imagination* (Delhi: Oxford University Press, 2001).
66 Chakrabarty, *Rethinking Working-Class History*.
67 Chatterjee, *The Nation and its Fragments*.
68 I first initiated and elaborated issues arising from such dispositions in Dube, *Stitches on Time*. They have been a critical component of my work of research, writing, and teaching ever since.

69 A distinct work that actually avows the productivity of power is a case in point. Gyan Prakash has approached modernity as an authoritative apparatus that ever engenders critical alterity. In his reading, the terms of modernity as expressed in the work of science find form and assume substance in the productivity of power of colonialism and nationalism. At the same time, content with having established the presence of alterity, Prakash barely stays any longer with the burden of such difference, particularly in the post-colony. Here, authority engenders alterity, yet such alterity intimates only an interstitial space-time whose principal logic is to be, well, *different* from the matrix of power in which it is embedded. Prakash, *Another Reason*. On the other hand, the productivity of power, including "governmentality," finds rather distinct configurations in the recent writings of Partha Chatterjee, a testimony to the formative heterogeneity and shifting emphases of subaltern studies. See, for example, Chatterjee, *The Politics of the Governed*.

70 Stephen K. White, *Sustaining Affirmation: The Strengths of Weak Ontology in Political Theory* (Princeton, NJ: Princeton University Press, 2000), pp. 3–4. Consider too the move toward a "strategic practice of criticism" in Scott, *Refashioning Futures*, pp. 3–10, 17–18.

71 de Certeau, *The Practice of Everyday Life*, p. ix.

72 I borrow this notion – and that of "unrecuperated particulars," which follows – from John McGowan, *Postmodernism and its Critics* (Ithaca, NY: Cornell University Press, 1991).

73 *Ibid.*

3

Maps of modernity: antinomies and enticements

This chapter considers aspects of the interplay of modernity and history, as entailing pervasive procedures of the temporalization of space and the spatialization of time. We have seen that these protocols have twin dimensions: on the one hand, they entail routine projections of historical time as necessarily homogeneous and yet founded on inaugural spatial ruptures; on the other, they involve antinomian blueprints of social space as innately split but ever along a singular temporal hierarchy. The configurations bind each other. At stake, actually, are oppositions and enchantments of modernity. And so, it is through the "oblique" perspective of the enchanted antinomies of modernity – rather than the dominant motif of its innate disenchantment – that this chapter approaches anew modernity's constitutive terms and their interplay with time and space, the past and the present.

Overture

The idea of modernity rests on rupture. It brings into view a monumental narrative: the breaching of magical covenants, the surpassing of medieval superstitions, and the undoing of hierarchical traditions. The advent of modernity, then, insinuates the disenchantment of the world: the progressive control of nature through scientific procedures of technology and the inexorable demystification of enchantments through powerful techniques of reason. Indeed, it is possible to argue – along with Martin Heidegger, for example – that the privileged dispensation of legislative reason within regimes of modernity gathers together nature and humanity as conjoint attributes of a disenchanted world.

Yet processes of modernity create their own enchantments. Here are to be found enchantments that extend from the immaculately imagined origins and ends of modernity through to the dense magic of money and markets; from novel mythologies of nation and empire through to hierarchical oppositions between myth and history, emotion and reason, ritual and rationality, East and West, and tradition and modernity. Intensely spectral but concretely palpable, forming tangible representations and informing forceful practices, the one bound to the other, such enticements stalk the worlds of modernity's doing and undoing. The enchantments of modernity give shape to the past and the present by ordering and orchestrating these terrains, at once temporally and spatially.[1]

The first chapter discussed the proposition that the developmental idea of a supersession of the past is crucial to modern imaginaries. This is true of academic assumption and everyday understanding, and also underlies the mutual articulations of modernity, modernization, and modernism. Such splitting of the past from the present is simultaneously temporal and spatial. Here the singular temporal trajectory and the exclusive spatial location of an overweening imagined yet tangible West together map the history and the here and now of all existing arenas, projecting their problems and possibilities as always lying along an a priori axis of space and time.[2] These images of historical temporal ruptures alongside their hierarchical, spatial distinctions have crystallized into constitutive hegemonic representations of modernity. Forming dominant persuasive presumptions of the modern, they underscore mutual oppositions between tradition and modernity, ritual and rationality, myth and history, the magical/medieval and the modern, community and state, and East and West. Such matrices intimate the abiding enticements of modernity: assiduously woven into formidable fabrics of empire, nation, and globalization, their presumptions and representations are, unsurprisingly, acutely articulated by historical subjects in their quotidian construal and everyday experience of space and time. This is to say that at stake are ruptures and representations, antinomies and assumptions, enchantments and apprehensions that form key conditions of knowing under modernity.

To pose matters in this manner is to register the salience of modernity's oppositions but without reifying them, to think through the enchantments of modernity yet without attempting to exorcise them. Indeed, my arguments do not propose a general solution to the oppositions and enchantments of modernity. Thus, I eschew readings that relentlessly seek foundations of such oppositions and enchantments in Enlightenment principles and post-Enlightenment traditions, only to abandon from imagination and understanding diverse human energies and enormous historical passions that have claimed these antinomies and animated these enticements. Rather, my effort is to work toward carefully questioning and critically exploring social worlds, particularly their scholarly apprehensions, in view of the place and persistence of modernity's oppositions and enchantments in academic and everyday temporal and spatial understandings.

All of this further suggests specific overlapping dispositions to analytical categories and social worlds (which were discussed in the previous chapters, yet which I emphasize again). On the one hand, modernity and its stipulations do not appear in this book as mere objects of knowledge, out there, at a distance, awaiting discovery, confirmation, or refutation. They intimate instead conditions of knowing, entities and coordinates that shore up the worlds we inhabit, demanding critical articulation. On the other hand, in deliberating the authoritative terms and the pervasive enchantments of modernity, my efforts do not simply cast these as ideological aberrations and mistaken practices. In necessarily different ways, they recognize, rather, their dense ontological dimensions, which simultaneously name and work upon the world in order to remake it.

This registered, it still remains to state some of the ways in which my arguments address other scholarly articulations of modernity's enchantments. As Bruce Knauft has suggested, from around the last decade of the twentieth century, the excesses of the "post" in postmodernism have led scholars across a range of disciplines "back in a significantly new key" to the study of modernity.[3] Here, critical considerations of modernity have unsurprisingly entailed imaginative analyses of the magic of the modern.

In the air for long now, the notion of the magic of modernity has found interesting articulations, especially in critical anthropology and cultural studies, during recent years. An important role here has been played by the ideas of Marx on commodity fetishism and the magical nature of money and markets, including the extension of these ideas to other terrains. In the past, analytical endeavor – especially using filters of "critiques of ideology" and those of "false-consciousness" – subsumed such suggestions of Marx to his related emphases on reification and alienation. But the newer writings register modernity's magic – and the interplay between the magical and the modern – as more critically constitutive of social worlds.[4] Important strands of such work have focused on the magic of capitalism and/or on the fetish of the state.[5] Still other exercises have moved toward the simultaneous evocation and defacement of power, pointing to the sacred character of modern sovereignty, in order to re-enchant modernity through surrealistic representation and writing and ecstatic thought and theory.[6]

Here, I consider it important to critically crystallize such consideration of the magic and/or the modern by placing the magical formations of money and markets as well as the fetish of state and sovereignty as part of the wider enchantments of modernity. I have noted that the enchantments extend from immaculate notions of origins and ends of modernity through to monumental mythologies of empires and nations, further encompassing modernity's hierarchical oppositions that split social worlds while holding them together. Now, the present work registers these enchantments as formative of modern worlds. That is to say, once again, I approach the enchantments of modernity not merely as objects of knowledge but as conditions of knowing. In these ways, I eschew the lingering tendency to variously dismiss the representations and foundations of modernity having once uncovered their contradictions and conceits. It only follows that, while learning from surrealist, Dada-like scholarly unmasking of modern power, my work as a whole points to the need to look beyond uneasy yet ready answers to history and modernity. My bid is to patiently and prudently stay longer instead with critical questions arising in these terrains, especially by unobtrusively endorsing a new ongoing "ontological" turn in political and social scholarship, which was indicated earlier.[7]

Abiding antinomies

There is something uncannily haunting, unerringly close to home, about modernity's enchantments, now drawing in and reaching beyond scholarly understandings. Consider the manner in which the term "medieval" bears enormous import for delineations of modernity, an issue that I have discussed elsewhere in relation to imperatives of contemporary politics.[8] The point here is that specters of the medieval – think of the Taliban, of Al-Qaeda, of ISIS, among other examples – darkly delineate practices, beliefs, cultures, faiths, and histories as at once a prior spatial presence *and* an ongoing temporal horror in the mirrors of modernity. They hover in the present in ominous ways.

Why should this be the case? I began by noting that as an idea, ideal, and ideology modernity and the modern appear as premised upon fundamental spatial-temporal ruptures: a surpassing of tradition, a break with the medieval.[9] Time after time, in this vision of the past, present, and posterity, an exclusive, imaginary, and bloated West has morphed into history, modernity, and destiny, realized or unrealized, for each society, any culture, and every people.[10] Even more widely, assiduously plotted against the horizon of a singular modernity, along the axis of an exclusive time and its hierarchical spaces, distinct meanings, practices, and institutions appear primitive or progressive, lost or redeemable, savage or civilized, barbaric or exotic, ever behind or almost there, medieval or modern.

These peoples have missed the temporal-spatial bus of universal history, or they hang precariously from one of its symmetrical sides. Patiently or impatiently, they still wait for the next vehicle plying the road of modernity. Comfortably or uncomfortably, they now sit within this transportation of historical time, this vehicle traversing social space. Their distance from the modern registers redemptive virtue or their falling behind on this route reflects abject failure.[11] Rather more than ideological errors, awaiting their inexorable exorcism through superior knowledge, such mappings circulate as structures of feeling, instituted as categorical entities, intimating the measures and the means of the modern, which is to say they are abiding enchantments of modernity.

From where do such hierarchal oppositions and their immense enchantments arise? For a long time now, formidable antinomies between static traditional communities and dynamic modern societies have played an important role in understandings of history and culture.[12] At first, the spatial-temporal duality might seem to be little more than an ideological plank of modernization theory, counterposing primarily non-Western tradition with chiefly Western modernity. But the antinomy has wider implications and deeper underpinnings.[13] It is not only that the duality has animated and articulated other enduring oppositions, such as those between ritual and rationality, myth and history, community and state, magic and the modern, and emotion and reason. It is also that as a lasting legacy of developmental temporal ideas of universal natural history and of aggrandizing spatial representations of an exclusive Western modernity, such oppositions have found varied expressions among the distinct subjects that they have named, described, and objectified since at least the eighteenth century.[14] At stake, indeed, are mappings of time and orderings of space, which substantialize both (space and time) in antinomian ways.

Representations emanating from the European Enlightenment have played a key role here. Now, it would be hasty and erroneous to see the European Enlightenment of the seventeenth and eighteenth centuries as all of a piece. From contending strains of rationalism in France and empiricism in Britain through to different conceptions of universal and natural history, it is more useful to speak in the plural of *Enlightenments*.[15] Here were to be found, too, challenges to rationalist procedures through varieties of *Counter-Enlightenments*, which shaped the Enlightenment.[16] Despite such plural procedures, it has been generally accepted that the period of the Enlightenment was accompanied and marked by ideas and processes of the secularization of Judeo-Christian time.[17] Actually, such secularization of Judeo-Christian time during the Enlightenment was an emergent and consequential idea, but a circumscribed and limited process.[18]

In this context, discrete yet overlaying developmental schemes underwrote grand designs of human history, from the rationalist claims of Voltaire and Kant through to the historicist frames of Giambattista Vico and Johann Gottfried von Herder. There was profound contention among such schemas, yet in different ways they each projected developmental blueprints of universal history, turning on space and time.[19] Such contrary strains and convergent emphases were bound to the fact, many times overlooked, that the Enlightenment was as much historical as philosophical, as much about the rewriting of history as about the rethinking of philosophy. The consequences were limited yet significant. On the one hand, throughout the nineteenth century but also afterwards Judeo-Christian and messianic time, temporality, and *telos* – and the spatial imaginaries on which they rested – did not lose their influence in Western worlds.[20] On the other, by the second half of the nineteenth century, at the very least in the Protestant West, secularized time could acquire a naturalized aura and developmental thought was distilled (uncertainly yet potently) as historical progress, each seeking to transform spatially segregated worlds in its image and wake.[21]

It followed that time and space, articulated in tandem, came to be increasingly mapped in hierarchical ways to plot peoples and cultures in the movement of history that was primarily projected as the passage of progress. Frequently articulated by the *Ur*-opposition between the primitive and the civilized, in place here nonetheless was neither a singular Western "self" nor indeed an exclusive non-Western "other." Rather, at play in this terrain were the spatial severalty of Western selves and the temporal hierarchies of non-Western otherness. In this scenario, many peoples (for example, Africans, African-Americans, and indigenous groups in the Americas and across the world) were still stuck in the stage of barbarism and savagery with few prospects of advancement. Other societies (for example, those of India and China) had reached the ascending steps of civilization yet lacked the critical foundations of reason. Still other people (chiefly of Western European stock) had evolved to the higher reaches of humanity through advantages of race and rationality and propensities of history and nationality. Indeed, it was the past and the present of this last set of people, comprising the enlightened European elect, that was seized on and rendered as a looking glass at large. In this mirror was envisioned the universal history of human destiny, a destiny represented as groups and societies caught in warps of space and vortexes of time, either failing before or rising to the stage of modernity that was ever cast as spatial and temporal apex.

It was registered earlier that dominant notions and pervasive narratives of modernity involve a break with the past, a carving up of space: here, stories of modernity ever intimate ruptures with ritual and magic and breaches with enchantment and tradition, setting to work procedures of the temporalization of space and the spatialization of time. Following authoritative understandings, as an epochal concept, modernity has been seen as embodying a distinct and new status from preceding periods. Two immensely influential contemporary discussions explicating the critical attributes of modernity should suffice here.

The philosopher Jürgen Habermas has suggested that under modernity the notion of the "new" or the "modern" world loses a "merely chronological meaning" to take on instead "the oppositional significance of an emphatically 'new' age." It follows from this that the normative order of modernity has to be ground out of itself, rather than drawing its dispositions from models offered by other, obviously earlier, epochs.[22] Similarly, the historian Reinhart Koselleck has argued that, starting in the eighteenth century, the regimes of historicity under modernity have entailed a series of homologous disjunctions between the past and the present, prophecy and prediction, and eschatological imaginings and secular visions. This is to say that modernity innately insinuates novel orientations to the past, present, and future.[23]

These are persuasive arguments that carry their own truths. But they also principally present modernity in idealized terms, overlooking also their own implicit articulations of time and space. At the same time, precisely for these reasons, the understandings are acutely representative. None of this should be surprising, for the persuasions and truths of such arguments and their presentation of modernity in idealized terms are inextricably entwined with each other. Indeed, at stake here is nothing less than the abiding enchantments of modernity.

First, influential and commonplace explications of modernity have for a very long time now proceeded by locating its constitutive terms as being entirely internal to an imaginary yet tangible space-time called Europe/West. This is to say that they have understood modernity as phenomena generated purely internally within the West. Produced within this spectral yet palpable Europe, it was only later that modernity was variously exported to other parts of humanity. Now, precisely this measure serves to override dynamics of colonizer and colonized, race and reason, Enlightenment and empire, and indeed space and time, dynamics that been constitutive of the terms and textures of modernity as history.[24]

Second, the protocols of modernity have all too frequently been approached through a resolute sieving of the necessarily uneven historical processes that have attended the emergence(s) and development(s) of the phenomena. Across disciplines, from history to sociology to philosophy, modular designs of modernity are assumed in place more or less a priori. These frames and filters then provide the means with which to approach, analyze, and apprehend the causes, characteristics, and consequences – as well as the terms, terrains, and trajectories – of modernity, including its expansion across the world in predetermined ways.[25] This has served to subordinate the everyday manifestations and critical margins of modernity – entailing of course key coordinates of space, time, and their regular and irregular productions – further underplaying the contentions and contradictions of modernity in Western and non-Western worlds.

Third and finally, representations and definitions of modernity – and its attendant processes such as secularization as well as its cognate concepts such as liberty – have entailed a ceaseless interplay between their ideal attributes and their actual manifestations. This has meant not only that the actual has been apprehended in terms of the ideal, but that even when a gap is recognized between the two the actual is seen as tending toward the ideal with each shoring up the other. At stake are more than simple errors of understanding, since it is exactly the admixtures of the actual articulations and the idealized projections of modernity that have defined its worldly dimensions.[26] Taken together, these procedures announce salient registers of hierarchical mappings of time and space. In both conscious and inadvertent ways, such registers entail two simultaneous measures. Rehearsing the West as modernity, they equally stage modernity "*as* the West."[27]

The idea of modernity as a coming apart from the past rests on the imagination of ruptures within Western history, that prior terrain of the past intimating distinct (and often diminished) coordinates of time and space. But such an idea cannot help also turning on the importance of disjunctions of the West with non-Western worlds, a categorically distinct lower space-time, whether explicitly or implicitly. On the one hand, the caesura defined by modernity as the new beginning is shifted into the past, "precisely to the start of modern times" in Europe.[28] It is ahead of this threshold that the present is seen as being renewed in its vitality and novelty under modernity. On the other hand, exactly when the modern is privileged as the most recent period, the novelty and vitality of modernity confront specters of the "medieval," the "superstitious," the "prophetic," and the "spiritual" meandering in their midst. These spirits are a prior presence *and* an ongoing process. Each attempt to engage them in the present entails marking them as an attribute of the past. My reference is to the ways in which in dominant representations, the Taliban, Al-Qaeda, Hamas, or ISIS are simultaneously "coeval" and "medieval"; and the manner in which, in pervasive understandings, the importance today of "indigenous spirituality" and "local tradition" is at once contemporary yet anachronistic.

I am suggesting, then, that the meanings, understandings, and actions that fall outside the disenchantment-driven horizons of modernity have to be plotted as lagging behind this novel stage. Here, spatial mappings and temporal measurements of the West and the non-West come to rest on the trajectory of time, an axis that claims to be normatively neutral but in fact produces profoundly hierarchical spaces. This is to say that the precise notion of modernity as a rupture with the past carves up social and historical worlds into the traditional and the modern, further naming and animating other temporal-spatial oppositions such as those between ritual and rationality, myth and history, and magic and modernity.

Why should the antinomies of modernity have played an important role in the mapping and making of social worlds? These oppositions emerged embedded within formidable projects of power and knowledge, turning on Enlightenment, empire, and nation as well as within the challenges to these projects. These have been motivated if diverse projects "not simply of looking and recording but of recording and remaking" the world, as Talal Asad tells us.[29] Unsurprisingly, the oppositions themselves assumed persuasive analytical authority *and* acquired pervasive worldly attributes, variously articulated with dominant representations of modernity and its spatial-temporal trajectory as a self-realizing project of progress and a self-evident embodiment of history. As worldly knowledge, then, these neat proposals, abiding oppositions, and their constitutive presumptions entered the lives of historical subjects, albeit at different times and in distinct ways. Formidably if variously disseminated as ways of approaching and modes of apprehending social worlds, they have appeared equally instituted as tissues of affect and textures of experience, intricately articulated (in inherently heterogeneous ways) with the production and meaning of space and time within everyday practices. And so, it should not be surprising that, their critical questioning notwithstanding, these oppositions continue to beguile and seduce.[30]

Untangling modernity

The pervasive presence of modern oppositions, especially in intellectual arenas, derives in no small measure from the manner in which modernity is often elided with modernization, and at other times folded into modernism. As is generally known, the notion of modernization as expressed by its different theorists/theories refers to modular temporal-spatial projections of material, organizational, and technological – as well as economic, political, and cultural – transformation(s), principally envisioned in the looking glass of Western development. Here, different, often hierarchically ordered, societies are seen as succeeding (or failing) to evolve from their traditional (or pre-modern) states through linear stages of succession to become modernized (or capitalist) arenas.[31] Now, the simplistic, step-by-step, spatial schemas and the reductive, totalizing temporal templates of modernization theories have always been far too tendentious.[32] And so, too, have they been decisively questioned and firmly rejected by critical scholarship for some time now. Yet motifs of modernization have also crucially carried wide resonance, easily elided with mappings of modernity, such that each shores up the other.

Why should this be the case? To begin with, as was just discussed, a crucial characteristic of pervasive articulations of Western modernity has hinged on their positing of the phenomenon as marked by a carving up of space and time, a break with the past, a rupture with tradition, a surpassing of the medieval. In this scenario, the blueprints of modernization have actually distilled the designs of modernity, the aggressive spatial assumption of the latter holding in place the schematic temporal prognosis of the former. Taken together, modernity's discourses and modernization theories, inextricably entwined, the one with the other, have articulated an imaginary but palpable distended and aggrandizing Europe/West as history and modernity, the *telos* of time and space, for each society, culture, and people.

Yet there is more to the picture. Reaching beyond routine representations, in artistic, intellectual, and aesthetic arenas, each understood broadly, modernity has often appeared in intimate association with its cognate (or conceptual cousin), modernism. Modernism is also an enormously contentious term, which necessarily follows from the contested and contradictory character of the tendencies it describes. Here are to be found cultural movements, styles, and representations, going back to the mid-nineteenth century and extending into our own times, which have been diversely expressed and performed in different parts of the world. Following Theodor Adorno, modernism has been a principally "qualitative" rather than a merely "chronological" category,[33] but it is also the case that the internal endeavors within modernisms to surpass the past, articulate the present, and envision the future have been intrinsically heterogeneous ones. They have variously engaged and interrogated, accessed and exceeded Enlightenment thought and Romantic tradition, abstract reason and religious truth, surface coherence and tonal depth, Western representations and precolonial narratives, the certainties of science and the presence of God, and governmental authority and popular politics. All of this raises intriguing issues of the configurations of time and space within the ideational articulations and aesthetic practices of modernism(s).

On the one hand, from Charles Baudelaire's avowal of "the ephemeral, the fugitive, the contingent" through to modernist rejections of realism and replication in favor of discontinuity and disruption, and from Ezra Pound's invitation to art to "make new" through to the many manifestations of modernisms flowing from the mid-twentieth century (and earlier), a key characteristic of these cultural tendencies has been to emphasize the difference of the contemporary present from past epochs. On the other, as Peter Childs has argued, modernism has always involved "paradoxical if not opposed trends towards revolutionary and reactionary positions, fear of the new and delight at the disappearance of the old, nihilism and fanatical enthusiasm, creativity and despair."[34] Now, to hold together the discourses of modernity and the articulations of modernism is not only to trace the interleaving yet distinct ways in which they each offer a cessation and overcoming of the past, it is also to register that the constitutive contradictions and contentions of modernism(s) can hold a mirror up to the characteristics, contingencies, contentions, and coordinates, especially of space and time, of that acutely authoritative universal: modernity.

To approach the entanglements between modernity, modernism, and modernization in this manner, where the one is not simply folded into the other yet their mutual linkages are adequately acknowledged, might have critical consequences. Building on my prior proposals, modernity is now understood not only as a forceful idea and ideology, but as also entailing heterogeneous histories and plural processes.[35] These imaginings and procedures extend back to the last five centuries and interlock in critical ways, such that both models of modernization and movements of modernism appear as crucial components, yet small parts, in the broader articulation of modernity. There are at least two faces to the phenomenon, each insinuated in the other. Intrinsic to each is the importance of querying pervasive procedures of the temporalization of space and the spatialization of time.

On the one hand, as part of a familiar picture, constitutive of modernity are processes of reason and science, industry and technology, commerce and consumption, nation-state and citizen-subject, public spheres and private spaces, and secularized religion(s) and disenchanted knowledge(s). Here, it warrants emphasis that vigilance is required regarding the endless unfolding of these developments as inexorable heroic histories, which themselves segregate space and hierarchize time through the assumption of a (readily) simple "before" and a (necessarily) complex "after," a beginning and an end, of these processes. Indeed, instead of teleological tales of the march of modernization/modernity, such stories require to be unraveled as rather more checkered narratives, even as models of modernization are registered as part of the protocols of modernity.

On the other hand, although this is often overlooked, at the core of modernity are also processes of empire and colony, race and genocide, resurgent faiths and reified traditions, disciplinary regimes and subaltern subjects, and the seductions of the state and enchantments of the modern. Lessons learned from the split, Janus-faced nature of modernism assume salience here. This is to register at once that ceaseless portrayals of modernity as embodying a singular seamless trajectory are actually shored up by hierarchical presumptions and antinomian projections of space and time; *and* that procedures of modernity have been contradictory, contingent, and contested – protocols that are incessantly articulated yet also critically out of joint with themselves.[36]

It is precisely these procedures that emerge, expressed by subjects of modernity. Here, my reference is to historical actors who have been active participants in processes of modernity: social actors who have been both *subject to* these processes but also *subjects shaping* these processes. Over the past few centuries, the subjects of modernity have included, as was noted in the introductory chapter, peasants, artisans, and workers in South Asia that have diversely articulated processes of colony and post-colony; indigenous communities in the Americas under colonial and national rule; peoples of African descent not only on that continent but in different diasporas across the world; and, indeed, subaltern, marginal, and elite women and men in non-Western and Western theaters. Unsurprisingly, these subjects have registered within their measures and meanings the formative contradictions, contentions, and contingencies of modernity.

I am suggesting that at stake in this discussion of subjects of modernity are key questions of heterogeneous yet coeval temporalities and overlapping but contending productions of space. First, it is well known that conceptions of modernity generally proceed by envisioning the phenomenon in the image of the European and Euro-American (frequently implicitly male) modern subject.[37] On the contrary, I am indicating the inadequacy of conflating the *modern subject* with the *subject of modernity*. Is it perhaps the case, then, that my articulation of subjects of modernity productively widens the range of address for modernity and its participants? And that it does this by querying the hierarchies and antinomies of time and space that underlie formidable projections of a routinely timeless tradition and an endlessly dynamic modernity?

Moreover, mine is not a chronological claim that everyone living in the modern age counts as a modern subject. For subjects of modernity have revealed, again and again, that there are different ways of being modern, now accessing and now exceeding the stipulations of the Western modern subject. Yet, all too often, in fashioning themselves, subjects of modernity have also scarcely bothered with the Western modern subject exactly while articulating the enduring terms of modernity. What are the implications of such recognition for weaving in distinct textures and transformations of affects and subjectivities – including inherently plural experiences, articulations, and elaborations of time, space, and their enmeshments – in considerations of modernity?[38]

Finally, it bears emphasis that there are other modern subjects besides Western ones, embodying formidable heterogeneity yet coevality of the temporal and the spatial, the affective and the subjective. Does this not suggest the need in discussions of modernity to rethink exclusive images of the modern subject in the past and present, across non-Western arenas and Western ones, and through space and time?[39]

Distinctions of modernity

Let me turn, then, to some of the distinctions of subjects of modernity and modern subjects, all the while keeping in view modernity's enchantments. I begin with questions of religion and politics under regimes of modernity. Here, the presumption sharpening the immaculate image of modernity is the following: since the Protestant Reformation, at least in the modern West religion has undergone a profound transformation, becoming a largely tolerant and broadly private affair with processes of secularization encompassing the "private" intact autonomy of religion.

When I write critically of this presumption, please do not get me wrong. Mine is not the silly suggestion that processes of secularization over the past few centuries are only a fiction, a lie. Nor am I simply proposing that there is an unavoidable discrepancy between the ideal of secularism and its realization in history, an inevitable distance between preaching and practice, thereby casting the story of secularization as an incomplete narrative yet to arrive at its immanent resolution. Rather, my point concerns how the force and reach of this presupposition, not unlike the *telos* of progress, another monumental enchantment of modernity, constitute the very basis of our worlds, their inherited and internalized verities lying at the core of commonplace conceptions and authoritative apprehensions of religion and politics.[40]

Among the consequences, enormously pertinent is the excision of distinct intermeshing(s) of religion and politics in the modern West.[41] Here apprehensions of the interplay between the categorical terrains of religion and politics in, say, the United Kingdom or the United States of America – as part of a reified West – usually rest upon a readily proffered putative gap between the ideal and the real. The former, the doctrinal ideal, is the true norm while the latter, the not-perfect reality, is merely a deviation.[42] This underplays the manner whereby the ideal and the actual – of the separation between religion and politics – mutually shape and reshape one another, each apart yet ever entwined, both much more than mere straw figures. It also means that distinct intermeshing(s) of religion and politics in Islam or Hinduism or Buddhism, in Afghanistan or India or Mexico, in modern times usually appear as figures of absence, lack, and failure, imperfect images in the mirror of an immaculate secular West. Such projections insinuate once more the abiding enchantments of modernity.

There are weighty elisions at stake here. Let us briefly consider the interplay between authoritative traditions and monumental histories at the core of the modern self-fashioning(s) of state and nation, especially in recent times. I have implied earlier that representations of modernity imbue categories and arenas with a distinct salience. One such category/arena is the concept-terrain of tradition.[43] This has meant that in the business of negotiating and enacting modernity as image and practice, subjects of modernity – from the first world through to the fourth – have unraveled particular traditions as constitutive of their specific identities. Such moves have been characteristic as much of "local" communities as they have of nation-states, acutely intensified under conditions of contemporary modernity.[44] Indeed, the burden of authentic traditions and authoritative identities in such distinct yet overlapping terrain – from the "local" to the "national" to the "global" – emerges intimately bound to the hierarchical, spatial-temporal oppositions of modernity, figures of endless enchantment.

Here novel construal and institutionalization of hoary traditions of peoples and territories has gone hand in hand with newer construction and sedimentation of monumental histories of state and nation. This has happened over the short run and in the long haul, from the altering faces of national civilization in India to the changing destinies of the Mestizo nation in Mexico to the shifting fortunes of the multicultural state in Western democracies. Yet, this should hardly surprise us. For quite as the performative and the pedagogical imperatives of the nation entail one another, so too is the nation configured simultaneously through its past traditions and its present distinctions – history as imagined and instituted on a monumental scale. This is to say that terms and visions of monumental history lie at the heart of narratives and practices of the modern state and nation, albeit assuming critically different forms.[45]

In presenting this picture in broad and rapid strokes, I am aware of the dangers of bringing into existence newer modular designs of modernity while overlooking critical dimensions of its prior understandings. For example, am I disregarding key processes of secularization, individualization, and the separation of private and public domains, privileging rather exclusive enactments of monumental histories as constitutive of modernity? Well, actually, not at all.

On the one hand, I have earlier pointed to processes of secularization and formations of the private and the public as among the important attributes attending modernity. Yet I have also implied that it is important to look beyond an exclusive pathway of secularization and individualization, recognizing precisely the diverse articulations of the "private" and the "public" across time, space, and their enmeshments while registering the immaculate image of these processes in the unfolding of modernity. For to do otherwise, might be to endlessly endorse the hierarchical, spatial-temporal oppositions of modernity or to merely reiterate the empirical complexity of modern history as restlessly defying analytical categories, or indeed to be simultaneously bound to the one move and the other measure.

On the other hand, I also admit to the salience of thinking through the distinctions of monumental histories of state and nation, which come in different shapes and sizes, divergent hues and patterns. At the same time, my point is that we encounter in such distinct expressions of monumental history plural, disjunctive articulations of modernity, which is as true of secular states as it is of regimes that reject principles of secularization, individualization, and the separation of the private and the public. After all, for very long now, antimodernist propositions – including, critically, positions that refuse claims made on behalf of the secular – appear enmeshed with authoritative terms, enduring oppositions, of modernity. Similarly, the negotiation and rejection of a dominant Western modern within enactment(s) of monumental history bear critical consideration. Taken together, at stake is nothing less than concatenations of distinct coeval temporalities and productions of overlapping heterogeneous spaces that variously straddle and scramble the hierarchies and oppositions of modernity.

Other moderns

Posing matters in this manner clarifies that presumptions projecting India as a land of endless tradition, recently rising from its slumber in the wake of globalization to truly embrace a Western modernity, share common ground with the pictures of the past few decades portraying the Indian subcontinent as combining the traditional with the modern. Both arguments rest upon exclusive, temporal blueprints and hierarchical, spatial oppositions of an essentially Western modernity and an innately Indian tradition. Instead, I am suggesting that the processes of modernity, including their contentions, on the Indian subcontinent over the past two centuries need to be understood as being shaped by diverse subjects of modernity as well as by distinct modern subjects.

Consider the case of anticolonial political nationalism on the subcontinent, which had its beginnings in the late nineteenth century.[46] On the one hand, subaltern initiatives in the wider terrain of Indian nationalism were the work not of modern subjects but of subjects of modernity. These endeavors participated in procedures of the modern nation by articulating specifically subaltern visions of freedom and their own initiatives of independence. Here are to be found frames of meaning and idioms of struggle that accessed and exceeded the aims and strategies of a generally middle-class nationalist leadership. It is not only that the supplementary nature of subaltern practices straddled their particular renderings of the nation and their distinct politics of nationalism, it is also that subaltern nationalisms carried forward agendas of the peasant insurgent in nineteenth-century India, an insurgent who was not a "pre-political" subject but one entirely coeval with, a contemporary and a constituent of, politics under modern colonialism and colonial modernity.⁴⁷ In each case, Indian subalterns engaged and expressed modern processes as subjects of modernity.

On the other hand, middle-class nationalism in India, the work of Indian modern subjects who were rather different from their Western counterparts, expressed its own distinctions. Drawing upon Enlightenment principles and the post-Enlightenment traditions of the West, it did not simply replicate but reworked these in distinct ways. Here were to be found translations and transformations of the ideals of the sovereign nation and the free citizen of Europe through grids of the subjugated homeland and the colonized subject in India. Such emphases only received a distinct twist in the politics of Mahatma Gandhi, who drew on various strains of modern Romanticism and Indian philosophies to construe thereby his own "critical traditionalism." Gandhi's radical critique of liberal politics and modern civilization was in fact thoroughly expressive of modernity, particularly its contestations, enchantments, and disenchantments.⁴⁸ In each instance, at stake were the fashioning and formation of the Indian modern subject, who drew upon yet went beyond images and ideas of the Western modern subject, telling us once more that there are different ways of being modern.⁴⁹

The discussion above suggests that processes of modernity in India, as elsewhere, have been characterized at once by contrariety and contention as well as ambiguity and ambivalence, a key claim of this book. This is as true of the present as it was of the past. Therefore, I now raise a few questions concerning the ways in which modernity is being articulated and debated in political and intellectual fields in India today, especially seeking to draw out critical implications for understanding its enchantments and oppositions, temporal and spatial.

Over the last hundred years, the politics of the Hindu nationalist Right, which has been thoroughly modern, nonetheless intimates a profound ambivalence toward modernity. This is expressed, for example, in its recent articulations of an alternative Hindu universalism, which is not a mere critique of the West. As Thomas Hansen has argued, this alternative universalism forms "part of a strategy to invigorate and stabilize a modernizing national project through a disciplined and corporatist cultural nationalism that can earn India recognition and equality (with the West and other nations) through assertion of difference."[50] Within Hindu nationalism, the fetish of the modern nation stands closely connected to such ambivalence, at once animating and utilizing ideological control and disciplinary strategies.[51] The assertion of the difference and purity of Hindu civilization and the salience of a strong and powerful modern nation go hand in hand.

Conversely, in recent years a variety of intriguing perspectives has served to open up questions of modernity in India.[52] Extending from the antimodernist "critical traditionalism" of Ashis Nandy through to the philosophical provocations of Dipesh Chakrabarty and on to wide-ranging histories/ethnographies, they provide valuable lessons provided we are willing to learn imaginatively and critically.[53] To begin with, we are reminded that the very meanings of modernity, delineations of democracy, and purposes of pluralism cannot be separated from inherently different formations of social subjects in inescapably heterogeneous worlds, shaped by the past and emergent in the present. It is in the practices of these subjects that there inhere ethics and politics for realizing and/or rejecting the possibilities of modernity, plurality, and democracy.

Next, it follows that to recognize the assiduous production of traditions by subjects of modernity is not to cast these – traditions and subjects – as somehow erroneous, faulty, or insubstantial. Instead, it is to acknowledge the enormous burden of such traditions in dominant projects of state and nation *and* the ethical force of particular claims upon community and tradition. At the same time, in each case this admission further entails exploring how signs of state come to lie at the heart of traditions and communities, authoritative traces that communities and peoples yet work upon to engender distinct meanings of nation and modernity, the unknown and the familiar.

Finally, it is becoming clear that to register the contingency and plurality of modernity across the world is not merely to harp on about "alternative modernities." Rather, it is to reconsider modalities of power, formations of difference, and their restless interplay at the heart of processes of modernity. Indeed, this also means not turning way from, but prudently unraveling, the exclusive images of Western modernity as shaping the concatenations and contentions of every modernity, while further recognizing that such stipulations are differently worked upon by social subjects to yield expected outcomes and unexpected consequences. Modernity as history is intimately bound to images of modernity.

Such considerations are further clarified by turning to discussions of modernity in Latin America. Intimations of modernity have long haunted Latin America, generally reflecting the phantasms of a reified yet tangible Europe. The region has itself been envisioned, uneasily yet readily, as part of the Western world, albeit with specific lacks and within particular limits. All of this is a result of dominant mappings and authoritative "metageographies,"[54] which have split the world into the Occident and the Orient, the West and the East, shored up by discourses of Orientalism[55] and Occidentalism[56] formidably present in aesthetic and everyday expressions.[57]

In Latin America, as in most of the world, dominant blueprints have rested on the modern stipulation decreeing that modernity had already happened somewhere else.[58] If this has generated among Latin American moderns the anxiety of looking unoriginal, it has also led them to a variety of searches for a distinctively national modern, modernism, and modernity, as one poised between the West and the Rest. (Unsurprisingly, diverse "indigenist" and "primitivist" discourses and representations have often played a critical role here.) In early and mid-twentieth-century Mexico, for example, we only need to think of the works and lives not merely of Diego Rivera and Frida Kahlo but also of "Los Contemporáneos" such as Jorge Cuesta and Salvador Novo (and, somewhat later, of the "Grupo Hiperión"). The point is that discussions of modernism – in their simultaneously republican and authoritarian, political and aesthetic, governmental and everyday avatars – have provided some of the most sustained understandings of narratives of modernity in Latin America.[59] This tendency continues into the present.[60]

It is against this background, then, that we need to register the broad sets of recent discussions of modernity in Latin America, which have all put a question mark over facile polarities between prolific modernisms and deficient modernization in the region as expressed by influential authors.[61] Two of these tendencies we have discussed already. The first concerns the critique of modernity implied by perspectives on the "coloniality of power" and "decolonial knowledge." The second involves recent work on Latin America and the Caribbean that has provided fresh meanings to discussions of the magic/insanity of capitalism and colonialism[62] and of the fetish/reification of state and nation.[63] To these we need to add a variety of writings on Latin America (and the Caribbean) that have imaginatively explored critical issues of modernity and its margins.

Such questions have found multiple expressions in discussions of architecture and the built form,[64] peasant and popular politics,[65] space and territoriality,[66] culture and consumption,[67] and representation and subalternity.[68] At stake are writings that have explicitly engaged historical and contemporary terms, textures, and transformations of modernity. In this terrain, the explorations have ranged from influential considerations of the hetero-temporal coordinates of national time-space[69] through to mutual mediations of modernity and nation.[70] They have engaged issues of piety, intimacy, embodiment, and image under entwined regimes of modernity and religion;[71] modernity in its Baroque formations[72] and its vernacular configurations;[73] finally, the wide-ranging acute contradictions and contentions of modernity.[74]

Taken together, here are to be found works focusing on different articulations of modernity as historically grounded and culturally expressed, articulations that query a priori projections and sociological formalism underpinning the category-entity.[75] Indeed, in Latin America and elsewhere, formations and elaborations of modernity are increasingly being discussed and debated today as contradictory and contingent processes of culture and power, as checkered and contested histories of meaning and mastery. The spirit and substance of these writings shore up my efforts in *Subjects of Modernity*.

Coda

I began this chapter by declaring that to adopt the oblique perspective of enchantment is a possible means of understanding modernity in newer ways. Now it remains to be stated that, for me, the enchantments *that endure* are also enchantments *to endure*, in order to better query their shadow and substance in the past and the present. For consider the irony and the travesty if our task consisted of merely demystifying – whether through the ruse of aggrandizing reason or the expedient of the critique of ideology – the enchantments of modernity. These enchantments constitute the formative entities and key coordinates of our worlds, which are not worlds or entities to presciently and pointedly disenchant. Rather, these are worlds to carefully question and ethically articulate, even worlds to re-enchant.[76] These tasks are taken up in distinct registers in the chapters that follow.

Notes

1   Indeed, precisely recognizing the worldly (or ontological) dimensions of the enchantments (and disenchantments) of modernity, I do not offer here a consideration of the different theories of modernity. Rather, I provide a provocative account of modern disenchantments and their enchantments, raising critical questions around these categories-entities as well as highlighting wider issues of the intricate interplay of history and modernity, time and space, and pasts and communities.

2   Yet, as was also noted, historical ruptures equally insinuate stubborn knots, which no less braid the temporal and the spatial. Here, prior times/places, at once anachronistic yet entirely coeval, are tangible specters at the core of contemporary stages/spaces. This announces the tangles, tatters, and textures of the past and the present, the spatial and the temporal.

3   Bruce Knauft, "Critically modern: an introduction," in Bruce Knauft (ed.), *Critically Modern: Alternatives, Alterities, Anthropologies* (Bloomington: Indiana University Press, 2002), pp. 1–54. Knauft provides

an able, extended, and critical survey of recent discussions of modernity. Consider also Bhambra, *Rethinking Modernity*.

4   Alex Owen, *The Place of Enchantment: British Occultism and the Culture of the Modern* (Chicago, IL: University of Chicago Press, 2004); Edward LiPuma, *Encompassing Others: The Magic of Modernity in Melanesia* (Ann Arbor: University of Michigan Press, 2001); Birgit Meyer and Peter Pels (eds.), *Magic and Modernity: Interfaces of Revelation and Concealment* (Stanford, CA: Stanford University Press, 2003); Simon During, *Modern Enchantments: The Cultural Power of Secular Magic* (Cambridge, MA: Harvard University Press, 2004). From the perspective of history writing, see the rich survey offered by Michael Saler, "Modernity and enchantment: a historiographic review," *American Historical Review*, 111 (2006): 692–716. See also Michael Saler, *As If: Modern Enchantment and the Literary Prehistory of Virtual Reality* (New York: Oxford University Press, 2012).

5   Jean Comaroff and John Comaroff (eds.), *Millennial Capitalism and the Culture of Neoliberalism* (Durham, NC: Duke University Press, 2001); Coronil, *The Magical State*.

6   Taussig, *The Magic of the State*; Michael Taussig, *Defacement: Public Secrecy and the Labor of the Negative* (Stanford, CA: Stanford University Press, 1999).

7   S. K. White, *Sustaining Affirmation*; see also Chapter 1 above.

8   Saurabh Dube, "Historical identity and cultural difference: a critical note," *Economic and Political Weekly*, 36 (2002): 77–81.

9   This is not deny the complex pasts of the term "modern," whose "conceptual history" in Western Europe, for example, Hans Ulrich Gumbrecht traces in interesting ways – a history that makes clear the articulations of the "modern" with the "ancient," the "classical," and the "romantic." Rather, it is to stay longer with the moment of Gumbrecht's understanding where the concept of "modern" yields to the category of "modernity," while recognizing that a purely "internal" account of a concept can elide its multiple hierarchies, played out in distinct registers. Hans Ulrich Gumbrecht, "A history of the concept 'modern,'" in Hans Ulrich Gumbrecht, *Making Sense in Life and Literature*, trans. Glen Burns (Minneapolis: University of Minnesota Press, 1992), pp. 79–110.

10 This pervasive, "meta-geographical" projection appears elaborated in several ways, from the evidently aggressive to the seemingly benign, embedded of course in "modernization" theory, yet also long lodged within the interstices of Western social and political thought. The way all this might come together is evident in the following statement by Gumbrecht: "From our perspective at least, modernization in the underdeveloped countries is … taking *place somewhere between* decolonization and our own present." The "stagist" presumptions of time and space here are not so far apart from the wide-ranging elisions of authoritative accounts – for example, by Anthony Giddens and Jürgen Habermas – that see modernity as a self-generated, European phenomenon. As I discuss later, the projection also finds contradictory articulations within discrete expressions of "tradition" that question "modernity" by reversing the moral import of its constitutive hierarchies and oppositions. To consider the enchantments of modernity is to think through such oppositions, hierarchies, and elisions. *Ibid.*, p. 108, emphasis added; Anthony Giddens, *Consequences of Modernity* (Stanford, CA: Stanford University Press, 1990); and Jürgen Habermas, *The Philosophical Discourse of Modernity: Twelve Lectures*, trans. Frederick G. Lawrence (Cambridge, MA: MIT Press, 1987).

11 Even as prior enchantments can appear as an antidote to a disenchanted modernity, so too logics of "exclusion" and terms of "inclusion" bind each other within the temporal and spatial hierarchies of modernity. While keeping this in view, I have found especially useful: Mehta, *Liberalism and Empire*; Chakrabarty, *Provincializing Europe*; and Comaroff and Comaroff, *Ethnography and the Historical Imagination*. See also Taussig, *Shamanism, Colonialism, and the Wild Man*.

12 This section draws upon and develops further arguments first presented in Dube, "Anthropology, history, historical anthropology," pp. 1–31.

13 For a wider discussion of the mappings of the traditional and the modern, see Dube, *Stitches on Time*.

14 This is not to deny prior formations of the modernity of the Renaissance and the New World, issues discussed, for example, in Dube and Banerjee-Dube, *Unbecoming Modern*.

15 Roy Porter, *The Creation of the Modern World: The Untold Story of the British Enlightenment* (New York: Norton, 2001); J. G. A. Pococok, *Barbarism and Religion: Volume Two, Narratives of Civil Government*

(Cambridge: Cambridge University Press, 1999); and Donald R. Kelley, *Faces of History: Historical Inquiry from Herodotus to Herder* (New Haven, CT: Yale University Press, 1998). See also Sankar Muthu, *Enlightenment against Empire* (Princeton, NJ: Princeton University Press, 2003); Sunil Agnani, *Hating Empire Properly: The Two Indies and the Limits of Enlightenment Anticolonialism* (New York: Fordham University Press, 2013); and, from a rather different direction, the implications of Jonardon Ganeri, *The Lost Age of Reason: Philosophy in Early Modern India* (Oxford: Oxford University Press, 2011).

16 Isaiah Berlin, *Against the Current: Essays in the History of Ideas* (Princeton, NJ: Princeton University Press, 2001), pp. 1–24; Darrin M. McMahon, *Enemies of the Enlightenment: The French Counter-Enlightenment and the Making of Modernity* (New York: Oxford University Press, 2002).

17 See, for example, Fabian, *Time and the Other*, especially pp. 26–7, 146–7.

18 I discuss these issues in much greater detail in Dube, "Anthropology, history, historical anthropology," although even in terms purely of eighteenth-century Enlightenment thought consider the emphases of Carl L. Becker, *The Heavenly City of the Eighteenth-Century Philosophers* (New Haven, CT: Yale University Press, 1932).

19 Put differently, not only rationalist, analytical schemes but also contending historicist, hermeneutic traditions articulated in distinct ways the terms of developmental, universal history, its projections of time and space. Kelley, *Faces of History*, pp. 211–62.

20 Concerning only the United States and its Puritan model of the secularization of the world, consider R. Laurence Moore, *Touchdown Jesus: The Mixing of Sacred and Secular in American History* (Louisville, KY: Westminster John Know Press, 2003); and Vincent Crapanzano, *Serving the Word: Literalism in America from the Pulpit to the Bench* (New York: New Press, 2000).

21 I am neither attributing an inexorable quality to these developments nor denying that such processes have possessed contradictory and critical pasts. See, for example, Fabian, *Time and the Other*, pp. 12–16.

22 Habermas, *Philosophical Discourse of Modernity*, p. 5.

23 Reinhart Koselleck, *Futures Past: On the Semantics of Historical Time*, trans. Keith Tribe (Cambridge, MA: MIT Press, 1985), especially pp. 3–20.

24 Consider that in some ways this problem continues to characterize Charles Taylor's sensitive and suggestive, truly remarkable recent opening-up of the terms, terrains, and trajectories of modernity. Charles Taylor, *Modern Social Imaginaries* (Durham, NC: Duke University Press, 2005).

25 Instead of providing instances of the seemingly endless writings that embody such procedures in straightforward ways, let me take up a more critical example. In their influential text on history writing, Joyce Appleby, Lynn Hunt, and Margaret Jacob adopt a dryly ironic, gently mocking tone toward what they call "a heroic model of science" of the Enlightenment – one they see as shaping and structuring modern knowledge, especially history. Yet, not only do these authors insufficiently probe the plurality of Enlightenment traditions, actually, for the most part, their own understanding of knowledge schemes rests upon the heroic model that they pillory. Here are to be found exactly the enchantments of modernity under discussion. Joyce Appleby et al., *Telling the Truth About History* (New York: W. W. Norton, 1995). Such difficulties extend from history through to philosophy, and I discuss the place of modular assumptions of modernity as shoring up the important, critical work of Habermas in Dube, *After Conversion*.

26 Considering the active interchange between the "ought" and the "is," the "ideal" and the "real," especially in relation to propositions of the secularization of the world, rather than approaching either as a mere straw figure, it is important to track how the interlacing of these propositional forms has undergirded not only academic and everyday understandings, but also the social worlds that they seek to explain.

27 Timothy Mitchell, "The stage of modernity," in Timothy Mitchell (ed.), *Questions of Modernity* (Minneapolis: University of Minnesota Press, 2000), p. 15, emphasis in the original.

28 Habermas, *Philosophical Discourse of Modernity*, p. 5. Saliently, Habermas is summarizing significant historical and philosophical writings here.

29 Asad, *Genealogies of Religion*, p. 269.

30 A cautious clarification is in order at this point. While it is entirely salient to register the place of the abiding oppositions of modernity in the molding of social worlds, it is equally important to attend to the contending elaborations of the analytical, ideological, and everyday separation between enchanted or traditional cultures and disenchanted

or modern societies, turning on space and time. The contentions are present at the core of post-Enlightenment thought and non-Western scholarship, each including critiques of the West in the past and the present. Indeed, the actual elaborations of the hierarchical oppositions of modernity have imbued them with contradictory value and contrary salience. Here are to be found ambivalences, ambiguities, and excesses of meaning and authority. All of this is registered by the *particular* unraveling of divergent traditions of understanding and explanation at the heart of modernity as ideology and history. My reference is to the opposed tendencies that have been described as those of "rationalism" and "historicism," of the "analytical" and the "hermeneutical," and of the "progressivist" and the "romantic." It is critical to track the frequent combination in intellectual practice of these tendencies in order to trace the contradictions and contentions and ambivalences and excesses of modern knowledge(s). Some of these questions are discussed in the next chapter.

31 Here, especially influential statements included W. W. Rostow, *The Stages of Economic Growth: A Non-Communist Manifesto* (Cambridge: Cambridge University Press, 1960); David E. Apter, *The Politics of Modernization* (Chicago, IL: University of Chicago Press, 1965).
32 I acknowledge that reassessments of modernization have emphasized the place of "tradition" in elaborations of "development," for example. But such understandings continue to be based on the enduring oppositions – and teleological templates of space-time – of discourses of modernity.
33 Theodor Adorno, *Minima Moralia: Reflections from Damaged Life*, trans. E. F. N. Jephcott (London: Verso, 2005), p. 218.
34 Peter Childs, *Modernism: The New Cultural Idiom* (New York: Routledge, 2000), p. 17.
35 See, for example, Dube, *Stitches on Time*; Dube, *After Conversion*; and Dube, *Enchantments of Modernity*.
36 Dube, *Stitches on Time*, particularly p. 11.
37 I am developing here ideas that were first initiated in Dube, *Stitches on Time*, p. 11.
38 Indeed, all of this is to emphasize, too, the importance of affect and subjectivity – long privileged within modernism(s) – in explorations of modernity. Yet, it is to do so while refusing to approach affect(s) as the

repressed other of the modern as well as eschewing an understanding of subject(s) as "sovereign" ones.

39 These various modern subjects in the West and the non-West are also subjects of modernity. But, once more, not all subjects of modernity are modern subjects, of course. At any rate, I hope it is clear that the dispositions to modernity that I am outlining do not claim to comprehensively define this category, entity, and process. Rather my bid is to open up spaces and suggest resources for discussing procedures of modernity and their many persuasions.

40 See, particularly, Asad, *Genealogies of Religion*. See also Russell McCutcheon, *Manufacturing Religion: The Discourse on Sui Generis Religion and the Politics of Nostalgia* (New York: Oxford University Press, 1997). The teleological cast of such a narrative of secularization bears connections with what Charles Taylor has called a "subtraction story." Charles Taylor, *A Secular Age* (Cambridge, MA: Harvard University Press, 2007).

41 See, for example, Peter van der Veer and Hartmut Lehmann (eds.), *Nation and Religion: Perspectives on Europe and Asia* (Princeton, NJ: Princeton University Press, 1999).

42 Against the grain of what such assertions insinuate regarding the stipulations of secularization in everyday life, consider the implications of Crapanzano's explorations of the dense presence of "literalism" in religion and the law in the US today. Crapanzano, *Serving the Word*.

43 To state matters in this way is not to foreclose the category of "tradition." Rather it is bring into view distinct horizons for carefully considering the possibilities of "tradition" as expressed, for example, in Alasdair MacIntyre, *After Virtue* (Notre Dame, IN: University of Notre Dame Press, 1983); and Stephen Watson, *Tradition(s): Refiguring Community and Virtue in Classical German Thought* (Bloomington: Indiana University Press, 1997).

44 I discuss these issues – in dialogue with part of the wide literature they have spawned – in Dube, *Stitches on Time* and Dube, "Terms that bind."

45 I am suggesting that critical attributes of monumental history variously lie at the core of what Hansen and Stepputat not so long ago classified as three "practical" languages of governance and three "symbolic" languages of authority that are "particularly relevant" for understanding the state. (The former consist of the state's "assertion of territorial

sovereignty by the monopolization of violence," "gathering and control of knowledge of the population," and "development and management of the 'national economy.'" The latter consist of "the institutionalization of law and legal discourse as the authoritative language of the state," "the materialization of the state in series of permanent signs and rituals," and "the nationalization of the territory and the institutions of the state through inscription of a history and shared community on landscapes and cultural community.") Clearly, monumental history articulates the institution of the nation as an "imagined community," the labor of anti-colonial nationalist difference, and everyday configurations of state and nation. Thomas Blom Hansen and Finn Stepputat, "Introduction: states of imagination," in Thomas Blom Hansen and Finn Stepputat (eds.), *States of Imagination: Ethnographic Explorations of the Postcolonial State* (Durham, NC: Duke University Press, 2001), pp. 7–9. Consider also Benedict Anderson, *Imagined Communities: Reflections on the Origin and Spread of Nationalism* (London: Verso, 1983); and Chatterjee, *The Nation and its Fragments*.

46 A wider discussion of Indian nationalism, based on recent writings on the question, is to be found in Dube, "Terms that bind."

47 Chatterjee, *The Nation and its Fragments*. See also Chapter 2 above.

48 See, particularly, Ajay Skaria, *Unconditional Equality: Gandhi's Religion of Resistance* (Minneapolis: University of Minnesota Press, 2016).

49 To argue for such disjunctions and distinctions at the core of Indian anti-colonial nationalisms is not to posit that, whether in their subaltern incarnation or their middle-class avatar, such endeavors embodied innocent and immaculate alterity. The picture is muddier and murkier, an issue discussed in Dube, "Terms that bind."

50 Hansen, *Saffron Wave*, pp. 90, 231.

51 It might be argued that Narendra Modi's current straightforward developmental discourse betrays no ambivalence at all toward modernity. Yet the internal tensions within the Hindu Right as regards his corporatist leadership – and Modi's own stance on history and Hinduism – are acutely indicative of such ambiguity and ambivalence.

52 These critical perspectives on modernity in India are discussed in detail in Dube, *After Conversion*.

53 Nandy, *Intimate Enemy*; *Traditions, Tyranny, and Utopias*; *Savage Freud*; *An Ambiguous Journey to the City*. In a related vein, consider Vinay Lal, *The History of History: Politics and Scholarship in Modern India* (New Delhi: Oxford University Press, 2003). Chakrabarty, *Provincializing Europe* and *Habitations of Modernity*. From within a significant corpus that addresses questions of modernity in South Asia, implicitly and explicitly, see, for example, Hansen, *Saffron Wave*; Veena Das, *Critical Events: An Anthropological Perspective on Contemporary India* (Delhi: Oxford University Press, 1995); Akhil Gupta, *Red Tape: Bureaucracy, Structural Violence, and Poverty in India* (Durham, NC: Duke University Press, 2012); Gupta, *Postcolonial Developments*; Axel, *Nation's Tortured Body*; Appadurai, *Modernity at Large*; Emma Tarlo, *Unsettling Memories: Narratives of India's "Emergency"* (New Delhi: Permanent Black, 2003); C. J. Fuller and Véronique Bénéï (eds.), *The Everyday State and Society in Modern India* (New Delhi: Social Science Press, 2000); Thomas Blom Hansen, *Wages of Violence: Naming and Identity in Postcolonial Bombay* (Princeton, NJ: Princeton University Press, 2001); Laura Bear, *Lines of the Nation: Indian Railway Workers, Bureaucracy, and the Intimate Historical Self* (New York: Columbia University Press, 2007); Amanda J. Weidman, *Singing the Classical, Voicing the Modern: The Postcolonial Politics of Music in South India* (Durham, NC: Duke University Press, 2006); Sanjay Seth, *Subject Lessons: The Western Education of Colonial India* (Durham, NC: Duke University Press, 2007); Nicholas Dirks, *Castes of Mind: Colonialism and the Making of Modern India* (Princeton, NJ: Princeton University Press, 2001); Peter van der Veer, *Imperial Encounters: Religion and Modernity in India and Britain* (Princeton, NJ: Princeton University Press, 2001); Manu Goswami, *Producing India: From Colonial Economy to National Space* (Chicago, IL: University of Chicago Press, 2004); Anand Pandian, *Crooked Stalks: Cultivating Virtue in South India* (Durham, NC: Duke University Press, 2009); Anupama Rao, *The Caste Question: Dalits and the Politics of Modern India* (Berkeley: University of California Press, 2009); Ajantha Subramanian, *Shorelines: Spaces and Rights in South Asia* (Stanford, CA: Stanford University Press, 2009); Véronique Bénéï, *Schooling Passions: Nation, History, and Language in Contemporary Western India* (Stanford, CA: Stanford University Press, 2008); and Ritu

Birla, *Stages of Capital: Law, Culture, and Market Governance in Late Colonial India* (Durham, NC: Duke University Press, 2009). Questions of modernity, especially those concerning the terms of a distinctively Indian modernist aesthetics, have been raised in several ways in the practice and discussion of art and cinema in India. See, for example, Geeta Kapur, *When was Modernism: Essays on Contemporary Cultural Practice in India* (New Delhi: Tulika, 2000); and Gulammohammed Sheikh (ed.) *Contemporary Art in Baroda* (New Delhi: Tulika, 1997). Concerning anthropological and historical perspectives related to the presence and play of the "visual" as variously part of the colonial and the national, the postcolonial and the modern, see, for instance, Christopher Pinney, *Camera Indica: The Social Life of Indian Photographs* (Chicago, IL: University of Chicago Press, 1998); William Mazzarella, *Shoveling Smoke: Advertising and Globalization in Contemporary India* (Durham, NC: Duke University Press, 2003); and Tapati Guha-Thakurta, *Monuments, Objects, Histories: Art in Colonial and Post-Colonial India* (New York: Columbia University Press, 2004).

54 Martin W. Lewis and Kären Wigen, *The Myth of Continents: A Critique of Metageography* (Berkeley: University of California Press, 1997).

55 Said, *Orientalism*.

56 Fernando Coronil, "Beyond Occidentalism: toward nonimperial geohistorical categories," *Cultural Anthropology* 11 (1996): 51–87.

57 For example, Octavio Paz, *Vislumbres de la India* (Barcelona: Seix Barral, 1995).

58 Meaghan Morris, "Metamorphoses at Sydney Tower," *New Formations* 11 (1990): 5–18.

59 Ángel Rama, *La ciudad letrada* (Hanover, NH: Ediciones del Norte, 1984); Doris Sommer, *Foundational Fictions: The National Romances of Latin America* (Berkeley: University of California Press, 1991); Julio Ramos, *Desencuentros de la modernidad en América Latina: literatura y política en el siglo XIX* (Mexico: Fondo de Cultura Económica, 1989); Jean Franco, *Plotting Women* (New York: Columbia University Press, 1989); and Jean Franco, *Critical Passions: Selected Essays* (Durham, NC: Duke University Press, 1999).

60 Tracey Hedrick, *Mestizo Modernism: Race, Nation, and Identity in Latin American Culture, 1900–1940* (New Brunswick, NJ: Rutgers University

Press, 2003); Jean Franco, *The Decline and Fall of the Lettered City: Latin America in the Cold War* (Cambridge, MA: Harvard University Press, 2002); Roberto González Echevarría, *Mito y archivo: una teoría de la narrativa latinoamericana* (Mexico: Fondo de Cultura Económica, 1998).

61 For example, Octavio Paz, *El ogro filantrópico: historia y política, 1971–1978* (Mexico: Joaquín Mortiz, 1979); José Ignacio Cabrujas, "El estado del disímulo," in José Ignacio Cabrujas, *Heterodoxia y estado: 5 respuestas* (Caracas: COPRA, 1987), pp. 7–35.

62 Michael Taussig, *My Cocaine Museum* (Chicago, IL: University of Chicago Press, 2004); Taussig, *Shamanism, Colonialism, and the Wild Man*; and Price, *The Convict and the Colonel*.

63 Coronil, *The Magical State*.

64 Valerie Fraser, *Building the New World: Modern Architecture in Latin America* (London: Verso, 2001); Jean-François Lejeune, *Cruelty and Utopia: Cities and Landscapes of Latin America* (Princeton, NJ: Princeton Architectural Press, 2005).

65 Florencia E. Mallon, *Courage Tastes of Blood: The Mapuche Community of Nicolás Ailío and the Chilean State, 1906–2001* (Durham, NC: Duke University Press, 2005); Steve Stern, *Remembering Pinochet's Chile: On the Eve of London 1998* (Durham, NC: Duke University Press, 2006); Steve Stern, *Battling for Hearts and Minds: Memory Struggles in Pinochet's Chile, 1973–1988* (Durham, NC: Duke University Press, 2006). See also Mark Thurner, *From Two Republics to One Divided: Contradictions of Postcolonial Nationmaking in Andean Peru* (Durham, NC: Duke University Press, 1997).

66 Ana María Alonso, "Territorializing the nation and 'integrating the Indian': 'Mestizage' in Mexican official discourses and public culture," in Thomas Blom Hansen and Finn Stepputat (eds.), *Sovereign Bodies: Citizens, Migrants, and States in the Postcolonial World* (Princeton, NJ: Princeton University Press, 2005), pp. 39–60; Sarah A. Radcliffe, "Imagining the state as a space: territoriality and the formation of the state in Ecuador," in Hansen and Stepputat, *States of Imagination*, pp. 123–45.

67 George Yúdice, *The Expediency of Culture: Uses of Culture in the Global Era* (Durham, NC: Duke University Press, 2004).

68 Beverley, *Subalternity and Representation*; Rodríguez, *Latin American Subaltern Studies Reader*; José Rabasa, *Writing Violence on the Northern*

Frontier: The Historiography of Sixteenth-Century New Mexico and Florida and the Legacy of Conquest (Durham, NC: Duke University Press, 2000); Roger Bartra, *El salvaje en el espejo* (Mexico: UNAM, 1992); Mark Thurner and Andrés Guerrero (eds.), *After Spanish Rule: Postcolonial Predicaments of the Americas* (Durham, NC: Duke University Press, 2003); Gareth Williams, *The Other Side of the Popular: Neoliberalism and Subalternity in Latin America* (Durham, NC: Duke University Press, 2002).

69 Néstor García Canclini, *Culturas híbridas: estrategias para entrar y salir de la modernidad* (Mexico: Grijalbo, 1989).

70 Claudio Lomnitz-Adler, *Exits from the Labyrinth: Culture and Ideology in the Mexican National Space* (Berkeley: University of California Press, 1993); Claudio Lomnitz-Adler, *Modernidad indiana: nueve ensayos sobre nación y mediación en México* (Mexico: Planeta, 1999); Mauricio Tenorio-Trillo, *Artilugio de la nación moderna: México en las exposiciones universales, 1880–1930* (Mexico: Fondo de Cultura Económica, 1998); María Josefina Saldaña-Portillo, *The Revolutionary Imagination in the Americas and the Age of Development* (Durham, NC: Duke University Press, 2003); Mark Overmyer-Velázquez, *Visions of the Emerald City: Modernity, Tradition, and the Formation of Porfirian Oaxaca, Mexico* (Durham, NC: Duke University Press, 2006).

71 Rebecca J. Lester, *Jesus in Our Wombs: Embodying Modernity in a Mexican Convent* (Berkeley: University of California Press, 2005); Pamela Voekel, *Alone Before God: The Religious Origins of Modernity in Mexico* (Durham, NC: Duke University Press, 2002); Serge Gruzinski, *Images at War: Mexico from Columbus to* Blade Runner *(1492–2019)* (Durham, NC: Duke University Press, 2001).

72 Bolivar Echeverría, *La modernidad de lo barroco* (Mexico: UAM, 1998).

73 Joanne Rappaport, *Intercultural Utopias: Public Intellectuals, Cultural Experimentation, and Ethnic Pluralism in Colombia* (Durham, NC: Duke University Press, 2005); Coronil, *The Magical State*; Michel-Rolph Trouillot, "North Atlantic universals: analytical fictions 1492–1945," in Dube (ed.), *Enchantments of Modernity*, pp. 45–66.

74 Stephan Palmié, *Wizards and Scientists: Explorations in Afro-Cuban Modernity and Tradition* (Durham, NC: Duke University Press, 2002); Sibylle Fischer, *Modernity Disavowed: Haiti and the Cultures of Slavery in the Age of Revolution* (Durham, NC: Duke University Press, 2004); Peter

Redfield, *Space in the Tropics: From Convicts to Rockets in French Guiana* (Berkeley: University of California Press, 2000); David Scott, *Conscripts of Modernity: The Tragedy of Colonial Enlightenment* (Durham, NC: Duke University Press, 2005).

75 For such writings in other contexts, see Rofel, *Other Modernities*; Ferguson, *Expectations of Modernity*; Donald Donham, *Marxist Modern: An Ethnograhic History of the Ethiopian Revolution* (Berkeley: University of California Press, 1999); Piot, *Remotely Global*; Comaroff and Comaroff, *Of Revelation and Revolution*; Harootunian, *Overcome by Modernity*; Chakrabarty, *Provincializing Europe*; Chakrabarty, *Habitations of Modernity*; Dube, *Stitches on Time*; Dube, *Postcolonial Passages*; Dube (ed.), *Enchantments of Modernity*; and Saurabh Dube (ed.), *Modern Makeovers: Handbook of Modernity in South Asia* (New York: Oxford University Press, 2011).

76 For different expressions of such procedures, see S. K. White, *Sustaining Affirmation*; Chakrabarty, *Provincializing Europe*; and William E. Connolly, *The Ethos of Pluralization* (Minneapolis: University of Minnesota Press, 1995). See also Taussig, *Defacement*.

Figure 1 Savindra Sawarkar, "Untouchable, Peshwa in Pune," etching, 35 × 29 cm.

Figure 2 Savindra Sawarkar, "Untouchable with Dead Cow," dry-point, 26 × 19 cm.

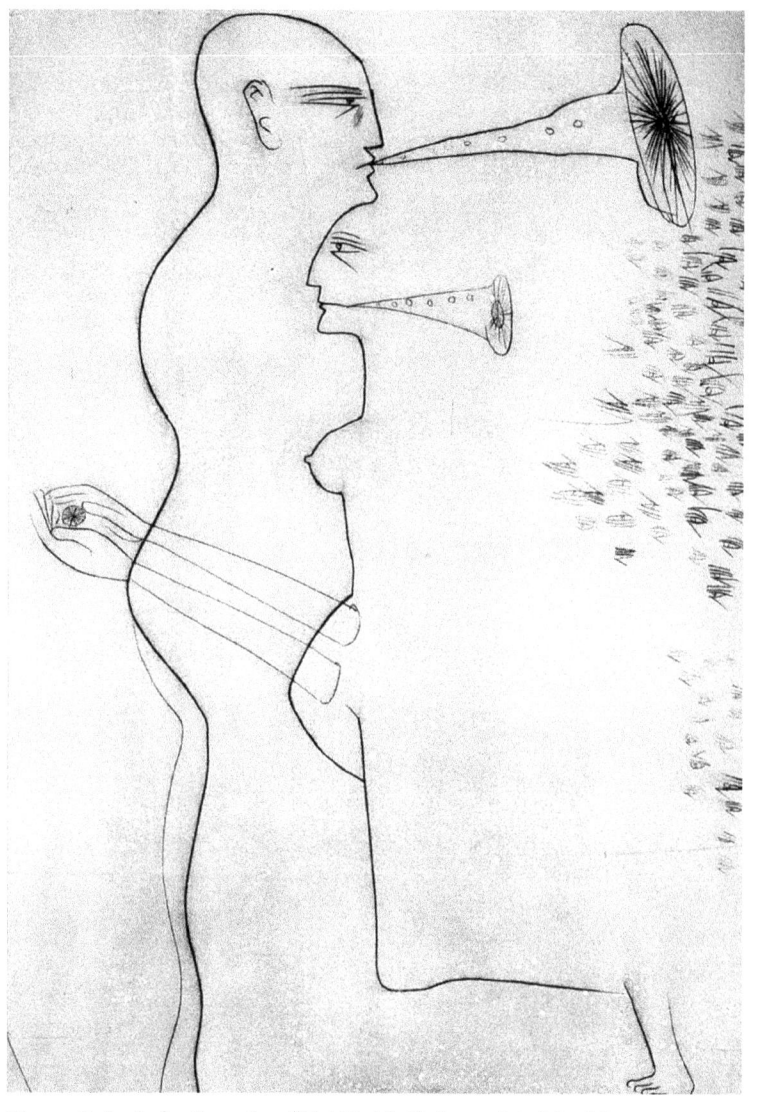

Figure 3 Savindra Sawarkar, "Untitled 0.9," dry-point, 36 × 28 cm.

Figure 4 Savindra Sawarkar, "Devadasi with pig voice," drawing on paper, 20 × 26 cm.

Figure 5 Savindra Sawarkar, "Introspecting Buddha," line drawing, 23 × 30 cm.

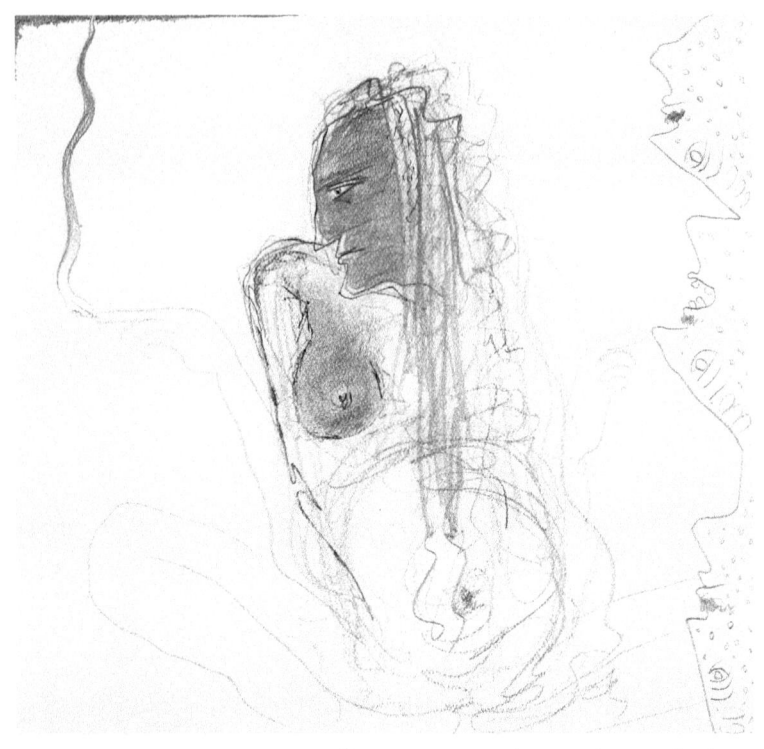

Figure 6 Savindra Sawarkar, "Pregnant Devadasi with upside-down Brahman," mixed media on paper, 18 × 18 cm.

4

Disciplines of modernity: entanglements and ambiguities

This chapter discusses aspects of the interplay between the disciplines and modernity, as mediated by temporal-spatial imperatives. It focuses on the relationship between anthropology and history in order to discuss formations of modern knowledge as themselves forming critical subjects and crucial procedures of modernity. On the one hand, I explore the mutual interchange of time and space as at once segregating yet binding these knowledge formations, whose implications reach far beyond their purely disciplinary configurations. On the other, I consider the presence of ambivalence and ambiguity at the core of recent renovations of anthropology and history, often overlooked by presumptions of progress in explanations of disciplines and their makeovers. At stake in this discussion are the contradictions and contentions of modernity, ever shaped by configurations of time and space, from the braiding of analytical and hermeneutic orientations to the making of historical anthropology.

Anthropology and time

For a very long time now, anthropological understandings have displayed varied dispositions toward issues of temporality and history, from willing disregard and uneasy elision to formative ambivalences and constitutive contradictions. Yet time itself has never been absent from such comprehensions. Today, there is wide acknowledgment of the epistemic violence that attended the birth and growth of modern anthropology. Here were to be found temporal sequences, based on evolutionary principles and racist presuppositions, which projected hierarchical stages of civilizations, societies, and peoples. At the same time, it is worth considering whether such hierarchically ordered evolutionary mappings of cultures and societies – turning on the "savage" form and the "primitive" figure – were excised from disciplinary formations with the emergence of fieldwork-based "scientific" anthropology in the first half of the twentieth century.

First, the apparent ruptures of functionalist and structural-functionalist anthropology with evolutionist (and diffusionist) principles on the grounds of their speculative procedures had wider consequences. They entailed a wider suspicion toward, the placing of a question mark on, history as such within the discipline.[1] Now the practice of anthropology could proceed in contradistinction to the writing of history. Second, these tendencies were conjoined with the influence of Durkheimian sociology in the shaping of structural-functionalist tenets. Such conjunctions led to pervasive presuppositions that societal arrangements were better understood in abstraction from their historical transformations. They called forth and rested on analytical oppositions between "synchrony" and "diachrony" or "statics" and "dynamics," where in each copula the former term was privileged over the latter concerning the object of anthropology. Third, these emphases were further bound to wider anthropological predilections toward seeking out continuity and consensus, rather than change and conflict, in the societies being studied. Fourth and finally, the ambivalence toward the temporal dimensions of structure and culture within the discipline was implicitly founded on broad disjunctions between Western societies grounded in history and reason, on the one hand, and non-Western cultures held in place by myth and ritual, on the other.[2]

Such premises came to underlie particular protocols of salvage anthropology, also shoring up formative dispositions of the ethnographic enterprise. These procedures and orientations have been imaginatively summarized by Bernard Cohn. His words have been quoted often, yet they bear repetition. Cohn writes:

The anthropologist posits a place where the natives are authentic ... and strives to deny the central historical fact that the people he or she studies are constituted in the historically significant colonial situation, affirming instead that they are somehow out of time and history. This timelessness is reflected in the anthropologist's basic model of change, what I would term the "missionary in the row boat" model. In this model, the missionary, the trader, the labour recruiter or the government official arrives with the bible, the mumu, tobacco, steel axes or other items of Western domination on an island whose society and culture are rocking along in the never-never land of structural-functionalism [tradition], and with the onslaught of the new, the social structure, values and life-ways of the "happy" natives crumble. The anthropologist follows in the wake of the impacts caused by Western agents of change, and then tries to recover what might have been. The anthropologist searches for the elders with the richest memories of days gone by, assiduously records their ethnographic texts, and then puts together between the covers of their monographs a picture of the natives of Anthropologyland. The peoples of Anthropologyland, like all God's Children got shoes, got structure ... These structures the anthropologist finds have always been there, unbeknownst to their passive carriers, functioning to keep the natives in their timeless spaceless paradise.[3]

Although Cohn's statement primarily criticizes structural-functionalism, its ironic edge carries wider implications. The statement not only underscores pervasive procedures of anthropological practice that have forged a tendentious timeless "tradition" through narrative techniques and analytical projections of a lasting "ethnographic present." It also arguably points toward intrusive presumptions that have sharply separated the dynamic time of the ethnographer's society from the static temporality of anthropological objects. Together, in widespread ethnographic orientations, change and transformation usually entered native structure in exogenous ways.

All of this has critical ramifications. Johannes Fabian has pointed to the repeated ways in which anthropological inquiry has construed its object as the irremediable other through measures turning on temporality: the ethnographic object is denied the "coevalness of time" with the instant of the anthropologist subject.[4] In other words, the (observing) subject and the (observed) object are precisely separated through time to inhabit distinct temporalities, the historical time of the former always ahead of the mythic time of the latter. Here, the temporal divide has meant that not only anthropological objects but ethnographic practice have emerged as being out of time, albeit in ambivalent and disjunctive ways. On the one hand, the temporal dimensions of anthropological writing have appeared effaced through their elision with both the taken-for-granted time and space of the modern subject and the objective time of scientific knowledge. On the other, the temporality of anthropological others – their time/timelessness – could only emerge as being external to and lagging behind the space and time of the writing of ethnography.[5] All of this has defined the "savage slot" and the "native niche" of anthropology that have been constitutive of the discipline.[6]

None of this is to deny that such schemes have been attended by contentions and exceptions within the discipline. These are exactly related to the formations and tensions of anthropology, incisively articulated by George Stocking, Jr.:

> The greatest retrospective unity of the discourses subsumed within the rubric "anthropology" is to be found in the substantive concern with the peoples who were long stigmatized as "savages," and who, in the nineteenth century, tended to be excluded from other human scientific disciplines by the very process of their substantive-cum-methodological definition (the economist's concern with the money economy; the historian's concern with written documents, etc.) … to study the history of anthropology is to … describe and to interpret or explain the "otherness" of populations encountered in European overseas expansion. Although thus fundamentally (and oppositionally) diversitarian in impulse, such study has usually implied a reflexivity which reencompassed the European self and alien "other" within a unitary humankind. This history of anthropology may thus be viewed as a continuing (and complex) dialectic between the universalism of "anthropos" and the diversitarianism of "ethnos" or, from the perspective of particular historical moments, between the Enlightenment and the Romantic impulse.[7]

At stake, then, are attempts to reconcile tensions between "generic human rationality" and "the biological unity of mankind," on the one hand, with the enormous variation of cultural formations, on the other, issues to which I shall return. The immediate point is that the constitutive presuppositions and procedures concerning time-space within the ethnographic enterprise require staying with longer. They intimate the persistent influence of evolutionist understandings on contemporary anthropology.[8] At the same time, beyond purely disciplinary considerations, they insinuate pervasive "meta-geographical" projections. Turning on time and space, such projections draw on developmental visions of history of academic bents, quotidian persuasions, and their persistent interchanges. Authoritatively, if ambiguously, temporally and spatially they carve up social worlds into enchanted terrains of tradition and disenchanted domains of modernity.

Under issue in fact is nothing less than the hierarchical ordering of time-space as part of the wide-ranging interplay between modern knowledge, anthropological understandings, historical blueprints, and their quotidian configurations. Consider the manner in which patterns of history and designs of culture have been understood in the past and the present through formidable antinomies between static enchanted communities and dynamic modern societies. This was discussed at length in the previous chapter under the rubrics of the enchantments and oppositions of modernity. Indeed, I hope to have underscored there the salience of registering the place of the spatial-temporal oppositions of modernity in the molding of social worlds.

My point now is that it is equally important to attend to the contending elaborations of the analytical, ideological, and everyday separation between enchanted or traditional cultures and disenchanted or modern societies. The contentions are present at the core of post-Enlightenment thought and non-Western scholarship, each including critiques of the West in the past and the present. Indeed, the actual elaborations of the hierarchical oppositions of modernity, turning on time and space, have imbued them with contradictory value and contrary salience. Here are to be found ambivalences, ambiguities, and excesses of meaning and authority. All of this is registered by the *particular* unraveling of divergent traditions of understanding and explanation at the heart of modernity as ideology and history. I am writing of the opposed tendencies that have been described as those of rationalism and historicism, of the analytical and the hermeneutical, and of the progressivist and the romantic.[9] It is critical to track the frequent combination in intellectual practice of these tendencies in order to trace the contradictions and contentions and ambivalences and excesses of modern knowledge(s), as part of processes of modernity. Together, such interleaving expressions reveal that the terms of modernity are assiduously articulated, but that they are also out of joint with themselves.

Ethnography and temporality: key protagonists

In tune with these considerations, let me turn to some of the contradictions and contentions that have characterized ethnographic orientations to time and temporality, which further carry critical connotations of space and spatiality. I shall first focus on aspects of the work of Franz Boas, E. E. Evans-Pritchard, and Pierre Bourdieu, three masters of the anthropological craft who represent different historical moments, explanatory efforts, and epistemological styles from the discipline's pasts. My choice of these scholars has much to do with their particular engagements with temporality. Then, I shall bring home these deliberations by discussing an ethnographic study from India, located on the cusp of colony and nation, which intimates the acute articulations of time-space with the anthropological enterprise at large.

We have noted the racial assumptions that underlay evolutionary anthropology in the later nineteenth and early twentieth centuries. Franz Boas (1858–1942) issued the single greatest early disciplinary challenge to such schemes and presuppositions.[10] At the beginning of the twentieth century, Boas defined anthropological knowledge as consisting of "the biological history of mankind in all its varieties; linguistics applied to people without written languages; the ethnology of people without historic records; and prehistoric archaeology."[11] Across his career, he added to all these forms of inquiry. At the same time, Boas's distinctive contribution to anthropology derived from his insistence on the diachronic dimensions of the discipline.[12] As George Stocking, Jr., has argued, "For Boas, the 'otherness' which is the subject matter of anthropology was to be explained as the product of change of time," an insistence that covered his unifying definition of the discipline.[13] Here was to be found his critique of evolutionary assumption, "a neo-ethnological critique of 'the comparative method' of classical evolutionism."[14]

Today there is appreciation not only of how Boas constructed a domain of inquiry mostly free of biological determinism to lay the basis for the modern disciplinary conception of culture as pluralistic and relativistic, but also of how his particular turn to the diachronic, the historical, and the temporal signified a road mainly not taken by anthropology during most of the twentieth century.[15] Indeed, Boas's orientation to anthropological knowledge can emerge in current commentaries as primarily building on nineteenth-century romantic and hermeneutic traditions in European science, philosophy, and history.[16] Yet it would not do to simply celebrate Boas's critique of evolutionary and racialist presuppositions from the vantage point of our present. Nor would it be enough to emphasize only the romantic underpinnings of his anthropology. In fact the work of Boas is best understood as straddling the dualism between progressivist and romantic traditions, at once braiding together while retaining a tension between these opposed tendencies. Here is to be found the salient entwining of contending schemes of modern knowledge, which have variously shored up anthropology and which reveal ambivalent articulations of time-space, as key components of worlds of modernity.

On the one hand, in the work of Boas, the progressivist stance was profoundly manifest in key nineteenth-century liberal beliefs, which stressed scientific knowledge and individual freedom. They expressed Boas's broader historical vision and developmental viewpoint. He believed in a cumulative rational knowledge that underlay innate human progress. Here human progress was understood not in a generalized manner but as intimating specifically the growth of what Boas called "our own" Western modern civilization.[17] Indeed, this perspective was marked by a fatalistic attitude toward technologically based historical development as not only pushing forward Western civilization but confronting and vanquishing "technologically primitive cultures." At the same time, Boas's universalistic rationalism also led him to assert the existence of "general values" that were "cumulatively realized" in the history of human civilization and "variously realized" in different human cultures. Thus Boas's well-known questioning of his own Western civilization and his belief in the alternative values of other cultures went hand in hand with his lack of submission to cultural relativism and faith in a non-contingent realm of scientific truth.[18]

On the other hand, throughout Boas's career, crosscutting this optimistic, rationalist, and universalistic progressivist stance was a more pessimistic, affective, and particularistic romanticist disposition. Arguably, the latter sensibility could not but inform both Boas's dissatisfaction with Western civilization and the manner in which such "alienation" found expression in his anticipation of a pluralistic conception of culture that was itself based on recognition of "the legitimacy of alternative value systems." At stake in this sensibility was an aesthetic undercurrent – reinforced by Boas's life experiences, yet carrying wider resonances – that made him acutely "aware of the role of irrational factors in human life." These tendencies were articulated positively in the variety of human forms of culture, but they were expressed negatively in the way particular customs of determinate groups could be retrospectively rationalized as universal norms, including in the case of race. Unsurprisingly, Boas's lifelong devotion to the study of culture and race, especially the exclusivity they each defined, stressed the profoundly contingent conditioning by history of these phenomena.[19]

Boas's thought derived motive force from its relentlessly restless juxtaposition of wider progressivist and romantic tendencies, its almost inevitable interleaving of universalistic and rationalist orientations with particularistic and affective dispositions. Note the contrasts. Boas "retained all his life a rather idealized and absolutistic conception of science" that was unambiguously non-contingent, but he also granted a necessary, contingent value to specific cultural groupings.

Boas singularly conjoined human progress and technologically based historical process with Western civilization, but he equally defended the "mental capacity" of "primitive man" to participate fully in "modern civilization."[20] Boas exclusively envisioned rational advance in the image of Western civilization, but he crucially affirmed the values of non-European cultures and established thereby "a kind of Archimedian leverage point" for a critique of his own civilization.[21]

Thus, the anthropologist avowed dominant representations of time under modernity to construe Europe as the enshrined space of progress, rationality, and history, but he also implicitly admitted contingent, different formations of time-space as undergirding distinct cultures. Arguably, this interleaving of the progressivist and the romantic led Boas not only to passively enact but to actively produce discrete notations of the temporal and the spatial as part of his anthropological practice. According to established disciplinary lore, Boas's career had a dramatic end. At a luncheon in New York, Boas had just begun to say, "I have a new theory of culture ...," when he fell dead in mid-sentence. In death as in life, Franz Boas encapsulated not only the ambiguities but the ironies of anthropology – in an acute way, his own manner.

The contrary dispositions constitutive of the anthropological enterprise were no less characteristic of the work of the British anthropologist E. E. Evans-Pritchard (1902–73), widely known as "E. P." In conventional anthropological wisdom, the work of E. P. has been approached as consolidating the structural-functional inquiry initiated by A. R. Radcliffe-Brown. Here there is acknowledgment of E. P.'s earlier interactions with Malinowski and there is recognition that from the 1950s onward his work followed different pathways of theory and explication. The latter included E. P.'s famous endorsement of anthropology as a humanistic (and not natural-scientific) discipline as well as his assertions of the close linkages of anthropology with history.[22] They extended to the questions E. P. raised concerning the inability of anthropologists to enter the minds of the people they studied; the limits of their scholarly motivations that often mirrored ethnocentric assumptions of their own cultures, and the narrowness of biological, sociological, and psychological theories of religion.[23] At the same time, despite such avowals of the shifts in E. P.'s anthropology, the centerpiece of his contribution to the discipline is nonetheless often assumed to consist of his development of structural-functionalism, reflecting the hagiography of this paradigm.[24]

In the face of such currents, I would like to indicate a distinct understanding of E. P.'s work, an approach that turns on critically registering how his writings were shaped by their salient interleaving of hermeneutic strands and analytical strains, which intimate ambiguous articulations, curious constructions, and particular productions of time-space. Such an orientation to E. P.'s anthropology does not deny, for example, the place of his monograph on the Nuer people as a flagship endeavor of structural-functionalist analysis.[25] Nor does it overlook the fact that E. P.'s work bore close connections with the formative presuppositions of both structural-functionalism and functionalism that have society as an integrated system. Rather, the disposition being outlined seeks to open up the terms of understanding of E. P.'s arguments and analyses.

In his discussion of time E. P. drew upon the work of both Durkheim and Malinowski.[26] In *The Nuer*, as well as in an essay on time-reckoning among this people, E. P. famously developed the notion of "oecological" time.[27] This notion emerged closely bound to time-reckoning concepts, conveying "social activities" or a "relation between activities to one another."[28] Here time's passage is perceived through a lens of cultural concepts referring to activities – that is, through time-reckoning systems – rather than through an actual immersion in activities.[29] Yet for E. P. time also consists of the "rhythm" of basic activity cycles linked to natural cycles: daily cattle movements and seasonal passages between villages and camps as well as the distinctive tempo of each season. In this sense, time appears as socio-spatial motion or process and not simply static units or concepts of reckoning time.[30] Together, two sets of emphases – turning on time-reckoning yet also concrete activity – work in tandem in E. P.'s elaboration of oecological (or everyday) time.

Conversely, when E. P. turns to long-term, structural time his gaze entirely shifts away from activities, which, recall, provide a sense of concrete movement. Rather E. P. now comes to focus exclusively on conceptual frames. This is to say that structural time is not about an incremental movement, but rather it is fundamentally non-cumulative so that the genealogical grid of the Nuer creates only an immobile "illusion" of time.[31] Drawing on the insights of Nancy Munn, I am suggesting that E. P.'s structural time is not qualitative and concrete, but quantitative and geometrical. It is a static version and vision of time that occludes the concrete and lived space of activities.[32]

At stake here is a constitutive split, a formative discrepancy. On the one hand, in *describing* oecological time E. P. brings to bear on his discussion key spatio-temporal activities, including, for example, phased movements between village and camp. This is, broadly speaking, the hermeneutic moment in E. P.'s understanding(s) of time. On the other hand, precisely this "co-constitution" of time and space in activity is ignored and suppressed within E. P.'s formalist frames, so that structural time appears as an abstract geometry of social distance.[33] This might be broadly spoken of as the analytical moment in E. P.'s conception(s) of time.

Needless to say, the hermeneutic and analytical tendencies are profoundly entwined in E. P.'s anthropology. Indeed, it is such entwining that provides E. P.'s considerations of time-space with their motive force and their critical limitations. The Nuer people in E. P.'s hermeneutic hands have their own concrete everyday time-space. The move serves to found the temporal and the spatial in the image of social diversity and cultural heterogeneity, implicitly opening up thereby pervasive common sense and taken-for-granted terms of time and space as, respectively, a simply homogeneous measurement and a merely given backdrop, each with no qualitative distinctions. But the Nuer people according to E. P.'s analytic also do not have long-term time. The measure raises key questions regarding his analytical framework as bearing the profound impress of dominant representations and lasting projections, discussed earlier, of primitive places (the Nuer and their oecological time) and modern spaces (the West and its long-term time).

The interplay between hermeneutic dispositions and analytical tendencies – as well as the opposition of the enchanted and the modern – no less marks the influential corpus of the French sociologist-philosopher Pierre Bourdieu (1930–2002). Bourdieu combines phenomenological,

Weberian, and Marxian dispositions to underscore the temporal-spatial dimensions of social practices and practical actors, arguing that totalizing frameworks of fixed "rules" of action take temporality out of spatial "practice." Yet, precisely such hermeneutic moves crucially crisscross in Bourdieu's work with analytical orientations that bring into play implicit oppositions between the "traditional" and the "modern," collective rhythms and individual action, and "space" and "time." Here, in framing time through agent-oriented filters, Bourdieu spatially-temporally contrasts precapitalist traditional Algeria as marked by "foresight" only of the immediate future (already "implicit in the directly perceived present") *with* capitalist modern societies where "forecasting" entails an indefinite future, "a field of possibilities to be explored … by calculation." Moreover, in his later work, the emphasis on exploring practices through a focus on both the irreversible, enduring time of socio-spatial activities and the agent's strategic manipulation of this time disappear when Bourdieu turns his gaze toward collective (calendric) rhythms and periodization, which are explained through symbolic homologies that now readily dissolve into a generalized "logic of practice." Finally, Bourdieu's writings not only do not escape the analytical oppositions of time and space but they principally privilege the former over the latter.[34] None of this is to suggest that a focus on the entwining of hermeneutic and analytical dispositions holds the exclusive key to understanding traditions within anthropology and history, but to regard it rather as a possible means of reconsidering the past and the present of the disciplines, especially their articulations of space and time.

Indeed, staying with and thinking through the formative ambivalences of ethnography make it possible to approach anew anthropology in non-Western worlds through temporal-spatial considerations.[35] Here, I shall take up only one instance that brings home such considerations: the anthropologist S. C. Dube's first monograph, *The Kamar*.[36] This developed from the self-trained Indian ethnographer's PhD dissertation, the thesis and the manuscript being written and revised in the second half of the 1940s. Now, the study can be criticized as a variety of salvage anthropology in the colonial frame, denying temporality to its object – the Kamar hunter-gatherers and shifting cultivators living in the southern part of the Raipur district in the Chhattisgarh region – through the means of evolutionary assumption, which places these people as inhabiting primitive places, savage spaces. At the same time, I would like to critically open up *The Kamar* toward other readings, which stay with the tensions that have been formative of anthropology on the subcontinent (and at large). To be found is the ambiguous yet pervasive play in such scholarship of temporality and history – and of empire and nation – that at once does and undoes hierarchical social spaces. This requires further examination.

The Kamar lies on the cusp of the end of colonial rule and the arrival of Indian independence. The study was shaped by assumptions of the prior primitive, the savage slot, and the native niche within colonial/modern ethnography, presuppositions and projections that we encountered earlier. Yet the book equally referred to Kamar lifeways as embedded within wider societal processes. The work cast its subjects as caught within the larger terms of nationalist transformation. Nonetheless, it constantly returned to an essential Kamar tradition. The point is that such tension is not merely a shift of accent in the study between portions written before and after Indian independence, nor is the tension simply disabling. Rather, the tension is formative of the book, running through its chapters. *The Kamar* captures and contains the ambiguities and ambivalences of S. C. Dube's thought and writing – themselves indicative of the anxieties of his discipline – at a critical juncture, uneasily braiding anthropological demand and nationalist desire.

It should not be surprising that the formative tensions and the productive ambiguities of *The Kamar* are bound to the style, structure, and sentiment of the work. Dube considered that primitive cultures were not static but dynamic, especially since culture itself was an adaptive mechanism. Here the notion of the primitive entailed twin registers. On the one hand, it signified historical backwardness upon an evolutionist axis of time-space, a self-explanatory schema, assumed in place a priori, the dominant vision of anthropology and nation at the time. On the other, it registered cultural difference, coeval with the ethnographer, in the space-time of the nation, which invited empathetic understanding. Thus in the study the imperative to describe the Kamar way of life before it changed crisscrossed with the impulse to record the changing way of life of the Kamar, the dual dispositions pulling apart but also coming together.[37]

Now mine is not the suggestion that Dube' first ethnographic monograph prematurely reconciled these contrary tendencies. Rather, the point is that the text is the site where such contradictory pressures are visible, the terrain where these tensions were set in motion. This serves to further reveal and unravel the conjunctions and disjunctions between anthropological frames and nationalist formulations, the distinct construal of time and space as part of ethnographic practice. In turn, all of this raises key questions for critical considerations of social-scientific traditions, particularly of scholarship construed in the shadow of empire and nation, as productive of disjunctive spatial-temporal configurations.

History and culture

Time and temporality are usually projected as the stuff of history, quite as culture and tradition are implicitly understood as subjects of anthropology. At the same time, as was noted, just as terms of time and temporality have been differently present at the core of anthropology, so also the writing of history has variously entailed projections of culture and tradition. It is to the latter issue that I now turn. Here it is important to reiterate that, no less than anthropology, history writing has borne the profound impress of the hierarchical oppositions of modernity as well as acutely expressed the contentions of modern knowledge, each turning on space and time. This has underscored also the reciprocity of these inquiries.

First, processes of the institutionalization of the discipline in the Euro-American world in the nineteenth century – as also their significant antecedents – meant that history writing emerged as bearing the flag of the nation. Not only could the discipline be endlessly, ethnocentrically inward-looking, but it was shaped by sharp distinctions between the civilized and the backward concerning peoples and nations, metropolis and colony. Second, it followed that in Western arenas the relatively few historical accounts that were undertaken of distant, generally colonial, territories frequently presented such pasts as footnotes and appendices to the history of Europe. Third, the histories construed in colonized countries and newly independent nations were themselves often envisioned in the image of a progressive West, albeit using for their own purposes the temporal hierarchies and spatial oppositions of an exclusive modernity.[38] Fourth and finally, important strands of history writing could express hermeneutic, historicist, and Counter-Enlightenment impulses, but their relationship with an exclusive, hierarchical Western modernity was double-edged. Such histories acutely articulated notions of culture, tradition, and the *volk* (folk), generally of the nation, to critically question the conceit of an aggrandizing reason that they saw as the leitmotif of the Enlightenment. Conversely, such articulations of hermeneutic, historicist, and Counter-Enlightenment tendencies themselves could not escape, as we have seen, the developmental schemes of a somewhat singular history centered on Europe.[39] In different ways, on offer were distinct configurations of exclusive hierarchical time and segregated hierarchized spaces.

What about more contemporary history writing? Turning to Indian examples, here also the notions of culture and tradition can find rather particular manifestations, including their being turned into empty placeholders or their being articulated in all too tendentious ways. Consider now historical accounts that are principally unreflexive about their presuppositions and/or that frame themselves in primarily analytical modes. In two important essays, Gyanendra Pandey has focused on the failure of modern history writing to adequately address the pasts of sectarian religious violence in colonial and postcolonial India, particularly the violence that constituted the Partition of the subcontinent.[40] He sees this lack as a larger problem of historiography that subordinates the everyday experience of violence and pain to histories of transition – of state, modernity, reason, and progress.

We could agree or disagree with Pandey's sweeping condemnation of history – or, following Foucault, of "historian's history" – that is rendered as "History," the dark and ominous reflection, in the resolutely antimodernist mirror held up by these essays, of "Modernity."[41] Yet it is important to register that Pandey points toward how pervasive blueprints of modernity and progress, state and nation, and reason and civilization are built into the tune and *telos* of diverse historical narratives. These arrangements not only orchestrate the existence and the experience of everyday and extraordinary moments of violence, but they do so by at once naturalizing and excising the transformations of culture(s) and tradition(s) in which the violence is embedded. Here, violence, culture, and tradition are ghosts, specters that history writing attempts to exorcise, but phantasms whose haunting presence is constitutive of the historian's narrative.[42]

Pandey shows how in these numerous historical accounts the exact articulations of violence, culture, and tradition are ignored yet assimilated – as inconsequential episodes and inconvenient aberrations – into endless narratives of inevitable transitions. Thus, colonial representations of "native" unrest and nationalist writings on "communal" conflict share common ground since each offers explanations cast in terms of the criminality, backwardness, primitive passions, and ready unreason of the people. Equally, there are close connections between modern historians of different ideological persuasions in their depiction of the violence, for example, of the Partition of the subcontinent into India and Pakistan. There is little room in these accounts – constituted, variously, by a quest for underlying structures, a privileging of impersonal forces of history, and a preoccupation with the actions of great men – for discussing the trauma or meaning of sectarian violence, including critical considerations of the terms and transformations of cultures and traditions of which they form a part. Unsurprisingly violence and pain – and their mutual entailments with culture and tradition – are relegated here to the realm of "otherness," an otherness that formatively haunts history writing and the Indian subcontinent.[43] Here a singular temporality, centering on subterranean transitions of nation-states and hidden determinations of economic structures, speaks of a certain sameness of history, a regularity that is yet undergirded by split spaces of "reason" and "unreason."

Anthropology: ambiguities and reconfigurations

In recent years the writings of anthropologists and historians have shaped incisive readings of meaning and power in the past and the present. Indeed, over the last three decades it has become a matter of critical orthodoxy that, beginning in the 1970s, a vigorous emphasis on practice, processes, and conflict has replaced the prior privileging of structure, rules, and consensus within ethnography. Similar claims can be found today concerning history's immaculate embracing of anthropology. Such understandings point toward important disciplinary transformations over the past four decades. At the same time, such overplaying of the uniqueness of ethnography and history in our own times not only underplays the difference and diversity in the pasts of these disciplines, but it is beset by two other problems.

On the one hand, by bearing the impress of the *telos* of progress, such emphases cast the disciplines as necessarily unfolding from strength to strength. On the other, exactly at the moment such wider social imaginaries are drawn upon, the disciplines are understood as entirely autonomous, framed by their exclusive internal logics, tacitly bracketed from the historical transformations in which they are embedded. At stake, of course, are implicit expressions of dominant representations of historical temporality, which then shore up quiet presumptions regarding the separate spaces and the autonomous times of the disciplines. However, consider now that from the 1940s to the 1970s transformations within ethnography were influenced by processes of counter-colonialism, decolonization, and other struggles against imperialism and racism. This context shaped emergent critiques of reigning paradigms within the discipline.[44] Here was an interchange between the autonomy and logic governing continuities and changes within disciplinary traditions *and* processes of history and politics affecting inherited understandings of the world.

Some of this is clarified by examining the vexed relationship between action and structure, especially within functionalism, structuralism, and the questioning of these theoretical traditions.[45] As is well known, functionalism and structuralism have been prominent paradigms within the social sciences, the former till the 1960s and the latter till the 1970s.[46] The two traditions have understood "structure" differently. Yet both have accorded primacy to the object(s) of structure over the subject(s) of history, emphases that worked in tandem with their privileging of synchrony over diachrony. All of this defined the atemporal predication of human action upon underlying structure in these theoretical traditions, which overlooked the interleaving of structure and agency through time.[47] Over the past three decades, the interrogations of these traditions have resulted in vigorous emphases on practice, process, and power in anthropology, including through articulations of historical materials.[48]

My point here is that the questioning of such paradigms – where social action was predicated on sociological structure – should not be approached as an inexorable disciplinary process set in motion only after the late 1960s. Consider, for example, the discrepancy between classical functionalist apprehensions of social action and the emphatic agency of non-Western subjects as witnessed in counter-colonial movements, nationalist struggles, and other practices of colonized subalterns. Arguably, this gap called forth diverse shifts existing within British anthropology since at least the 1930s. These included the efforts of the Rhodes Livingstone Institute in Africa to move the locus of ethnographic inquiry from tribes to proletarians.[49] They extended to the emergent interrogation of functionalism within British anthropology, especially its many Manchester variants, which formed part of attempts to understand anew conflict, process, and action in social orders. In this terrain, questions of structure and practice appeared in newer ways in theories of (individual) action and analyses of (collective) processes, particularly from the 1950s.[50] At stake were varied endeavors to grapple with the shifting contexts of anthropology, to respond to wider political and historical transformations affecting the discipline, and to think through the autonomy of analytical traditions.[51] Such efforts could not simply shake off the long shadow cast by functionalist schemes. At the same time, they announced critical engagements with inherited visions and models of social action and anthropological practice.[52]

Ambiguities and contradictions were equally characteristic of efforts to reconfigure the anthropological discipline after the experiences of the 1960s. Recall that this decade saw the intense articulation of antiracist and civil rights movements and of anti-imperialist and radical student actions, which found varied expressions in Western and non-Western worlds. At the very least implicitly, such events and processes pointed once more to tensions between the somewhat abstract focus on underlying structures within influential scholarship and the clearly palpable nature of human action in social worlds. At the same, the late 1960s and the 1970s also saw the immense success in sociology and anthropology of explanatory frameworks according precedence to the unfolding of structures and systems in understandings of history and society. This was the case with "world systems" and "dependency" theories that projected the irrevocable logic of world capitalism as orchestrating and overwhelming the conduct of historical actors in the metropolis and the colony.[53] In such schemas the exact avowal of history/power could go hand in hand with a ready privileging of structure/system and an unsteady undermining of action/practice. To reiterate, such ambiguities and contradictions must be kept in view while considering the turn within anthropology to practice, process, and power, intimating reconfigurations of the discipline.

The 1970s saw critical explorations of the linkages between structure and practice, formulations that thought through the acute enmeshments of social reproduction and cultural transformation. Such efforts could take the form of critical sociological reflection; they could also imaginatively conjoin ethnography and theory to rethink issues of structure and practice, rules and processes.[54] It followed that, by the beginning of the 1980s, ethnographic and sociological scholarship increasingly turned to practice as a key category, a concept that helped to mediate the oppositions of society and individual as well as of social structure and historical action.

The emergent emphasis on practice appeared linked with a heightened sensitivity to temporal processes and historical considerations in anthropological inquiry. Such tendencies derived impetus from world systems theory and Marxist models, including their structuralist variants. Yet they extended to distinct dispositions of ethnographic practice, especially considerations of the temporal textures of cultural configurations, spatial formations, and societal transformations.[55] Salient anthropological writings that engaged the historical record focused on non-Western subjects of colonialism and capitalism. Here the meanings and practices of these subjects did not emerge as simple responses to colonial projects and capitalist processes. Rather such actions and apprehensions were explored as critical attributes of the contradictory elaboration of colonialism and capitalism, themselves understood as historically and culturally, temporally and spatially, layered fields, in apparently marginal arenas. Far from cut-and-dried spatial-temporal distinctions between Western and non-Western worlds, here were to be found discussions of sustained interchanges between these terrains.[56] Above all, such scholarship could involve implicit and explicit recognition that not merely social processes, but anthropological analyses were enacted through time, located in space, putting a question mark over a hierarchizing temporality and its split spaces.

Much of this diverse scholarship highlighted the presence of power and its negotiation in configurations of meaning and practice. In emergent yet critical ways, under challenge were procedures of ethnographic practice that framed their objects of inquiry as contained within, and themselves insinuating, bounded and coherent entities, especially by drawing pervasive temporal-spatial distinctions between traditional orders and modern societies. Actually, nothing better illustrates the shifts within anthropology on account of the freshly laid emphasis on relationships of power – and on terms of practice and process – than the rethinking, revaluation, and reworking of the concept of culture, a category of categories in ethnography, especially in its American avatar.[57]

Three broad interconnected criticisms of earlier anthropological orientations that totalized culture assume importance here. First, such dispositions frequently presented culture not only as essentially coherent in space and time, but also as virtually autonomous from diverse modalities of power, including in characterizations of "stateless" societies. Such procedures thereby underplayed formations of dominance, contentions of authority, and terms of dissonance *within* arrangements of culture, critical distinctions that entailed, for example, power relations of community and gender and race and office. Second, it followed that culture often appeared here as inescapably discrete and inexorably bounded. This is to say that non-Western culture was marked off from broad patterns of societal change – involving, for instance, articulations of colonialism, capitalism, nation, and modernity – and it was envisioned as sets of imaginings that chiefly looked inward, spatially and temporally turning only on themselves. Third and finally, these problems were connected to the fact that authoritative ethnographic understandings did not approach the values, beliefs, symbols, and rituals that they examined as embedded within temporal-spatial processes, themselves formed and transformed by historical subjects. Rather, the elements of culture were rendered as principally untouched by the shifts and mutations, ruptures and continuities, which have shaped the past and the present.[58]

History: ambiguities and reconfigurations

I have noted that narratives describing anthropological endeavors from the 1970s onward as breaking with the past – by being increasingly oriented to practice, process, and power – can be too exclusive in focus and scope. Similar problems can underlie singular storylines of the heroic rise of social/cultural history, which function most pervasively as pedagogical frameworks, manifest in the classroom and the seminar. Here are to be found projections of such disciplinary histories as becoming more and more democratic, progressively inclusive of hitherto marginalized subjects (both research themes and human constituencies) of the past, and consequently as ever more embracing of other disciplines, especially anthropological methods. Once more implicit articulations of historical progress, which then fabricate an autonomous space-time of disciplines, are at work here.

Such narratives frequently start off with the privileged place of politics in the institutionalization of history as a discipline from the second half of the nineteenth century onwards, and emphasize that in such scholarship social and cultural history writing had a residual role, including as the practice of history with the politics left out. Next they focus on major breakthroughs in historical scholarship that progressively expanded the subject matter of history from the 1930s onward to draw in wide-ranging dynamics of society and culture, also including in their fold subaltern subjects, while initiating a dialogue with the social sciences, especially anthropology, sociology, and psychology. Discussions of "masters" and "schools" marking such breakthroughs involve mention particularly of the work of the Annales in France;[59] the erstwhile British Communist Group of Historians;[60] cultural historians of Europe and scholars of African-American slavery based in the US;[61] and prominent historical tendencies on the Continent, especially Italian "micro-history" and German "Altagsgeschichte" (history of everyday life).[62] Finally, it is against this backdrop that such storylines sketch the problems and potentialities of social/cultural history, including the dialogue with anthropology or sociology, in diverse institutional contexts in the here and now.

Once more, the difficulties with such storylines are not that they are simply wrong, but that they are highly tendentious. Construed from the vantage point of the present and implicitly cast in teleological molds, they overlook the constitutive ambivalences and contradictions, silences and tensions, and problems and possibilities at the core of developments in the discipline of history: from the privileged place of political and diplomatic history in the past to the greater prominence of cultural and social history in the present. At stake are persistent contentions and excesses of history writing as a form of modern knowledge, including contrary articulations of temporal-spatial matrices, ever constitutive of modernity.

To begin with, prior and present political histories have carried their own varied articulations of culture and society and tradition and modernity. These can entail key conjunctions of hermeneutic and analytical tendencies and of romanticist and progressivist sensibilities. Such conjunctions have formed part of the institutionalization of the historical discipline, including the privileging of an exclusively demarcated domain of the "political," but they have also resisted the turning of historical knowledge into a merely subordinate ally of overwrought social-scientific schemes: I provide a single example here.

The writings of the early nineteenth-century French philosopher-historian Jules Michelet have been criticized as the work of a mere "romantic," one that poetically idealized a popular "people" in his account of the French Revolution. Or they have been celebrated for uncovering a new object-subject of history, turning on collective mentalities and anonymous forces in the unfolding of the past. Yet such readings ignore Michelet's actual procedures of research and writing, which arguably recast both "hermeneutic" and "scientific" methods in order to create a genuinely "modernist" historical scholarship. Michelet's history writing, Jacques Rancière has argued, brought to the fore the salient but repressed "subject of history," also intimating the requirements of historical research to live up to its threefold contract – "scientific, political, and literary" – with modern political democratic constituencies.[63] Indeed, precisely by ignoring Michelet's "method" and assimilating his writing into prefigured schemes, modern historians were "able to continue the age-long tradition of keeping the 'the poor' in their place – outside of history – and of pretending to be relating nothing but facts – and ignoring their meanings."[64] To read a historian such as Michelet (or figures such as Herder or Ranke, and many, many others) without succumbing to inherited historiographical schemas is to begin to track the pathways that have been opened up yet mainly forgotten within historical practice, disciplinary genealogies.[65] It is also to think through the unthought predilections and underenunciated assumptions of history writing, shored up by a singular temporality of a progressivist provenance, which precisely permit the disciplinary delineation of its autonomous time-space. Together, at stake are particular configurations of temporality and spatiality as part of everyday enactments of modern historiography, issues that require further deliberation.

It should also not be surprising, then, that ready projections of the triumphant rise of social and cultural history are often insufficiently critical, especially regarding their invocations of "schools" and "masters" of the historical craft. They do not adequately probe the constitutive conceits of such traditions. Consider the Annales School of history writing in France, which has existed since at least 1929 into the present, and was important in breaking with earlier event-based narratives of political history. Drawing on wide sociological considerations and especially impressed with the formulations of Emile Durkheim, the Annales not only suggestively, vastly opened out the scope and subject of history writing, but also created influential versions of long-term "structural" history.

At the same time, it is important to ask whether the histories crafted by Lucien Febvre and Fernand Braudel, two of the formative figures of the Annales School, did not deprive Western "history of its human subject, its links to a generally political and specifically democratic agenda, and its characteristic mode of representing its subject's manner of being in the world, namely, narrative."[66] It is equally worth reflecting on how Braudel's seminal writings have not only rendered entire regions of the Mediterranean world as islands floating outside the currents of civilization and history, but further cast as ahistorical the sphere of everyday "material culture," especially when compared with the historical dynamism of early modern mercantilism.[67] At work here are weighty distinctions between the "backward" and the "civilized," entailing hierarchical mappings of time and space that we encountered earlier.

Similarly, it is crucial to recognize that the work of the British socialist historian E. P. Thompson has imaginatively explored the contours of culture and consciousness of the "plebian public" in eighteenth-century England, including the transformations of time among these subjects with the advent of the measurement of time-in-labor as part of new regimes of capitalist and industrial manufacturing processes.[68] Yet, it is critical to register that Thompson's writings tend to locate eighteenth-century plebian culture along an irrevocable axis of historical modernization that sets up too solid an opposition between the "tradition" bound moral economy of the plebian public and the market-driven economy of "modern" capitalism.[69] This axis further governs Thompson's construal of spatially segregated non-Western orientations to time in the second half of the twentieth century, which are seen simultaneously as lagging behind the time of the West and as insinuating a haplessly traditional space waiting to be inevitably overcome by modern history.[70] Clearly, we are faced with apparently normatively neutral, but actually profoundly ideological, temporal-spatial, hierarchical oppositions of modernity.

To be sure, none of this is to deny the profound transformations of history writing in the past few decades. Rather, it is to approach such changes by cautiously considering the unstated, uncritical assumptions and the formidable, underlying conceits of the discipline. Here the enduring extension and palpable prominence of social/cultural history in more recent times need to be understood as part of the wider expansion after World War II of the historical discipline of the patterns of academic growth that have been true of anthropology and sociology too. The expansion has included an increase in professional specialization and a significant growth of job opportunities, which have shored up the delineation and development of identifiable social and cultural fields of history writing. At the same time, such spreading out of social/cultural history has been no less the result of abiding yet manifold intellectual interests, archival engagements, cross-disciplinary concerns, and political commitments, including impulses toward the democratization of history writing.[71]

While tracking the reconfigurations of history, including distinct articulations of time and space, it is especially important to register endeavors that have focused on subjects hitherto marginalized from the historical record.[72] This has been accompanied by at least two related developments: the presence of attempts to seek out distinct archival materials and to read historical sources in innovative ways – also opening up questions of the varieties, veracities, and validities of "sources" of history – especially considering the paucity and perversity of the record of the pasts of marginal subjects; and the place of necessary conversations with other disciplines, from anthropology and sociology to demography and psychology, which have also led historiography in new directions.

At the same time, it is worth considering that these new modes of history writing emerged principally, albeit in different ways, as alternative articulations of the history of the nation. The works of Christopher Hill and E. P. Thompson attempted to recast authoritative understandings of

English history by bringing to the fore, respectively, patterns of popular, radical religious dissent in the seventeenth century and frameworks of meaning and practice of the plebian public in the eighteenth century, each scholar tracing the approbation and interrogation of authority among such subordinate subjects.[73] The writings of Eugene Genovese and Lawrence Levine sought to restore to African-American slaves their own modalities of culture and action, consciousness and agency, in order to critically rethink the history of the US nation, which in its conservative and liberal renderings had overlooked the experiential textures of slavery and cast the slave population as objects rather than subjects of (national) history.[74] The central task that the subaltern studies collective set itself was to explore *"the failure of the nation to come into its own,"* especially focusing on the place of the subaltern in the history of the Indian nation that had failed its dispossessed peoples.[75] These historiographical tendencies imaginatively extended the terms of the dominant coupling of history and nation under modernity, but they were also unable to simply break with these bonds.

Rather than being disabling, the ambiguities have been productive. Indeed, the developments in history writing discussed above have been followed over the past three decades by an even wider opening up of critical histories. As in the case of anthropology, shifting political contexts, the "linguistic" and "affective" turns in the social sciences, and key crossovers with antifoundational perspectives have influenced these transformations. The consequences have been wide-ranging: from the expansion of imperatives of "minority" histories through to new historical accounts of colony and nation, body and sexuality, and affect and imagination; and from critical reconsiderations of concepts-entities of modernity and the state through to the radical rethinking of the terms of theory and the disciplines, including history and anthropology.

At the end

The reconfigurations of history and anthropology that I have discussed have been crucial for the emergence of historical anthropology. Indeed, several of my emphases in this chapter have themselves emerged from within such critical expressions of history, anthropology, and historical anthropology. Here, the first phase of historical anthropology was shaped by renewed emphases on practice and process, concerned with acting subjects and social domination, and sometimes influenced by Marxian political economy.[76] This was followed by newer considerations of the interplay between culture and power, especially as foregrounded in the writings of Michel Foucault. Here were also to be found crucial conversations with postcolonial perspectives, subaltern studies, and critical theory, among other orientations. Now colonial cultures, imperial evangelism, nations and nationalisms, and communities and their histories came to be critically examined as embodying authority as well as alterity, meaning as well as power.[77] The third ongoing stage builds upon these prior emphases of historical anthropology. At the same time, there is now a greater critical reflexivity regarding histories and anthropologies of the disciplines themselves as well as a simultaneous engagement with social theory and political philosophy. Under discussion are not only newer studies of empire and nation, modernity and neoliberalism, frontiers and politics, and public cultures and governmental anxieties. Rather, also at stake are understandings of how modern regimes of state, nation, and bureaucracy have shaped the disciplines as well as the recognition that, for example, ethnographies of Christianity must in some ways equally be anthropologies of the secular.[78]

In other words, on offer are critical questions, posed as provocations here: Why and how are archives, fields, and disciplines organized in the ways that they are? What does this tell us about their very nature? Should not more of contemporary anthropology turn away from the endless difference, often deferred, of recursive formations – traditional or hybrid or modern – to rather become the study of subjects of modernity, which include modern subjects? Should not more history writing critically query the routine sameness of the modern subject in order to explore instead the presence of heterogeneous yet coeval temporalities in worlds of modernity and many others? What exactly do we mean by "history" and "anthropology" and why do we study them in the first place? The spirit and substance of these questions informs my explorations of identity and modernity, acutely entailing issues of space and time, in the next chapter.

Notes

1 I distinguish between "functionalism" (of, for example, Malinowski) and "structural-functionalism" (of, for instance, Radcliffe-Brown) as analytical procedures, but also consider together the shared orientations of these traditions to time-space in the practice of anthropology. See Bronislaw Malinowski, *Argonauts of the Western Pacific: An Account of Native Adventures in the Archipelagoes of Melanesian New Guinea* (London: Routledge, 1922); A. R. Radcliffe-Brown, *Structure and Function in Primitive Society* (Glencoe, IL: The Free Press of Glencoe, 1952); S. N. Eisenstadt, "Functionalist analysis in anthropology and sociology: an interpretive essay," *Annual Review of Anthropology*, 19 (1990): 243–4; Adam Kuper, *Anthropologists and Anthropology: The British School, 1922–1972* (London: Allen Lane, 1973), pp. 92–109; Vincent, *Anthropology and Politics*, pp. 155–71; and George Stocking, Jr., *After Tylor: British Social Anthropology, 1888–1951* (Madison: University of Wisconsin Press, 1995), pp. 233–441.
2 This discussion brings together arguments offered by varieties of critical engagements – going back at least to the 1950s – with functionalist analyses. Rather than provide numerous citations, it should suffice to say that my criticisms would be widely accepted in critical anthropology today.
3 Cohn, "History and anthropology," p. 199. On the critical significance of Cohn's statement for historical scholarship, see Hans Medick, "'Missionaries in the rowboat'? Ethnological ways of knowing as a challenge to social history," in Alf Lüdtke (ed.), *The History of Everyday Life: Reconstructing Historical Experiences and Ways of Life*, trans. William Templer (Princeton, NJ: Princeton University Press, 1995), pp. 41–71.
4 For Fabian in anthropological analyses the work of time brings into play projections of space through procedures of visualization, taxonomy, and

classification. While I have learned much from Fabian's critique of naturalized "Time-Space," as should be evident in this book, my arguments also intimate somewhat different emphases, especially concerning the everyday production of time and space, heterogeneous yet overlaying temporal and spatial formations, and an unwillingness to succumb to the distinction between "real" and "representational" (or ideological) space. Fabian, *Time and the Other*.

5   Here I am once again engaging and extending Fabian (*ibid.*).
6   On the notion of the "savage slot" of anthropology, see Michel-Rolph Trouillot, "Anthropology and the savage slot: the poetics and politics of the otherness," in Richard Fox (ed.), *Recapturing Anthropology: Working in the Present* (Santa Fe, NM: School of American Research Press, 1991), pp. 17–44. On the "native niche" of the discipline, see Dube, *Stitches on Time*.
7   George Stocking, Jr., *The Ethnographer's Magic and Other Essays in the History of Anthropology* (Madison: University of Wisconsin Press, 1992), p. 347.
8   Thomas, *Out of Time*.
9   Each of these copulas is broadly homologous to the other. Rationalist and progressivist dispositions – privileging the capacity of reason and seeking to remake the world in its image – have emerged as often bound to the analytical model: "the analytical (*analysis* being basically a mathematical and logical term), requiring the selection and isolation of factors, political or economic … [that are] given privileged explanatory status." In contrast, the hermeneutical model has entailed "interpretation on the analogy of reading a text in its literary and philological fullness (as distinguished from logical analysis)," treating history itself as "a matter not of seeing, as tradition and etymology would have it, but rather of reading, deciphering, and interpreting" (Kelley, *Faces of History*, pp. 247, 262). Hermeneutical protocols have been frequently linked to expressions of historicism. Here historicist procedures have variously played out: critiques of an abstract and aggrandizing reason; reassertions of the centrality of language and historical experience; the principle of individuality (while often pursuing a universal history); and acute inclinations toward hermeneutical understandings. This is to say also distinct formations and discrete intimations of what Isaiah Berlin has notably described as the "Counter-Enlightenment," "the great river of romanticism" running from the eighteenth into the

nineteenth centuries, its waters no less overflowing into the times and terrains that have come after. Berlin, *Against the Current*.
10 Stocking, *The Ethnographer's Magic*, pp. 94–8.
11 Franz Boas, "The history of anthropology," in George Stocking, Jr. (ed.), *The Shaping of American Anthropology, 1883–1911: A Franz Boas Reader* (New York: Basic Books, 1974), p. 35.
12 Elsewhere, I have discussed the importance of exploring the work of Franz Boas rather than that of later Boasians (such as A. L. Kroeber or E. Sapir or P. Radin), which can be understood as more frontally expressing historical and historicist considerations. Dube, "Anthropology, history, historical anthropology," pp. 52–3, n. 33.
13 Stocking, *The Ethnographer's Magic*, p. 347.
14 *Ibid.*, pp. 352–3.
15 Stocking succinctly considers such disciplinary departure(s) from Boas's emphasis on the diachronic and the historical. Here are to be found transformations of key tendencies in Boasian anthropology as increasingly inclined from the 1920s onwards toward a synchronic study of integration of cultures and of the relation of "culture" and "personality" as well as a widening breach between British and US anthropology, albeit one where both traditions emphasized synchrony although with different emphases. *Ibid.*, pp. 353–7. See also Stocking, *After Tylor*, pp. 233–441.
16 For a hint of such a reading, see Marshall Sahlins, *Culture in Practice: Selected Essays* (New York: Zone Books, 2000), pp. 20–2.
17 Franz Boas, *Anthropology and Modern Life* (New York: W. W. Norton, 1928), p. 206.
18 Stocking, *The Ethnographer's Magic*, pp. 110–11.
19 *Ibid.*, p. 111.
20 *Ibid.*, pp. 110–12.
21 *Ibid.*, pp. 112–13.
22 See E. E. Evans-Pritchard, "Social anthropology" and "Social anthropology: Past and present," in E. E. Evans-Pritchard, *Social Anthropology and Other Essays* (New York: The Free Press of Glencoe, 1962), pp. 1–134, 139–57; E. E. Evans-Pritchard, *Anthropology and History* (Manchester: Manchester University Press, 1961).

23 E. E. Evans-Pritchard, *Theories of Primitive Religion* (Oxford: Clarendon Press, 1965).
24 This is far from denying that E. P.'s work has been read in other ways. See, for example, David F. Pocock, *Social Anthropology* (London: Sheed and Ward, 1961), pp. 72–82.
25 E. E. Evans-Pritchard, *The Nuer: A Description of the Modes of Livelihood and Political Institutions of a Nilotic People* (Oxford: Clarendon Press, 1940).
26 For a discussion of the ways in which E. P.'s articulations of time crystallized the "un-resolvable ambiguities" concerning time in the work of Durkheim (and his associates) and Malinowski see Munn, "Cultural anthropology of time," pp. 94–8. My arguments draw on Munn's brilliant essay, extending its insights through overlapping but distinct emphases.
27 Evans-Pritchard, *The Nuer*; E. E. Evans-Pritchard, "Nuer time reckoning," *Africa*, 12 (1939): 189–216.
28 Evans-Pritchard, *The Nuer*, pp. 96, 102.
29 Munn, "Cultural anthropology of time," p. 96.
30 *Ibid.*; Evans-Pritchard, *The Nuer*, pp. 98–103.
31 Evans-Pritchard, *The Nuer*, pp. 98–103, 105–8.
32 Here there is something of an implicit, unthought opposition between time and space in E. P.'s formulations. Munn, "Cultural anthropology of time," pp. 97–8.
33 *Ibid.*
34 Pierre Bourdieu, *Algeria 1960*, trans. Richard Nice (Cambridge: Cambridge University Press, 1979), p. 8 (first published in French in 1963); Bourdieu, *Outline of a Theory*; and Munn, "Cultural anthropology of time," pp. 106–9.
35 A wider discussion of these questions is contained in Dube, "Anthropology, history, historical anthropology".
36 S. C. Dube, *The Kamar* (Lucknow: Universal, 1951). Here my discussion draws on Saurabh Dube, "Ties that bind: tribe, village, nation, and S. C. Dube," in Patricia Uberoi, Satish Deshpande, and Nandini Sundar (eds.), *Anthropology in the East: Founders of Indian Sociology and Anthropology* (New Delhi: Permanent Black, 2007), pp. 444–95.
37 Consider that Dube wrote of the Kamars as "seriously talk[ing] about Gandhi Mahatma, *the king of all kings* … endowed with greater magical

powers to fight the white *sahibs*." Yet, he described the Kamars as "almost untouched" by the "great political awakening which has given a new national consciousness to India during the last sixty years." The narrative holds together, but it also strains at the seams. Dube, *The Kamar*, p. 166.

38 On this issue see Chakrabarty, "Postcoloniality and the artifice of history"; Frederick Cooper, "Conflict and connection: rethinking colonial African history," *American Historical Review*, 99 (1994): 1519–26; and Sarkar, *Writing Social History*, pp. 30–42. See also Prakash, "Subaltern Studies as postcolonial criticism." While registering certain exceptions, the surveys by Cooper and Sarkar both substantiate my claims.

39 The critical edge of my arguments notwithstanding, there is much to be learned anew from all these different tendencies of history writing. Specifically the distinct entwining of hermeneutical and analytical impulses in different modes of historical endeavor requires special attention. Equally, considering the "difference" introduced by non-Western histories, see Prachi Deshpande, *Creative Pasts: Historical Memory and Identity in Western India, 1700–1960* (New York: Columbia University Press, 2007); Dipesh Chakrabarty, *The Calling of History: Sir Jadunath Sarkar and His Empire of Truth* (Chicago, IL, and London: University Of Chicago Press, 2015); and Mark Thurner, *History's Peru: The Poetics of Colonial and Postcolonial Historiography* (Gainesville: University Press of Florida, 2011).

40 Pandey, "In defense of the fragment"; and Gyanendra Pandey, "The prose of otherness," in Arnold and Hardiman (eds.), *Subaltern Studies VIII*, pp. 188–221.

41 Pandey, "The prose of otherness."

42 Clearly, I am sieving Pandey's arguments and emphases through related yet distinct filters.

43 *Ibid.*; Pandey, "In defense of the fragment." On recent writings on the Partition seeking to redress such excision of terms of violence and pain in historical endeavor, see, for example, Urvashi Butalia, *The Other Side of Silence: Voices from the Partition of India* (New Delhi: Viking Penguin, 1998); Ritu Menon and Kamla Bhasin, *Borders and Boundaries: Women in India's Partition* (New Delhi: Kali for Women, 1998); and Pandey, *Remembering Partition*.

44 See, for example, Vincent, *Anthropology and Politics*, pp. 225–9, 308–14.

45 Dube, "Terms that bind," pp. 2-3.
46 Nonetheless functionalist tenets and structural analyses did not simply disappear from the academic scene after the 1970s. Rather they have continued to variously exercise their influence on anthropology, also being differently reconfigured in distinct disciplines. Eisenstadt, "Functionalist analysis," pp. 243-51; Sherry Ortner, "Theory in anthropology since the sixties," *Comparative Studies in Society and History*, 26 (1984): 127-32, 135-41; and Vincent, *Anthropology and Politics*, pp. 335-41.
47 Bourdieu, *Outline of a Theory*, particularly pp. 4-9.
48 Not only functionalism and structuralism but also other important anthropological traditions of the time could variously privilege structure over action, an issue discussed in Dube, "Anthropology, history, historical anthropology," pp. 1-31.
49 The political nature of the setting up of the Rhodes Livingstone Institute could combine imperial administrators' deep skepticism of anthropological work. See Kuper, *Anthropologists and Anthropology*, pp. 133-5. On the shifts in anthropological research initiated by the Institute see, Vincent, *Anthropology and Politics*, pp. 276-83; and for a more recent critical assessment of this research, see Ferguson, *Expectations of Modernity*.
50 See, for example, Edmund Leach, *Political System of Highland Burma: A Study of Kachin Social Structure* (London: G. Bell and Sons, 1954); Max Gluckman, *Order and Rebellion in Tribal Africa* (London: Cohen and West, 1963); F. G. Bailey, *Caste and the Economic Frontier: A Village in Highland Orissa* (Manchester: Manchester University Press, 1957); F. G. Bailey, *Stratagems and Spoils: A Social Anthropology of Politics* (Oxford: Basil Blackwell, 1969); Fredrik Barth, *Political Leadership among Swat Pathans* (London: Athlone Press, 1959); J. P. S. Uberoi, *The Politics of the Kula Ring: An Analysis of the Findings of Bronislaw Malinowski* (Manchester: Manchester University Press, 1962); and Victor Turner, *Schism and Continuity in an African Society* (Manchester: Manchester University Press, 1957).
51 It is as part of such wider rethinking of the discipline that we might consider the famous endorsement by E. P. of the intersections between anthropology and history. Evans-Pritchard, *Anthropology and History*.
52 Such transformations were also evident in anthropology in the US after World War II in the study of "complex civilizations," work in political

economy and on subordinate groups in a historical frame, and ethnohistory, all issues discussed in Dube, "Anthropology, history, historical anthropology."

53 Such models and theories interrogated the capitalist and imperialist continuities of Western domination in non-Western theaters through polarities of core and periphery, development and underdevelopment. See Wolfe, "History and imperialism."

54 For example, Bourdieu, *Outline of a Theory*; Abrams, *Historical Sociology*; Giddens, *Central Problems in Social Theory*; John Comaroff and Simon Roberts, *Rules and Processes: The Cultural Logic of Dispute in an African Context* (Chicago, IL: University of Chicago Press, 1981); Ortner, "Theory in anthropology"; and Marshall Sahlins, *Islands of History* (Chicago, IL: University of Chicago Press, 1985). See also E. P. Thompson, *The Poverty of Theory and other Essays* (New York: Monthly Review Press, 1978).

55 Fabian, *Time and the Other*; Renato Rosaldo, *Ilongot Headhunting 1883–1974: A Study in Society and History* (Stanford, CA: Stanford University Press, 1980); Sahlins, *Islands of History*; Cohn, *Anthropologist among the Historians*; Gerald M. Sider, *Culture and Class: A Newfoundland Illustration* (Cambridge: Cambridge University Press, 1986).

56 For instance, Jean Comaroff, *Body of Power, Spirit of Resistance: The Culture and History of a South African People* (Chicago, IL: University of Chicago Press, 1985); and Michael Taussig, *The Devil and Commodity Fetishism in South America* (Chapel Hill: University of North Carolina Press, 1980). See also Richard Price, *First-Time: The Historical Vision of an Afro-American People* (Baltimore, MD: Johns Hopkins University Press, 1983); June Nash, *We Eat the Mines and the Mines Eat Us: Dependency and Exploitation in Bolivian Tin Mines* (New York: Columbia University Press, 1979). In history writing such issues found expression in complementary yet distinct registers. See, for example, Guha, *Elementary Aspects*.

57 Of course shifting definitions of culture have characterized the pasts of anthropology. Writings that initiated recent critical considerations of culture include Talal Asad, "Anthropological conceptions of religion: reflections on Geertz," *Man* [n.s.], 18 (1983): 237–59; Gerald M. Sider, "The ties that bind: culture and agriculture, property and propriety in the Newfoundland village fishery," *Social History*, 5 (1980): 1–39; and Herman Rebel, "Cultural hegemony and class experience: a critical reading of

recent ethnological-historical approaches (parts one and two)," *American Ethnologist*, 16 (1989): 117–36, 350–65.
58 These critical considerations have been taken forward in distinct ways in recent decades. I have discussed elsewhere how questionings of anthropological articulations of culture emerged linked to various processes: the rethinking of the Marxist conception of culture; the place of the "reflexive" turn in the "experimental" ethnography of 1980s that brought forth questions of "authority" in the "representation" of culture; more recent calls for writing *against* culture, where culture is seen as implicated in dominant projects – from anthropological schemes to imperial regimes to nation-state routines – that make a fetish out of cultural difference; the interweaving of critical articulations of culture in anthropology today with a growing interest in transnational processes of empire, diaspora, and modernity; and, finally, the importance of not approaching culture as merely an analytical device but as a concept-entity that has been central to the imaginings and practices of the very people the notion has sought to define and describe. Needless to say, such disciplinary reconfigurations have been closely bound to wider changes in the world at large. All these issues are elaborated in Dube, "Anthropology, history, historical anthropology."
59 Lucien Febvre, *A New Kind of History: From the Writings of Febvre*, trans. K. Folca (London: Routledge, 1973); Marc Bloch, *The Historian's Craft*, trans. Peter Putnam (Manchester: Manchester University Press, 1954); Fernand Braudel, *The Mediterranean and the Mediterranean World in the Age of Philip II: Vols. I and II*, trans. S. Reynolds (London: Fontana/Collins, 1973); Emmanuel Le Roy Ladurie, *Montaillou: The Promised Land of Error*, trans. Barbara Bray (New York: Vintage Books, 1979); and Roger Chartier, *Cultural History: Between Practices and Representations*, trans. Lydia G. Cochrane (Ithaca, NY: Cornell University Press, 1993).
60 Thompson, *Customs in Common*; Christopher Hill, *The World Turned Upside Down: Radical Ideas during the English Revolution* (New York: Penguin Books, 1973); and Eric Hobsbawm, *Nations and Nationalism since 1780: Programme, Myth, Reality* (Cambridge: Cambridge University Press, 1993).
61 Natalie Z. Davis, *Society and Culture in Early Modern France: Eight Essays by Natalie Zemon Davis* (Stanford, CA: Stanford University Press, 1977);

Robert Darnton, *The Great Cat Massacre and Other Episodes in French Cultural History* (New York: Vintage, 1985); William H. Sewell Jr., *Work and Revolution in France: The Language of Labor from the Old Regime to 1848* (New York: Cambridge University Press, 1980); Genovese, *Roll, Jordan, Roll*; and Levine, *Black Culture and Consciousness*.

62 Carlo Ginzburg, *The Cheese and the Worms: The Cosmos of a Sixteenth Century Miller*, trans. John and Anne Tedeschi (Baltimore, MD: Johns Hopkins University Press, 1980); Edward Muir and Guido Ruggiero (eds.) *Microhistory and the Lost Peoples of Europe*, trans. Eren Branch (Baltimore, MD: Johns Hopkins University Press, 1991); and Lüdtke, *History of Everyday Life*.

63 Jacques Rancière, *The Names of History: On the Poetics of Knowledge*, trans. Hassan Melehy (Minneapolis: University of Minnesota Press, 1994). See also Jacques Rancière, *The Philosopher and His Poor*, trans. Andrew Parker et al. (Durham, NC: Duke University Press, 2004).

64 Hayden White, "Foreword: Rancière's revisionism," in Rancière, *The Names of History*, p. xvii. White is commenting on Rancière's reading of Michelet here.

65 See, for instance, John H. Zammito, *Kant, Herder, and the Birth of Anthropology* (Chicago, IL: University of Chicago Press, 2002). See also Thurner, *History's Peru*; and Chakrabarty, *Calling of History*.

66 H. White, "Foreword," p. xi; Rancière, *The Names of History*.

67 According to Braudel the history of mountainous regions, as worlds far removed from civilization proper, is to have no history. Braudel, *The Mediterranean*, vol. 1; Medick, "'Missionaries in the rowboat'?," pp. 42–4.

68 E. P. Thompson, "Patrician society, plebian culture," *Journal of Social History*, 7 (1974): 382–405; E. P. Thompson, "Eighteenth century English society: class struggle without class," *Social History*, 3 (1978): 133–65; E. P. Thompson, "Time, work-discipline and industrial capitalism," *Past and Present*, 38 (1967): 56–97; E. P. Thompson, "The moral economy of the English crowd in the eighteenth century," *Past and Present*, 50 (1971): 76–136.

69 On such questions see Hans Medick, "Plebian culture in the transition to capitalism," in Raphael Samuel and Gareth Stedman Jones (eds.), *Culture, Ideology and Politics* (London: Routledge and Kegan Paul, 1983), pp. 84–113.

70 Thompson, "Time, work-discipline and industrial capitalism."
71 I explore such issues in Dube, *Stitches on Time*, especially pp. 133–7.
72 Guha (ed.), *Subaltern Studies I–VI*; Chatterjee and Pandey (eds.), *Subaltern Studies VII*; Arnold and Hardiman (eds.), *Subaltern Studies VIII*; Shahid Amin and Dipesh Chakrabarty (eds.), *Subaltern Studies IX: Writings on South Asian History and Society* (Delhi: Oxford University Press, 1996); Gautam Bhadra et al. (eds.), *Subaltern Studies X: Writings on South Asian History and Society* (New Delhi: Oxford University Press, 1999).
73 Hill, *The World Turned Upside Down*; Thompson, *Customs in Common*.
74 Genovese, *Roll, Jordan, Roll*; Levine, *Black Culture and Consciousness*.
75 Ranajit Guha, "On some aspects of the historiography of colonial India," in Guha (ed.), *Subaltern Studies I*, p. 7. Emphasis in the original. For a wider discussion of such questions see Dube, *Stitches on Time*, ch. 5.
76 For example, Taussig, *The Devil and Commodity Fetishism*; David Warren Sabean, *Power in the Blood: Popular Culture and Village Discourse in Early Modern Germany* (Cambridge: Cambridge University Press, 1984); Dirks, *The Hollow Crown*; Rosaldo, *Ilongot Headhunting*.
77 A few indicative examples include Comaroff and Comaroff, *Of Revelation and Revolution*, vol. 2; Cooper and Stoler, *Tensions of Empire*; Rappaport, *Cumbe Reborn*; Axel, *Nation's Tortured Body*; Skaria, *Hybrid Histories*; and Dube, *Untouchable Pasts*.
78 For instance, Bear, *Lines of the Nation*; Jonathon Glassman, *War of Words, War of Stones: Racial Thought and Violence in Colonial Zanzibar* (Bloomington: Indiana University Press, 2011); Townsend Middleton, *The Demands of Recognition: State Anthropology and Ethnopolitics in Darjeeling* (Stanford, CA: Stanford University Press, 2015); and Dube, *After Conversion*. See also John Comaroff and Jean Comaroff, *Ethnicity, Inc.* (Chicago, IL: University of Chicago Press, 2009); and Bhambra, *Rethinking Modernity*. Needless to say, the emphases outlined above not only undergird this book, but are acutely embodied in Dube, "Formations of an evangelical modernity."

5

Margins of modernity: identities and incitements

This chapter focuses on questions and contentions of identity and modernity, entailing stipulations of time and space. Instead of approaching identity as an already given entity that is principally antithetical to modernity, in speaking of identities my reference is to wide-ranging processes of formations of subjects, expressing not only particular personhoods but also collective groupings. Upon such an understanding, then, identities comprise a crucial means through which social processes are perceived, experienced, and articulated. Indeed, defined within historical relationships of production and reproduction, appropriation and approbation, and power and difference, cultural identities (and their mutations) are essential elements in the quotidian constitution (and pervasive transformations) of social worlds. These are issues to which I shall return. The point now is that the account ahead explores the elaborations of identities within historical anthropology, including postcolonial perspectives and subaltern approaches. In these domains, identities have been articulated as part of critical considerations, at once theoretical and empirical, not only of colony and community and empire and nation, but also of modernity and history and their entanglements and contradictions, the subjects of this book.

Untangling identity

An apparent irony involving the past in our present turns on and draws together the terrains of history, modernity, and identity. Here is what the irony entails: exactly at the moment when formative procedures of disciplinary history writing have come under searing scrutiny in the academy, claims upon heritage and history have become combustible questions and burning issues in the wider worlds of citizens and subjects of modern rule – contemporary regimes of state and nation, race and reason, majority and minority, community and gender, and ethnicity and identity.

Now, insistent demands on historical identity as well as searching criticisms of disciplinary history writing have existed in the past. This has to do with the contradictions and contentions of modernity discussed in the last four chapters. On the one hand, critical strains of modern knowledge, including hermeneutic ones, have for a long time queried the claims of an aggrandizing reason and the conceits of historical progress – of modernity, nation, and the disciplines. On the other, processes of modernity have frequently imbued with a specific salience the categories-entities of tradition and culture, community and identity, turning them into the very stuff of heritage and history. Unsurprisingly, enunciations and denunciations of history and interrogations and entitlements of identity have loomed large, even monstrously, in modern projects of division and unity, from nationalisms and genocides through to fourth-world politics and minority endeavors. It is a formidable "contemporary arrogance" that overplays the uniqueness of our times.[1]

At the same time, however, critiques of (disciplinary) history and clamors over (cultural) identities have acquired urgency in our recent pasts. Actually, the contentions and claims form part of the same logic, turning on the subversions and seductions of the representations and ruptures of modernity. To begin with, as the first chapter noted, the questioning of dominant history writing in recent decades derives from at least three distinct yet overlapping critical dispositions. First, key challenges to pervasive protocols of universal history. Such moves have at once explored distinct pasts under wider intermeshed relations of power and queried the abiding imperatives of historical progress and the very nature of the academic archive, each envisioned as an intimate image of a reified West. Second, acute interrogations of dominant designs of a singular modernity, which have simultaneously revealed the contradictory and contingent nature of the phenomena as well as explored contending intimations of heterogeneous moderns. Finally, the placing of a question mark over the enduring oppositions of modern worlds. This has involved measures that have at once queried a subject-centered reason and a meaning-legislating rationality and challenged the analytical binaries of academic disciplines and wide-ranging representations of cultural otherness. Clearly, at stake here are the contentions not merely of modern knowledge, but of modernity at large.

All of this registered, it is to the other side of the apparent irony of the past in our present that I now turn. For, alongside such querying of authoritative history writing, consider the manner in which, over the same time period, terms such as culture, tradition, and identity have increasingly, assertively become much more than mere intellectual devices. Rather, these terms are ever more seized upon by their objects of analysis, the very people the concepts once purported merely to categorize, analyze, and describe. From impoverished indigenous communities to rich immigrant populations to various religious militants to formidable power brokers in the world at large, here are subjects who have zealously claimed identity and history, tradition and culture, articulating them in intriguing ways, including by living and dying in the name of these categories and entities. The point is that demands on pasts and identities have been central to such procedures, albeit in innately different ways. Unsurprisingly, representations of history and identity regularly find shifting yet salient configurations – as contested territory, ambivalent resource, ready motif, and settled verity – within public discourses. From the fourth world through to the first, there is no turning away from the specter of history, no simple shrugging off of the burden of identity.

This is to say further that the insistent and contending claims on history and identity in the here and now signal something specific about contemporary worlds. The point is that emphatic demands on the past – including especially escalating expressions of tradition, culture, and identity – are far from being primordial patterns or recalcitrant residues that modern and global processes of capital and consumption, reason and nation, and state and citizenship have been unable to stamp out. Rather, the pervasive presence of these concepts and resources indicates their renewed salience within schemes of modernity. Such salience and schemes are ever more expressed today by subjects of modernity – as well as by modern subjects – of distinct persuasions, as they articulate on the ground, in everyday spaces and public places, the West and the nation, history and globalization, the religious and the secular, and cultural politics and political cultures. To reiterate, none of this might be entirely new, but it has assumed exponential exigency today. At work, then, is nothing less than distinct manifestations and critical articulations of the configurations and consequences of modernity, identity, and history, as ideal and ideology and as process and practice.[2]

All of this indicates equally the importance of rethinking our usual understandings of identities and their implications. Now, when I write of identity in these pages, the reference is to processes of formations of subjects – processes, formations, and subjects that militate against persistent projections of sovereign "individuals" and primordial "communities." Instead, as indicated earlier, identities entail at once collective groupings and particular personhoods, where the one betokens the other. This is to say that as critical attributes of the constitution of subjects, identities form essential elements in the everyday production and reproduction of social life. They turn on simultaneously symbolic and substantive – and structured yet fluid – attitudes and imaginings, norms and practices, and rituals and dispositions. Here are to be found the resources through which social relationships within and between groups/classes/communities/genders are perceived, experienced, and articulated, including the construal of time and space as part of these processes.

Moreover, in the perspective that I am sketching, identities are defined within historical relationships of production and reproduction, appropriation and consumption, empire and modernity, and nation and globalization. They emerge critically mediated by shifting configurations of gender and class/caste, race and age, office and sexuality.

Such relationships and configurations, predicated upon power, involve diverse renderings of domination and subordination – as well as negotiations and contestations of authority – in distinct arenas. Constitutive of dominant and subaltern identities, here are to be found contradictory processes that are simultaneously characterized by the work of hegemony and the reworking of power, which form part of the same logic.[3] Unsurprisingly, on offer also are authoritative temporal and spatial representations and practices as well as their articulations in the production of space and time in everyday arenas.

Lastly, in such an orientation, identity neither spells a priori sameness nor indicates unchanging inventories of exclusive beliefs, bounded traditions, and distinct customs of particular peoples, groups, or communities. Rather, identities entail at once assertions of sameness and practices of difference. They turn upon the ways in which symbolic imaginaries and meaningful practices are implicated in and lived within human worlds, insinuated at the core of the entangled relationships and contentious processes of these terrains. Since these relationships, processes, and worlds change, makeovers and modifications are at the heart of identities, including the pervasive construal of heterogeneous yet overlaying spaces and times, entailing in turn authority as well as alterity.

It bears emphasis that I underscore the intersections between overlapping yet distinct processes of power, technologies of representation, relationships of production, and modes of reproduction as critical to the articulation of identities. This has important consequences, especially as each of these coordinates is rendered an integral part of historical practices. On the one hand, my efforts challenge pervasive, commonplace, reductive projections of identity, themselves founded on the putative ruptures of modernity. On the other, having learned from the critical ferment in contemporary thinking, but without necessarily submitting to its conceits that dissolve social subjects altogether, the moves clear the ground for explorations of the substantive mutual contributions of historical anthropology, subaltern studies, and postcolonial perspectives in understandings of identities.[4]

How does this chapter approach questions of time and space, their mutual enmeshment and active construal within these disciplinary perspectives? My efforts do not trace the particular ways in which each of the writings under discussion individually challenges (or reiterates) dominant temporal-spatial representations. Nor do I track notions and notations of space and time produced within the epistemic practice of this scholarship.[5] Rather, my bid is twofold. It reads historical anthropology, subaltern studies, and postcolonial perspectives into each other as together articulating colony and nation, community and history in a manner that, far from temporally-spatially segregating modernity and identity, understands their common construal in/of time and space. This further allows for the possibility of readings that can track the production of nonhierarchical hetero-temporalities and socio-spatial expression in these terrains.[6]

Colony and empire

Influential tendencies within postcolonial perspectives and subaltern studies have tended to treat colony and empire as totalized formations, spatially and temporally.[7] At the same time, important writings with newer sensibilities have also thought through postulates of overarching colonial structures and overriding imperial systems. Such rethinking has been led by seminal scholarship in historical anthropology.[8] Studies in this genre have explored the contradictory location and contending agendas of distinct colonizing peoples and diverse colonized groups in the creation of colonial cultures of rule. This has involved discussions of the representations and practices and the boundaries and contradictions of imperial agents, settler communities, and evangelizing missionaries in colonial locations. In brief, there have been critical examinations of not only colonized populations, but also colonizing peoples, even if the programmatic desire toward treating the colonizer and the colonized as parts of a single analytical field has sometimes receded into the background here. At any rate, such studies have revealed the persistent fault lines and the critical divisions between different agents of colonialism, diverse agendas of empire.[9] On the one hand, the racial mythologies and the homespun lifestyles of colonizers sought to blur such fault lines, often invoking an exclusive time-space of European (and Euro-American) folk. On the other, divisions between different colonialist groups also stood highlighted within everyday representations and quotidian practices in distinct contexts, betraying contending spatial and contentious temporal matrices among them.

It follows that the view of colonialism as a monolithic temporal venture, a homogeneous spatial project, stands severely tested today. At issue here are not only the variations in the colonial endeavors and imperial exertions of different nations and separate epochs, featuring diverse forms of production and exchange, all important distinctions recognized in earlier scholarship. Rather, recent ethnographies and histories have revealed that the conflicting interests and the contending visions of empire of differentially located interests and actors several times drove a single colonial project. At the same time, distinct colonial projects could draw upon each other's models and metaphors, while imbuing them with varied and contrary salience. Here were to be found jumbled, conflicting temporal and spatial processes.[10]

Three examples should suffice. In the case of colonial South Africa, Jean and John Comaroff have shown that the exact divisions and conflicts, bearing critical spatial-temporal dimensions, between British administrators, evangelical missionaries, and Dutch settlers led to the elaboration of race and empire.[11] My own work on the evangelical enterprise in central India underscores that American missionaries in the region borrowed from the governmental modalities and cartographic practices of Her Majesty's imperial administration in order to elaborate a rather distinct vision and practice, space and time, of "the Empire of Christ."[12] Finally, K. Sivaramakrishnan's study of the construal of the colonial state, the shaping of forests, and the making of "tribal" places in nineteenth-century woodland Bengal, eastern India, brings together several of the concerns outlined above.[13] Imaginatively intervening in debates in recent environmental studies and colonial discourse theory, he brings to bear on postcolonial and subaltern studies the perspectives of a critical historical geography, itself shoring up an innovative environmental history. On the one hand, Sivaramakrishnan attends to the construction of space as part of historical practice, transcending, too, facile distinctions between "metaphorical" and "material" spaces. On the other hand, his emphases further suggest the importance of tracking how the conflicting interests and the contending visions of empire of socio-spatially differentially located actors could coalesce in a single colonial project, shaped by different overlaying temporalities.

All this has underwritten close analyses of the relationship between the metropolis and the colony, which have queried pervasive projections of their inexorable spatial segregation based on a singular hierarchizing time. It has become increasingly clear that there were conjunctions and connections – and contentions and contradictions – between efforts to discipline and normalize subject groups at home and attempts to civilize and control subject populations in the colonies.[14] Such explorations have carried forward earlier examinations and contemporary discussions of imperial histories and colonial cultures as deriving from interactions between the colonizer and the colonized. They have crucially considered the mutual shaping of European processes and colonial practices in order to imaginatively analyze how developments in distant margins could influence metropolitan transformations of identity, how the impulses of empire and their reworking in the colonies brought about changes at the heart of Western history.[15]

Here, the explorations have included the incisive examination by Uday Mehta of the focal presence of the Indian colony in the shaping of the very premises of dominant political thought in nineteenth-century Britain, revealing the significance of empire in structuring the "anthropological" propensities of liberal theory. At stake are liberal thought's fundamental "strategies of exclusion," resting on projections of the (civilizational) "infantilism" and (inherent) "inscrutability" of Indians that placed them in the spatial-temporal "waiting room" of colonial history until they could be extricated from there by their (imperial) rulers and benefactors.[16] The analyses have extended to the imaginative excursus by Peter van der Veer into the interplay between religion and politics in the common constitution of empire and nation in Britain and India.[17] This highlights the differences of the modern state in these terrains, while also questioning the temporal-spatial binary of a secular West and a religious East.

Such recognition has further led to varied analyses of the many modes and diverse forms entailed by colonial processes. There have been remarkable studies of the colonization of space, time, language, and the body;[18] critical discussions of imperial travel, exhibitory orders, and museum collections;[19] deft analyses of colonial representations;[20] astute probing of the politics under empire of art, literature, culture, and consumption;[21] and striking work on sexuality, race, and desire as shaping the metropolis and the margins.[22] The historical identities spawned by colonial cultures have made a striking appearance on the stage of the humanities and the social sciences, inviting reconsiderations of space and time – and of territories and imaginaries – of empires and their subjects.

In several ways, this emphasis has provided a valuable corrective to reifications of an impersonal, exclusive world capitalist system and privileges accorded to abstract, singular colonial structures, each with their own subterranean temporal dynamic and irrevocable spatial logic, which characterized several influential writings in the past.[23] At the same time, the concerns of culture here do not necessarily discount considerations of political economy and aspects of state power. Rather, several significant studies in this new genre suggest the importance of tracking the interplay between forms of representation, processes of political economy, and imperatives of state formation in expressions of identity.[24] Here there is no a priori privilege accorded to any one of these heuristic domains on the grounds of meta-theory. Instead, the mutual determinations of these analytical arenas appear better articulated through histories and ethnographies that eschew rigorously formal frameworks and avoid resolutely abstract blueprints, also intimating thereby newer renderings of colonies and empires, their times and spaces.

Such nuanced understandings of culture and power have emerged bound to powerful reminders that gender and sexuality crucially inflected the temporal-spatial formations of identity under empire. Salient scholarship has underscored that the profound importance of gender identities for imperial formations extended very widely from the lifestyles of Euro-American peoples in the colony to the politics of colonial representations; from the tensions of empire to the implications of colonial civility; and from the divisions among the colonialists to varieties of material exchanges, museum collections, and exhibitory orders. Similarly, the key influence of sexual subjectivities in the conquest of space and time cut across truly broad, crisscrossing terrain from the mutual entailments of the metropolis and the margins to the colonization of language and bodies; from the contradictory location of colonial agents to the complex fabrication of imperial cartographies; and from definitions of space(s) of wilderness to delineations of time(s) of modernity. On the one hand, in each case the critical forces of gender and sexuality shaped and structured the different dynamics and diverse dimensions of colonialism's cultures and the identities these spawned. On the other, the intersections between race, class, and gender – as imaginaries and institutions – in the construal of identities acquired new meanings through their elaboration within/of colonial temporal imperatives and imperial spatial stipulations.[25]

The critical spirit of such work has been extended by two other developments. First, key discussions have rethought the past and the present of the disciplines, especially keeping in view their linkages with determinations of colony, nation, race, and gender. Of special significance here have been forceful considerations of the acute inequalities of knowledge and power between the West and the Rest, dominant visions and minority voices, and metropolitan histories and provincial pasts, inequities that carry critical spatial and temporal implications.[26] Second, the corpus of writings stressing the critical place of the colonial experience in the making of the modern world have not only reached beyond analyses focusing on the shaping of Europe by empire, but they have also put a different spin on configurations of time and space in the past and the present. In addition to perspectives on the coloniality/decoloniality of power/knowledge that were discussed earlier, important here have been distinct studies focusing on the linkages of the Enlightenment and empire, race and reason, the past and the present.[27]

Pasts and communities

All of this is equally indicative of the manner in which the critical rethinking of history, identity, and historical identities has been at the core of historical anthropology, subaltern studies, and postcolonial perspectives. On the one hand, members of the South Asian subaltern studies collective have pointed to the place of power in the production of the past.[28] Needless to say, they have done this alongside other intellectuals, focusing on diverse geopolitical areas.[29] Such measures have underscored the inherently political character of history writing while putting a question mark over the very nature of the academic historical archive. On the other hand, scholars of anthropology, history, and related disciplines have emphasized the socio-spatial plurality of cultural pasts, the manner in which history and temporality are differently approached and understood, seized upon and set to work by distinct social groups in conversation with their identities.[30]

Three overlaying emphases have played a crucial role in such considerations.[31] To begin with, it has been diversely admitted that forms of historical consciousness vary in their degree of symbolic elaboration, their ability to pervade multiple contexts, and their capacity to capture people's imaginations between and across socio-spatial groupings and their identities. Second, it has been increasingly noted that history does not just refer to events and processes out there, but that it exists as a negotiated resource at the core of shifting, temporal-spatial configurations of historical worlds and social identities. Third and finally, as was indicated earlier, there has been an opening up of critical questions considering the coupling of history writing with the modern nation and of the haunting presence of a reified "West" in widespread beliefs in historical progress, each shored up by the hierarchizing of social space through the ruse of singular time.

Together, in approaching the past and the present, such efforts toward critical history writing have often bound the impulse to cautiously probe and affirm social worlds with the desire to carefully narrate and describe them. The endeavors have truly taken seriously the requirements of evidence and fidelity to facts. Yet they have also sieved historical evidence through critical filters and construed unexpected facts, times, and spaces, which speak in the uneasy echoes of limiting doubt rather than deal in dead certainties.[32] It only follows that the emphases outlined above have not resorted to spatial-temporal, geometric oppositions involving cyclical notions of the past as characteristic of the East and linear conceptions of history as constitutive of the West. Nor have they approached the assertive appropriations and enunciations of the past in historical and contemporary worlds by submitting to views that each of these visions is equally true. Rather, they have precisely probed such overwrought blueprints and solipsistic schemes by tracking expressions of history as made up of interleaving, conflict-ridden processes of meaning and authority, time and space, ever entailing identity and authority, dominance and difference.[33]

In this terrain, the explorations have traced the variability and mutability that can inhere in the temporal perceptions and spatial practices concerning the pasts of cultural communities. They have tracked the uses of history and their contending validities in the making of social identities, turning on space and time, especially the play of power in the production of history. In elaborations of these conjoint emphases, particularly pertinent are Shahid Amin's innovative account of the interplay between governmental demands and subaltern desires in the spatial remembering and temporal monumentalizing of a critical event of Indian nationalism in a North Indian village across the twentieth century;[34] Ajay Skaria's thickly textured study of wildness, environment, gender, and politics among the Dangis of western India, especially as based on these people's narratives of "colonial" and "extra-colonial" times and spaces;[35] and Ishita Banerjee-Dube's imaginative inquiry into the unfolding of oral and written histories and sectarian and ascetic formations – each inflected by the presence of the law and the state, the temporal and the spatial – within a popular religious formation in eastern India from the mid-nineteenth century through to the present.[36]

All of these writings have variously combined historical fieldwork and ethnographic archival research. Unsurprisingly, they have been accompanied by analyses that have unraveled and interrogated dominant mappings of time and space: from the persistent oppositions between myth and history through to pervasive projections of the West and nation as history, modernity, and destiny for all people and every identity. Important examples of such work reside in the challenges posed by Dipesh Chakrabarty's forceful philosophical critique of the developmental premises of "historicist" thinking, discussed earlier, as well as by Gyanenendra Pandey's recent critical considerations of the formidable violence that is at once embodied and ignored, made routine and glossed over, by the modern coupling of nation and history.[37]

No less than in relation to history, the acute rethinking of identity in connection with community has been at the core of historical anthropologies, postcolonial perspectives, and subaltern endeavors. Here, too, there has been a braiding of two apparently incommensurable yet actually complementary emphases. On the one hand, several scholars associated with subaltern studies have underscored the key role of the community as an ethical formation in questioning and challenging projects of power – of colony and empire, nation and history – and thereby construing discrete notations of space and time.[38] On the other, distinct strands of critical scholarship have queried persistent, spatially-temporally static portrayals of the community as an ineluctably anachronistic, tightly bounded entity, one tending toward consensus in its expression, entailing allegiance to primordial tradition, and as broadly opposed to modernity. Together, communities have come to be understood as active participants in wider processes of colonialism and empire, nation and nationalism, state and citizen, and modernity and globalization, participants that imbue such processes – themselves made up of diverse relationships of meaning and power – with their own terms and textures, perceptions and practices, including of time and space.[39]

Writings in historical anthropology, subaltern studies, and postcolonial approaches have explored the many meanings of community construed by its members, especially their symbolization and elaboration of boundaries, necessarily socio-spatial-temporal, as providing substance to their differences and identities. To start with, this has involved examinations of the constitutive location of community within wide-ranging processes of power as well as of its internal divisions as expressed in terms of property, gender, law, and office.[40] Moreover, such efforts have been fortified by incisive accounts of communities as questioning and contesting dominant projects of meaning and power, including those turning on empire and nation as well as religion and race, unraveling their challenge to authority in a historically and ethnographically layered manner.[41] Finally, there have been diverse endeavors to write greater heterogeneity – across social space and cultural time – into the concept of community. Indeed, recent reconfigurations of the category have derived further support from the thinking through of the endless antinomy between community and state, moves that have queried the analytical binaries of modern disciplines, which are closely bound to totalizing temporal templates of universal history and exclusive spatial blueprints of Western modernity.

Some studies have combined these overlapping emphases. We have noted the work of Skaria on the Dangs in western India and of Banerjee-Dube on Orissa in eastern India.[42] In addition, consider my historical and anthropological exploration of an untouchable and heretical caste-sect formation of Chhattisgarh in central India over the past two centuries.[43] The account focuses on a large internally differentiated community in order to trace the endeavors of its members within changing relations of power and property under precolonial regimes and colonial rule in the region; track the group's negotiation and reproduction of ritual authority and gender hierarchies; and explore its articulations of caste and Hinduism, evangelism and empire, and state and nation, especially as these were played out in everyday arenas. Especially important in each of these steps were the explicit articulations of the community's perceptions and practices and the implicit intimations of its construal of cultural time and social space. Together, such writings suggest that prudent procedures in historical anthropology, postcolonial perspectives, and subaltern studies are at work in the rethinking not only of community and history, but also of nation-state, nationalism, and modernity.

Nation and modernity

Key departures in historical anthropology, subaltern studies, and postcolonial understandings have played an important part in reformulations of approaches to nation, nationalism, and the identities they spawn. Beginning with the critical rethinking of these concepts-entities within subaltern studies, the endeavors have extended in postcolonial scholarship to the highlighting of the pedagogical performances of the nation and unraveling(s) of the scandal of the state.[44] In explicit and implicit ways, issues of time and space lie at the core of these understandings of identities, broadly conceived.

Together, the writings in these arenas have thought through pervasive projections of nations, nationalisms, and national identities as expressing primordial temporal patterns and innate spatial designs, which turn upon each other, seamlessly and timelessly. They have also interrogated the ways in which various renderings of such identities can be differently yet intimately bound to authoritative – indeed, biographical – portraits of nation-states and nationalist endeavors, each understood as image and practice, especially entailing territorial-historical space-time. In such questioning, a key role has been played by the acute recognition that nations, nationalisms, and national identities are historical and social artifacts and processes, constructed temporally and spatially. This is to say that, although nations, nationalisms, and the identities they spawn are among the most consequential features of modern times, they nonetheless display attributes of what Benedict Anderson has called "imagined communities."[45] Following such recognition, there have been astute studies of socio-spatial and cultural-temporal productions of nations, nationalisms, and national cultures/identities as projects and processes of power and meaning. Here ethnographies and histories have come together with sociological discussions and literary explorations not only to query familiar understandings of these categories and entities, but actually to do this by tracking their varied creations and formidable fabrications.[46] At the same time, other related efforts have focused on how the ideological frames, pedagogical performances, and narrative techniques assiduously construing nation, nationalism, and nationalist identities insinuate rather more than mere ideational errors. Rather, such patterns and procedures – turning on articulations and reifications of time and space – each acquire a formidable presence in the world, assuming acute ontological attributes.[47]

These emphases have been accompanied by analyses stressing the socio-spatial differences and cultural-temporal distinctions at the core of nations, nationalisms, and the identities they beget, particularly considering the subaltern expressions, anticolonial manifestations, and gendered dimensions of these ensembles. We saw that the subaltern studies project and associated scholarly developments led to rich explorations of the idioms and trajectories of wide varieties of subaltern endeavors. Against the grain of nationalist propositions and instrumentalist projections concerning the politics and identities of the lower orders, these analyses have shown that, in the broader terrain of anticolonial politics, subaltern ventures followed a creative process of straddling and subverting the ideas, symbols, and practices defining dominant nationalism. Such initiatives thereby articulated a supplementary politics, intimating accompanying identities, with distinct visions of the nation and particular expressions of nationalism, entailing and engendering times and spaces, which accessed and exceeded the aims and strategies of a generally middle-class nationalist leadership.[48]

Unsurprisingly, extending the terms of these deliberations, it has been emphasized that middle-class anticolonial nationalisms and nationalist identities embodied their own difference and distinction, spatial and temporal, ahead of likenesses of the nation in the looking glass of Europe. In particular, by drawing on yet reworking European democratic and republican traditions and Enlightenment and post-Enlightenment principles, middle-class nationalist endeavors and identities translated and transformed the ideals of the sovereign nation and the images of the free citizen through forceful filters of the subjugated homeland and the colonized subject.[49] With distinct accents, other critical writings have unraveled the presence of gender and the place of women in formations of modern nations and articulations of nationalist identities. In place here have been astute explorations of the social mappings of space-time of the nation through identifications of domesticity; the gendered construal of the homeland as a feminine figure; women's participation and presence, involving tropes/times of family and kinship, in nationalist endeavors and identities; and the socio-spatially ambiguous identifications of gender that attend their definition as citizen-subjects. In this way, the analytic of gender has incisively interrogated the attributes of authority and alterity, of time and space, at the heart of nations and nationalisms in their dominant and subaltern incarnations.[50]

All of this has meant that salient recent work has probed the identities and differences embodied by nation and state, examining especially their intimate associations as well as contending connections with modern power and global transactions. Rather than accepting the spatial-temporal identifications of the nation-state as settled analytical coordinates, recent writings have explored the interplay of national and nationalist imperatives with transnational and global processes, critically examining how the one can be inextricably embedded in the other. Here are to be found explorations of the representation of historical images in the making of a diasporic "community" as well as analyses of the everyday production of the space-time of the nation that question the limitations of "methodological nationalism."[51]

Still other studies have focused on the nation-state as entailing sets of frequently conflicting disciplines to normalize and order society and identity, bringing to the fore what Hansen and Stepputat have summarized as three "practical" languages of governance and three "symbolic" languages of authority, which are together crucial for understanding state, nation, and identity.[52] The pedagogies, performances, and practices of state and nation – and the identities they engender – have been critically unraveled through scholarship that has focused on the quotidian configurations and everyday identifications of these concepts and entities. Such different yet interconnected emphases have clarified that across shifting contexts and terrains, propelled by distinct agendas and aspirations, nationalisms and nation-states have articulated wide varieties of spatial-temporal practice, disciplinary power, and cultural identity.[53]

At the same time, related work has pointed to distinct tensions at the core of the modern state. A single salient instance should suffice here. The political philosopher William Connolly has reminded us of the intensification in the present of a subterranean tension that has long resided at the core of modern pluralist democracies.[54] This tension inheres in how such polities, as Stephen White in his discussion of Connolly's ideas puts it, "by their very nature experience friction between the imperative of protecting the economic and cultural conditions of the distribution of identities existing at any given time, on the one hand, and the imperative of openness to the emergence of new identities, on the other."[55] Now, what happens under contemporary conditions of "late modernity" is that this tension is intensified, leading to two unrelenting, opposed, simultaneous socio-spatial responses: an acceleration toward more and more "cultural *pluralisation*" and, conversely, an increasingly "aggressive *fundamentalisation* of existing identities."[56]

Here, it seems to me, that to critically and carefully consider the entwining of these impulses – of the pluralization and fundamentalisation of identities – is to ask and explore how such entanglements straddle the state and its subjects, the nation and its representations, multiculturalism and its advocates, and global politics and their constituencies, including the spatial and temporal imperatives of the "minority" and the "majority." All of this further entails attention to enactments on the ground not only of stipulations of "modern pluralist democracies" – which are no longer only envisioned in the limited likeness, the exclusive experience of an abstract West – but equally of the rejection of democratic imperatives. Such enactments are mapped in terms of their distinct hetero-temporal articulations and socio-spatial expressions, characteristic of modernity as a global phenomenon.[57]

Unsurprisingly, incisive discussions in historical anthropology and critical ethnography have pointed toward the need for careful considerations of modernity and modern identities, their processes and persuasions. As has been noted already, there has been prescient probing in this terrain of the analytical abstractions and the formalist frames that endlessly attend apprehensions of these categories. It has become clear that ahead of their exclusive images, the divergent articulations of modernity and contending identifications of the modern have been linked to particular processes of history and culture, identity and difference, time and space.[58] Equally, such work has highlighted that the diverse spatial-temporal manifestations of modernity and modern identity have been frequently influenced by singular likenesses of Western modernity, where the singularity and universal cast of the latter are differently engaged by the plural and vernacular attributes of the former.[59] Precisely these distinct procedures shape, structure, and suture the terms, textures, and transformations of empire, nation, and globalization.[60]

Coda

At the end, let me point to how this discussion of identity and modernity suggests wider critical considerations. The point is simple. When inquiring into identities, it is crucial to query the pervasive antinomies between the "universal" and the "particular" and "power" and "difference." After all, it is much too easy to rail against the universality and power of modernity in order to simply celebrate the particularity and difference of identity. Instead, the more challenging task involves exploring the articulation of identities as expressing the shared entailments and mutual productions of power and difference, as interleaving the founding exclusions and constitutive contradictions of authority and alterity, entailing as well as engendering formations of space, notations of time. This further means that the productive possibilities of postcolonial emphases, subaltern studies, and historical anthropology – in this case concerning identities – inhere in constant vigilance against their self-projections as always subversive, already known modes of scholarly knowledge and political criticism. Rather, it is through the self-questioning of their formative presumptions and formidable limitations that these approaches can more adequately explore modernity, history, identity, and their interplay – as shaped by the concatenations of distinct yet coeval temporalities and of overlapping yet heterogeneous spaces. After all, such distinction and heterogeneity have been the soul, stuff, and substance of modernity and its subjects, of subjects of modernity and modern subjects. These are issues that run through the epilogue that follows.

Notes

1 Trouillot, "North Atlantic universals," p. 46.
2 See, for example, Dube, *Stitches on Time* and *After Conversion*.
3 This is to say that just as analytically fatal mistakes surround understandings of hegemony as a closed system of cultural and ideological control by dominant groups so also theoretically grave errors attend the reification of subaltern autonomy and agency, an issue discussed in Dube, *Stitches on Time*.
4 Following from this, it is important to register the heterogeneity at the core of subaltern studies, postcolonial perspectives, and historical anthropology. In basic terms, we might distinguish between two tendencies. On the one hand, strongly influenced by critical theory – especially the work of Michel Foucault and Jacques Derrida, but also the writings of philosophers and critics from Martin Heidegger to Edward Said – a key corpus has focused on formations and regimens of modern power. Such scholarship has especially tracked the discursive entailment and constitutive embedding of power in projects and provisos of, for example, empire, modernity, state, and nation. Here extraordinary efficacy has been accorded often to dominance and its dissonance, so that practices and processes construed by historical subjects have primarily appeared as encompassed by power and its productivity. On the other hand, distinct dispositions have focused on the contingent and contradictory elaborations of societal processes and cultural practices as enacted by historical subjects. Such practices, processes, and subjects have been explored as at once part of and themselves articulating relationships of power, but without turning power into a fetishized force and omnipresent totality. Here are to be found examinations of the vexed relationships between culture, structure, action, and event, including the ways each of these terms mediate history. Here are to be

discovered, too, discussions that cast the metropolis and the margins and the dominant and the subaltern as part of mutual analytical fields, including by tracking the transformations of time-space within anthropology and history.

5 As the previous chapters have indicated, these are potentially valuable endeavors, worth undertaking in their own right.

6 In taking these steps, I follow particular protocols of citation, an issue that was discussed in the Preface. Thus, in the references provided below, I juxtapose writings from distinct "areas" and different "disciplines" as part of a critical narrative. Here, specific studies are drawn on in a manner that articulates their wide analytical implications.

7 Dube, "Terms that bind"; Dube, "Anthropology, history, historical anthropology."

8 Jean Comaroff and John Comaroff, *Of Revelation and Revolution: Christianity, Colonialism, and Consciousness in South Africa*, vol. 1 (Chicago, IL: Chicago University Press, 1991); Comaroff and Comaroff, *Ethnography and the Historical Imagination*; Comaroff and Comaroff, *Of Revelation and Revolution*; Ann Laura Stoler, *Race and the Education of Desire: Foucault's History of Sexuality and the Colonial Order of Things* (Durham, NC: Duke University Press, 1995); Ann Laura Stoler, *Carnal Knowledge and Imperial Power: Race and the Intimate in Colonial Rule* (Berkeley: University of California Press, 2002); Ann Laura Stoler, *Along the Archival Grain: Epistemic Anxieties and Colonial Common Sense* (Princeton, NJ: Princeton University Press, 2008).

9 Ann Laura Stoler, "Rethinking colonial categories: European communities and the boundaries of rule," *Comparative Studies in Society and History* 13 (1989): 134–61; Comaroff and Comaroff, *Of Revelation and Revolution*. See also Patrick Wolfe, *Settler Colonialism and the Transformation of Anthropology: The Politics and Poetics of an Ethnographic Event* (London: Cassell, 1999); Ranajit Guha, "Not at home in empire," in Dube (ed.), *Postcolonial Passages*, pp. 38–46. For wider discussions, see Dube, *Stitches on Time*.

10 Stoler, "Rethinking colonial categories"; Stoler, *Carnal Knowledge and Imperial Power*; Thomas, *Colonialism's Culture*; Cooper and Stoler, *Tensions of Empire*.

11 John Comaroff, "Images of empire, contests of conscience: models of colonial domination in South Africa," *American Ethnologist*, 16 (1989): 661–85. Comaroff and Comaroff, *Ethnography and the Historical Imagination*.
12 Dube, *Stitches on Time*; Dube, *After Conversion*.
13 K. Sivaramakrishnan, *Modern Forests: Statemaking and Environmental Change in Colonial Eastern India* (New Delhi: Oxford University Press, 1999).
14 Anna Davin, "Imperialism and motherhood," *History Workshop*, 5 (1978): 9–65; Comaroff and Comaroff, *Ethnography and Historical Imagination*, pp. 265–95. See also Webb Keane, *Christian Moderns: Freedom and Fetish in the Mission Encounter* (Berkeley: University of California Press, 2007).
15 Cohn, *Colonialism and its Forms of Knowledge*; Edward W. Said, *Culture and Imperialism* (New York: Vintage, 1994); Mignolo, *Darker Side of the Renaissance*; Stoler, *Race and Education of Desire*; Antoinette M. Burton, *At the Heart of the Empire: Indians and the Colonial Encounter in Late-Victorian Britain* (Berkeley: University of California Press, 1998); E. M. Collingham, *Imperial Bodies: The Physical Experience of the Raj, c.1800–1947* (Cambridge: Polity Press, 2001). See also Piya Chatterjee, *A Time for Tea: Women, Labor, and Post/Colonial Politics on an Indian Plantation* (Durham, NC: Duke University Press, 2001); Simon Gikandi, *Maps of Englishness: Writing Identity in the Culture of Colonialism* (New York: Columbia University Press, 1996).
16 Mehta, *Liberalism and Empire*.
17 van der Veer, *Imperial Encounters*.
18 Nancy Rose Hunt, *A Colonial Lexicon of Birth Ritual, Medicalization, and Mobility in the Congo* (Durham, NC: Duke University Press, 1999); Timothy Mitchell, *Colonizing Egypt* (Berkeley: University of California Press, 1988); Johannes Fabian, *Language and Colonial Power: The Appropriation of Swahili in the Former Belgian Congo* (Cambridge: Cambridge University Press, 1986); Rabasa, *Writing Violence on the Northern Frontier*; David Arnold, *Colonizing the Body: State Medicine and Epidemic Disease in Nineteenth-Century India* (Berkeley: University of California Press, 1993); Megan Vaughan, *Curing Their Ills: Colonial Power and African Illness* (Stanford, CA: Stanford University Press, 1991); Collingham, *Imperial Bodies*; Goswami, *Producing India*. See also José Rabasa, *Tell Me the Story*

of *How I Conquered You: Elsewheres and Ethnosuicide in the Colonial Mesoamerican World* (Austin: University of Texas Press, 2011).

19 Fabian, *Out of Our Minds*; Inderpal Grewal, *Home and Harem: Nation, Gender, Empire, and the Cultures of Travel* (Durham, NC: Duke University Press, 1996); Mary Louise Pratt, *Imperial Eyes: Travel Writing and Transculturation* (London: Routledge, 1992); Annie E. Coombes, *Reinventing Africa: Museums, Material Culture and Popular Imagination in Late Victorian and Edwardian England* (New Haven, CT: Yale University Press, 1994); Tony Bennett, *The Birth of the Museum: History, Theory, Politics* (London: Routledge, 1995); Tony Bennett, *Pasts Beyond Memory: Evolution, Museums, Colonialism* (London: Routledge, 2004); Amiria Henare, *Museums, Anthropology and Imperial Exchange* (Cambridge: Cambridge University Press, 2009); and John M. MacKenzie, *Museums and Empire: Natural History, Human Cultures and Colonial Identities* (Manchester: Manchester University Press, 2010).

20 Vicente Rafael, *Contracting Colonialism: Translation and Christian Conversion in Tagalog Society under Early Spanish Rule* (Ithaca, NY: Cornell University Press, 1988); Guha, *Elementary Aspects*; David Scott, *Formations of Ritual: Colonial and Anthropological Discourses on the Sinhala Yaktovil* (Minneapolis: University of Minnesota Press, 1994); Wolfe, *Settler Colonialism*.

21 Gikandi, *Maps of Englishness*; Guha-Thakurta, *Monuments, Objects, Histories*; Saloni Mathur, *India by Design: Colonial History and Cultural Display* (Berkeley: University of California Press, 2007); Emma Tarlo, *Clothing Matters: Dress and Identity in India* (Chicago, IL: University of Chicago Press, 1996); Pinney, *Camera Indica*; Christopher Pinney, *Photos of the Gods: The Printed Image and Political Struggle in India* (London: Reaktion Books, 2004).

22 Mrinalini Sinha, *Colonial Masculinity: The "Manly Englishman" and the "Effeminate Bengali" in the Late Nineteenth Century* (Manchester: Manchester University Press, 1995); Mrinalini Sinha, *Specters of Mother India: The Global Restructuring of an Empire* (Durham, NC: Duke University Press, 2006); Lata Mani, *Contentious Traditions: The Debate on Sati in Colonial India* (Berkeley: University of California Press, 1998); Indrani Chatterjee, *Gender, Slavery and Law in Colonial India* (New Delhi: Oxford University Press, 1999); Lenore Manderson and Margaret

Jolly (eds.), *Sites of Desire, Economies of Pleasure: Sexualities in Asia and the Pacific* (Chicago, IL: University of Chicago Press, 1997); Stoler, *Carnal Knowledge and Imperial Power*.

23 For a wider discussion, see Dube, "Terms that bind."

24 Frederick Cooper, *Decolonization and African Society: The Labour Question in French and British Africa* (Cambridge: Cambridge University Press, 1996); Coronil, *The Magical State*; Birla, *Stages of Capital*.

25 McClintock, *Imperial Leather*.

26 Chandra Talpade Mohanty, *Feminism without Borders: Decolonizing Theory, Practicing Solidarity* (Durham, NC: Duke University Press, 2003); Chakrabarty, *Provincializing Europe*.

27 Ian Baucom, *Specters of the Atlantic: Finance Capital, Slavery, and the Philosophy of History* (Durham, NC: Duke University Press, 2005); Agnani, *Hating Empire Properly*; Fischer, *Modernity Disavowed*; Russel A. Berman, *Enlightenment or Empire: Colonial Discourse in German Culture* (Lincoln: University of Nebraska Press, 2004); Scott, *Conscripts of Modernity*; Audra Simpson, *Mohawk Interruptus: Political Life across the Border of Settler States* (Durham, NC: Duke University Press, 2014); and Derek Gregory, *The Colonial Present* (Oxford: Blackwell, 2007). See also Muthu, *Enlightenment Against Empire*.

28 Guha, *Elementary Aspects*; Guha, *Dominance without Hegemony*; Chakrabarty, *Provincializing Europe*; Pandey, *Remembering Partition*.

29 Trouillot, *Silencing the Past*; David William Cohen, *The Combing of History* (Chicago, IL: University of Chicago Press, 1994); Klein, *Frontiers of Historical Imagination*. See also Saidiya H. Hartman, *Lose Your Mother: A Journey Along the Atlantic Slave Route* (New York: Farrar, Straus and Giroux, 2007); and Hartman, *Scenes of Subjection*.

30 For example, Rosaldo, *Ilongot Headhunting*; Rappaport, *Cumbe Reborn*; Florida, *Writing the Past, Inscribing the Future*; David William Cohen and E. S. Atieno Odhiambo, *Siaya: Historical Anthropology* (Cleveland: Ohio University Press, 1989); Price, *First-Time*; Price, *Alabi's World*; Luise White, *Speaking with Vampires: Rumour and History in Colonial Africa* (Berkeley: University of California Press, 2000).

31 I develop these themes in Dube, "Anthropology, history, historical anthropology."

32 Redfield, *Space in the Tropics*; Dube, *Stitches on Time*.

33 Vinayak Chaturvedi, *Peasant Pasts: History and Memory in Western India* (Berkeley: University of California Press, 2007); Deshpande, *Creative Pasts*; Shail Mayaram, *Against History, Against State: Counterperspectives from the Margins* (New Delhi: Permanent Black, 2004); Price, *The Convict and the Colonel*; Ann Gold and Bhoju Ram Gujar, *In the Time of Trees and Sorrows: Nature, Power, and Memory in Rajasthan* (Durham, NC: Duke University Press, 2002); Dube, *Untouchable Pasts*; Trouillot, *Silencing the Past*.
34 Amin, *Event, Metaphor, Memory*.
35 Skaria, *Hybrid Histories*.
36 Ishita Banerjee-Dube, *Religion, Law and Power: Tales of Time in Eastern India, 1860–2000* (London: Anthem Press, 2007).
37 Chakrabarty, *Provincializing Europe*; Chakrabarty, *Habitations of Modernity*; Pandey, *Remembering Partition*; Pandey, *Routine Violence*; Ashis Nandy, "History's forgotten doubles," *History and Theory*, 34 (1995): 44–66.
38 Recall the discussion of these themes in Chapter 2.
39 For a wider discussion, see Dube, "Anthropology, history, historical anthropology."
40 Das, *Critical Events*; Malavika Kasturi, *Embattled Identities: Rajput Lineages and the Colonial State in Nineteenth-Century North India* (New Delhi: Oxford University Press, 2002); Dube, *Stitches on Time*; Charu Gupta, *Sexuality, Obscenity, and Community: Women, Muslims, and the Hindu Public in Colonial India* (New Delhi: Permanent Black, 2002).
41 Rao, *The Caste Question*; Shail Mayaram, *Resisting Regimes: Myth, Memory and the Shaping of a Muslim Identity* (New Delhi: Oxford University Press, 1997); David Hardiman, *The Coming of the Devi: Adivasi Assertion in Western India* (New Delhi: Oxford University Press, 1987); Guha, *Elementary Aspects*.
42 Skaria, *Hybrid Histories*; Banerjee-Dube, *Religion, Law and Power*.
43 Dube, *Untouchable Pasts*. See also the discussion in Chapter 2.
44 Homi K. Bhabha (ed.), *Nation and Narration* (London: Routledge, 1990), particularly pp. 291–322; Rajeswari Sunder Rajan, *Scandal of the State: Women, Law, and Citizenship in Postcolonial India* (Durham, NC: Duke University Press, 2003).
45 Anderson, *Imagined Communities*.

46 Guha, *Dominance without Hegemony*; Amin, *Event, Metaphor, Memory*; Chatterjee, *The Nation and its Fragments*; Pandey, *Remembering Partition*; Peter van der Veer, *Religious Nationalism: Hindus and Muslims in India* (Berkeley: University of California Press, 1994).

47 Ana María Alonso, "The politics of space, time, and substance: state formation, nationalism, and ethnicity," *Annual Review of Anthropology* 23 (1994): 379–400; Amin, *Event, Metaphor, Memory*; Butalia, *Other Side of Silence*; Pinney, *Photos of the Gods*; and Tarlo, *Clothing Matters*.

48 See Dube, "Terms that bind," for a broader discussion.

49 Chatterjee, *The Nation and its Fragments*. See also Prakash, *Another Reason*.

50 Tanika Sarkar, *Hindu Wife, Hindu Nation: Community, Religion, and Cultural Nationalism* (New Delhi: Permanent Black, 2001); Sinha, *Specters of Mother India*; Menon and Bhasin, *Borders and Boundaries*; Anupama Roy, *Gendered Citizenship: Historical and Conceptual Explorations* (Hyderabad: Orient Longman, 2005).

51 Axel, *Nation's Tortured Body*; Goswami, *Producing India*.

52 Hansen and Stepputat, "Introduction: states of imagination."

53 Tarlo, *Unsettling Memories*; Hansen, *Wages of Violence*; Bénéï, *Schooling Passions*; Gupta, *Postcolonial Developments*; Gupta, *Red Tape*; and Middleton, *Demands of Recognition*.

54 Connolly, *Ethos of Pluralization*; see also William E. Connolly, *Identity/Difference: Democratic Negotiations of Political Paradox* (Ithaca, NY: Cornell University Press, 1991).

55 S. K. White, *Sustaining Affirmation*, p. 120.

56 Connolly, *Ethos of Pluralization*, pp. 97, 100, emphasis in the original.

57 Following Connolly, *Ethos of Pluralization*, such sites open up spaces for political, ethical, and ontological reflection.

58 Comaroff and Comaroff, *Of Revelation and Revolution*; Achille Mbembe, *On the Postcolony* (Berkeley: University of California Press, 2001); Gilroy, *The Black Atlantic*; Dube, *Stitches on Time*.

59 Coronil, *The Magical State*; James Ferguson, *Expectations of Modernity*; Dube, *After Conversion*; Dube and Banerjee-Dube, *Unbecoming Modern*. See also Mitchell, "The stage of modernity"; Dube, *Enchantments of Modernity*; and Fischer, *Modernity Disavowed*.

60 Several of these emphases come together in Laura Bear's remarkable historical anthropology of the Indian railways and the Anglo-Indian community, a pre-eminent "railway caste." She brings to bear on worlds of modernity and identity issues of empire and intimacy, nation and difference, race and sexuality, citizenship and kinship, and subject and self-making. Bear's bid is to detail and describe the generative practices and constitutive meanings of these intermeshed processes by thinking them down to their expressions on the ground. Ever attentive to the spatial specificity and temporal tangibility, contention and contradiction, and ambiguity and murkiness of modernity and identity, her work also imaginatively interweaves the cautious querying, careful unraveling, and prudent affirmation of social worlds. See Bear, *Lines of the Nation*.

6
Modern subjects: an epilogue

This epilogue turns attention to salient subjects of a modernist provenance on the Indian subcontinent. Now, in South Asia, a certain haziness regarding modernism and modernity derives not only from the manner in which they can be elided with each other, but the fact that they are both frequently filtered through the optics of modernization. At stake is the acute, albeit altering, importance of being modern, as a person, a nation, and a people. This is true not only of quotidian common sense but of scholarly sentiments. Here, as was noted, modernization implicitly entails pervasive projections of material, organizational, and technological – as well as economic, political, and cultural – transformation(s), principally envisioned in the looking glass of Western development. In this scenario, tacitly at least, different, often hierarchically ordered, peoples are seen as succeeding (or failing) to evolve from their traditional circumstances to arrive at a modernized order. Indeed, motifs of modernization, carrying wide implication, readily draw together mappings of modernism, modernity, and (being) modern, such that each shores up the other.

Overture

Why should this be the case? To begin with, as this book has emphasized throughout, a crucial characteristic of dominant descriptions of the modern and modernity has hinged on their positing of the phenomena as marked by a break with the past, a rupture with tradition, a surpassing of the medieval. Here, through ruses of teleological historical progress, stages of civilization, and social evolutionist schemas, by the second half of the nineteenth century, across much of the world an exclusive West was increasingly presented as the looking glass for the imagining of universal history. As worldly knowledge, borne alike by empire and nation, oriented not merely toward ordering but simultaneously remaking the world, these neat proposals and their formative presumptions variously entered the lives of South Asian subjects. On the Indian subcontinent, across the twentieth century, such principles and presuppositions were first disseminated as ways of approaching social worlds and soon instituted as dimensions of experience and affect within everyday arenas, at the very least middle-class ones. In this scenario, the blueprints of modernization actually distilled the meanings of the modern, articulating an imaginary but palpable distended and aggrandizing West/Europe as modernity – for all those awaiting its second coming in prior places, anachronistic spaces, lagging in time.

In artistic, intellectual, and aesthetic arenas, modernism(s) in South Asia have variously, often critically, engaged with these projections and presuppositions: but they have also been unable to easily escape their long shadow.[1] Now, modernist tendencies on the subcontinent have formed part of diverse expressions across the world of modernism as contentious and contradictory movements, styles, and representations, going back to the mid-nineteenth century and extending into our own times. Here, if modernism has been a principally "qualitative" rather than a merely "chronological" category, it is also the case that on the subcontinent, as elsewhere, the internal endeavors within modernisms to surpass the past, articulate the present, and envision the future have been intrinsically heterogeneous ones.[2]

On the one hand, such initiatives have severally accessed and exceeded colonial representations and precolonial narratives, nationalist thought and nativist tradition, primitivism and futurity, abstract reason and religious truth, and governmental authority and popular politics. There are parallels here with modernist initiatives elsewhere. On the other hand, South Asian endeavors equally sieved such concerns through distinct expressions of modernism, at once querying the colonial connection with a (generally bourgeois) modern, articulating the national dynamic with an (often avant-garde) modern, exploring the critical contours of a (contending, "primitivist") modern, rethinking the content of tradition, and debating the nature of modernity. Imbued with specific spatial densities and tousled temporal energies, this has provided South Asian modernisms with their own twist, with discrete textures.

We have discussed that a key characteristic of modernism at large has been to emphasize the difference of the contemporary present from past epochs. Within South Asian modernisms, this claim of a surpassing of the past, turning on time and space, was variously inflected by the gravity of anticolonial and nationalist imaginaries, the weight of memory and history, the pull of the mythic and the primitive, and the burden of a violent independence and postcolonial politics. This is to say, these endeavors, inhabiting "multiple constellations throughout the twentieth century," appeared critically shot through by "a dialectical process of invoking, resisting, or negotiating questions of tradition, identity' and experience."[3] It followed, too, that ruptures with prior artistic moments within the subcontinental aesthetic landscape – alongside engagements with wider modernist imaginaries – instilled these tendencies with rather particular energies. All of this has meant that the paradoxical, even opposed, trends that have characterized modernisms at large acquired in South Asia a discrete cadence, unfamiliar attributes.

In what follows, I shall elaborate these first formulations by exploring issues of time and space, broadly understood, that informed distinct modernist moments, cutting across different forms of aesthetic production, in South Asia. Here, the temporal-spatial imperatives are culled from within modernist practices themselves, which filtered and reworked distinct influences through a self-directed aesthetic. Indeed, it warrants emphasis that my bid is to follow chronology in order to rethink chronology, and to use taxonomy in order to undo taxonomy, in an effort to foreground the multiple yet overlaying temporal articulations and spatial stipulations of modernisms in South Asia.

Genealogies

By the beginning of the twentieth century, British rule on the Indian subcontinent was 150 years old. This period had seen shifting layered entanglements and conflicts between the colonizer and the colonized: the suppression of dynamic yet contentious processes turning on indigenous authority and political economy; the containment of fluid borders between field and forest; and the subordination of the Indian economy to North Atlantic cycles of trade, profit-making, and consumption. On the one hand, the systematic destruction of forests, the conversion of commons into property, and the emphasis on increasing land revenue had led to the lineaments of an agrarian order consisting of settled agriculture and specialist commodity production, marked by relatively clear groupings of caste and community. This had lasting legacies for the nationalist and imperial imaginaries, including modernist ones: village, agricultural, and caste arrangements that had acquired their distinct terms and textures principally across the nineteenth century were now rendered as ageless, timeless, millennia-old, innate attributes of a spatially singular Indian civilization. On the other hand, this extended epoch had witnessed uneven yet acute articulations of colonial urbanism, entailing debates on the content of tradition and formations of gender on the subcontinent, religious negotiations of evangelical encounters, nationalist contestations of colonial claims, and varied experiments with European traditions in the letters, arts, and politics.

Against the backdrop of these broad-based, twin movements, crucial for formations of aesthetics in South Asia, I recount a vignette from the early twentieth century:

> On 7 May 1921 the Indian poet Rabindranath Tagore celebrated his sixtieth birthday in Weimar, and used the opportunity to visit the Bauhaus ... [soon], at Tagore's suggestion, a selection of Bauhaus works was shipped to Calcutta to be exhibited, in December 1922, at the fourteenth annual exhibition of the Society of Oriental Art ... Among the exhibits (which mysteriously never returned to Europe)

were two water colours by Wassily Kandinsky and nine by Paul Klee [and a larger number of other pieces by many different artists] … The exhibition was well received, but … what was perhaps even more important about it was that a number of Cubist paintings by Rabindranath's nephew Gaganendranath Tagore and folk-primitivist works by his niece Sunayani Devi were also shown on this occasion.[4]

At least three points stand out. First, at stake in the exhibition was a break with the formidable influence of prior nationalist art, especially the Orientalism of the Bengal School. If the Bengal School configured a counter-colonial, "pan-Asian" style of narrative painting as part of Swadeshi nationalism (1905–11), while opposing the academic naturalism of narrative art, now a newer disposition came to the fore.[5] Thus, one form of counter-colonial sensibility, appealing to bourgeois nationalists, was replaced by a modernist anti-imperial imaginary which would soon draw on the energies of the subcontinental popular, announcing shifts that were aesthetic and political, temporal and spatial.

Second, rather more than the ready influence of the Bauhaus (or of Europe/West at large), it is the experiments of Gaganendranath – and, in a different way, those of Sunayani – that appear as an inaugural moment of the modernist idiom in Indian art. None of this involved a mere imitation of European modernism. Actually, discussed as part of the quest for "artistic autonomy" in the modernist journals of the day, in Gaganendranath's work, "a dynamic, fluid, mysterious play of light and shade and colour" replaced "the relatively static geometry of analytical Cubism," revealing also "an imagination steeped in literature and myth," setting to work and itself construing a time-space that was prior yet present as idea and practice.[6]

Third, while Gaganendranath's work remained something of an exception in terms of its broader impact, the folk imaginary underlying the art of his sister Sunayani had wide implications. It not only affected the primitivist motifs of the artist Jamini Roy, a point usually acknowledged. The imaginary arguably also formed an integral part of larger expressions of primitivism and ruralism in modernist art in India, bearing acutely spatial-temporal dimensions while being shaped by distinct configurations of anticolonial nationalism on the subcontinent.

Until the end of the 1910s, Indian nationalism had remained a principally middle-class (and elite) phenomenon, despite some attempts during the Swadeshi period to draw in popular participation in nationalist agitation. All this was to change from the beginnings of the 1920s as Mahatma Gandhi took decisive steps to transform Indian nationalism, turning the Indian National Congress into a firm grouping with an organizational structure and regular membership (rather than a forum that met at the end of each year). Gandhi's political strategy was to draw in the participation of the Indian "masses," especially the peasants, yet to do so in a rigorously controlled manner, such that the subalterns obeyed and followed the Congress leadership. At the same time, the nationalist endeavor to "discipline and mobilize" was equally accompanied by Gandhian ideology and practice that struck an acutely antiindustrial, anti-urban note. Here were to be found an imaginatively counter-modern cadence, turning on a critique of Western civilization, a valorization of the village and tradition, and an innately moral politics, all arguably grounded in the reinvigoration of an unsullied space-time. The subaltern groups in turn came to articulate their own supplementary anticolonial politics and perceptions of nationalism and nation, founded in everyday practices, which acceded yet exceeded the official Congress understanding.[7]

All of this informed the aesthetic, spatial-temporal, expressions of folk and primitivist imaginaries in modernist Indian art.[8] There were different trajectories here. Nandalal Bose, who presided over the art school at Rabindranath Tagore's Santiniketan, conjoined folk styles, bold brushstrokes, and outdoor murals in an eclectic practice. This served to engender an aesthetic discourse rooted in a principally timeless community signifying the space of the nation, including through Bose's association with Gandhi, especially producing wall panels for the Haripura session of the Indian National Congress in 1938. Arguably, this association of nationalism, community, and (the insistence on) a formal clarity acquired distinct dimensions among Bose's students, even as their experiments bore testimony to the critical autonomy of aesthetic traditions. Thus, if the painter K. G. Subramanyan honed an expressive, imaginative, figurative style, the sculptor Ramkinkar Baij – a remarkable talent from a humble background and with scant formal education – represented the lives of the "adivasi" Santals, creating monumental outdoor sculptures of these subjects in cement, rubble, and concrete to showcase thereby a "subaltern modernism." Here was a modernism that imbued allegedly anachronistic subjects with formidable aesthetic and existential coevality, a temporal and spatial energy that was at once prior, acutely present, and entirely futural. Indeed, taken together, on offer was a querying of the colonial connection with a bourgeois modern, articulations of the national dynamic with an avant-garde modern, and explorations of the critical contours of a (contending) "primitivist" modern.

At the same time, the density and gravity of artistic interchanges often exceeded the formal influence – intellectual and ideological, aesthetic and political – of anticolonial nationalism in articulations of modernist, folk and primitivist, imaginaries in South Asia. Here, Jamini Roy's primitivism arrived at striking modernist brevity through a simplification of form and an elimination of details. Drawing on folk forms while rooting his work in local artisanal practice, Roy created an art at odds with colonial urban culture precisely through its intrinsic valorization of the communitarian in actual aesthetic practice. In a not unconnected manner, Rabindranath Tagore's own modernist internationalism was not only founded on critical intimations of the "illegitimacy of nationalism" but his forceful, mask-like, virtually totemic images were an acute expression of what Partha Mitter has described as "the dark landscape of the psyche." Finally, away from Bengal, painting in North India, Amrita Sher-Gill's primitivist art, at once formatively modernist and startlingly cosmopolitan – drawing comparisons with her Mexican contemporary, Frida Kahlo – far exceeded merely "indigenous" influences.[9] It intimated instead a politics of art that refused to be reduced to prescribed ideology. In each instance, at stake are formative configurations of space and time as parts of the reworking of tradition and the rethinking of modernity within Indian modernist artistic practice, issues which yet await fuller understanding.

Formations

From the 1920s onwards, anticolonial nationalism, drawing in popular participation, appeared accompanied by connected yet contending tendencies, socialism and communism, which could now form compelling friendships and now forge intimate enmities. These intellectual-political impulses had a profound impact on the arts – from painting to literature to theater to cinema – in the 1940s. The tumultuous times of famine and suffering, an antifascist war and subaltern struggles, the end of empire and intimations of independence saw the formations of progressive organizations such as the Indian People's Theatre Association (IPTA) and various artist groups. This left cultural movement sought to create in art a distinct "popular" – "national in form, socialist in content" – and in its wake, it brought together artists, writers, and performers on a common platform to fashion the idiom of a progressive art.[10]

Even as these initiatives were being expressed, the subcontinent gained independence from British imperial rule, itself accompanied by the Partition of its territories and subjects, each innately sociospatial, into two nations, India and Pakistan (West and East). The hopes and desires of the new citizens, the times-spaces of their habitation and imagination, were fragmented, even split, by the violence that marked their Partition. While estimates vary, between 200,000 and 1.5 million Muslims, Hindus, and Sikhs were killed in the violence, including reciprocal genocide; around 75,000 women were raped and/or abducted in the drawing and redrawing of the boundaries of these communities; and a little less than 15 million people were displaced, losing homes and belonging across new borders, as concrete as they were imaginary. Some of the split nature of these processes, which fabricated and jumbled terrible temporalities and shadowy spaces, was captured by Nehru, the formidable statesman-architect as well as ideologue-rhetorician of a modernist nationalism, in his "tryst with destiny" speech, delivered at the stroke of midnight on August 15, 1947.[11]

Yet much of this failed to convince modernist artists and authors. While the communist slogan "Yah azadi jhooti hai [this freedom is a lie]" did not prove persuasive, the recognition of a truncated freedom, a compromised independence, and Partition's violence, calling into question the space-time of the new nations, haunted the modernist imagination at large. Nor were these specters laid to rest as India embarked on a vigorous program of nation-building, based on a governmentally planned economy, state presence in heavy industry, and the building of large dams and other monumental public works. Indeed, what came to the fore was a nation and society lacking in soul and spirit. Against this were variously pitted issues of artistic autonomy, aesthetic independence, individual alienation, and social commitment in the quest for a modern that was avant-garde in expression yet Indian in essence – imagination and practice in which epic, legend, and myth, signifying uncommon spatial-temporal matrices, often played a critical role. Here, I provide a series of juxtapositions from different art forms.

In the wake of independence and Partition, modernisms in South Asia saw an acute overlaying of artistic technique and the force of the past, an incessant interchange between the density of aesthetic traditions and the urgency of the present, an acute interplay between claims on tradition and the construal of space-time. This past and present, technique and aesthetic, and time and space had to be made modern for the people, for the nation in the making with its flaws and fractures. Some of this is clarified by the terms of theater in the mid-twentieth century. The activities of the IPTA turned on progressive performances, realist drama, and social critique aimed toward a "cultural awakening" among the people of the subcontinent. At the same time, rather than being subsumed by a limited aesthetic-politics of agitation and propaganda, here were to be found innovations that drew upon the resources of realism in order to reveal rather other glimmers of modernist theater. Thus, in the terrain of theater in South Asia, the social impact drama of the 1940s was followed by cutting-edge developments which critically and imaginatively articulated the epic and the avant-garde, the myth and the contemporary, the legend and the present, the temporal and the spatial in expressions of modernism, developments that yet remain insufficiently conceptualized.

Unsurprisingly, in "progressive" endeavors in the plastic arts, questions of a practice that was adequate to an emergent era, an inviting internationalism, and a modern art came to be of critical import. In such a scenario, what was the precise place of a new nation, its spacetime, within a novel aesthetic? Did the nation implicitly uphold the aesthetical, providing also the context and support for key emergences? Or, did the nation-state hinder aesthetic autonomy? It followed that these artistic efforts could follow different directions, but none could escape the demands of avant-garde autonomy, ever on the edge of social space and transient time. Thus, the most influential of these artists' organizations, whose prominence came to virtually eclipse that of the others, was the Progressive Artists' Group (of Bombay), founded at the end of 1947 as a response to Partition, which spoke not only of a radical break from the past, but of the autonomy of the work of art itself: "Absolute freedom for content and technique, almost anarchic."[12]

At the same time, the articulations of such autonomy were deeply entangled with the density of myth and memory, intimations of palpable pasts and receding presents, sown into the landscape and adrift in the air. Indeed, these temporal-spatial resources could be a means of unraveling the pain of Partition, the puzzle of the nation, the ambiguity of identity, and the force of exile. Two salient examples, both emerging from the Progressive Artists' Group and each extending from the 1940s into our present, should suffice. In the work of M. F. Hussain, who came from a disadvantaged Muslim background, altered cubist configurations entered into conversations with prior traditions of Indian sculpture and miniature paintings, while he sieved the resources of epics and legends, gods and goddesses to create a distinctive modernist practice, construing novel idioms of space and time.[13] Similarly, the art of F. N. Souza, a Catholic, who fiercely guarded his autonomy in exile, conjures a formidable expressionism that is ever tied to the figures and forms of a haunting past and a spectral present, which signify space and create time. Here are to be found crucifixes and the (black) Christ, Last Suppers and erotic nudes, the mother and child, each drawing in the textures and tangles of a vernacular Christianity and an everyday aesthetic from Goa in western India. At the same time, all this is done and undone, spatially and temporally, by the conjuring of "a God, who is not a God of gentleness and love, but rather of suffering, vengeance and terrible anger."[14]

Consider now that literary modernisms in the mid-twentieth century engaged at once with related genres in the rest of the world while seeking also to express a specific modern on the subcontinent. This could reveal formative tensions and critical creativity, discrete insinuations of time, space, and their enmeshments, as suggested by the two most significant figures, Ajneya (S. H. Vatsyayan) and G. M. Muktibodh, of Hindi modernism. On the one hand, Ajneya stressed a "formalist universalism," concentrating on "poetic structure, rather than on social or historical problems," while emphasizing the immense isolation of the modern individual, a subject stalking an alienated temporality and a spatial indeterminacy.[15] On the other, Muktibodh's "intensely self-conscious, anguished poetic voice abandoned the high modernism of Europe and America for experimental, radical, sometimes surreal sequences that draw equally upon the Bhakti tradition of late medieval [early modern] India as upon other literatures of Asia, Africa, and Latin America," construing new configurations of the mythic and the epic, space and time.[16]

Finally, mid-twentieth-century cinema in the subcontinent straddled realist representations and innovative aesthetics that reached far beyond a mere "national allegory" and adroitly drew together the aural and the visual, sensibility and technique, dance and drama, the "old" and "new," and the temporal and spatial. Thereby, it cast alienated individuals at the center yet set them adrift, showed the finger to promises of progress, sieved the contradictions of imagined worlds, held up a mirror to the lies of nation, and looked into the eye of a living ghost, India's Partition and its intimate violence. Now the auteur and the actor, new *flâneurs* both, could grimly move through the restless scuttle of quotidian creatures – scattered spatially, temporally, and everywhere one looked – facing up to the immanent possibility of an unclimatic end. Here was cinema – of Ritwik Ghatak and Satyajit Ray, but also of Guru Dutt and Khwaja Ahmad Abbas, among many others – that recast mythology, rethought history, and reworked the contemporary in probing and unraveling the innocence and idea, the space and time, of India.[17]

Emergences

These mid-twentieth-century modernists had arguably anticipated the unraveling of the South Asian nations from the 1960s onwards. If in Pakistan such undoing entailed the central place of authoritarian governments and military regimes, in India the idealism of the past was replaced by a manipulative politics, cynical invocations of socialism, and attacks on democratic norms all in the name of the nation, unity, and progress. Unsurprisingly, the birth of Bangladesh, aided by India, was among the last gasps of Bandung-era third-world nationalism. What came to the fore were not only the governmental registers of a politics of violence, exemplified by the state of emergency (1975–77) in India, the execution of Z. A. Bhutto in Pakistan, and escalating ethnic conflicts in Sri Lanka, but increasingly newer openings/orientations toward corporate capital, the political-religious Right, and neoliberal common sense, all claiming and conjuring time and space in their own image. These developments have been accompanied by lower-caste assertions, subaltern struggles, armed Left militancy, popular democratic endeavors, and feminist (as well as alternative sexuality) interventions, signifying often rather different spatial and temporal assumption and imagination.

In front of these developments, salient tendencies have redefined issues of art and literature, aesthetics and politics, and time and space in modernisms in South Asia. Here are two examples. The first concerns the narrative moment (and "movement") from the 1970s onwards, which has posed critical questions of what constitutes properly modernist artistic practice in an independent India, a nation that had betrayed its dispossessed, both people and art, the one bound to the other. At stake are revisitations – by women and men artists – of epic and legend, myth and history, the past and the present in acutely temporally figurative and explicitly spatially narrative ways within the visual arts, including cinema. Needless to say, these procedures and representations have foregrounded critical questions of the majority and the minority, the body and pain, gender and sexuality, authority and alterity, and the entitled and the popular – in their diverse socio-spatial and hetero-temporal dimensions.[18] The second key development, which began in the 1950s but acquired formidable force a decade later, involves Dalit ("broken") literature and art, expressing the anguish, anger, and aesthetic of India's ex-untouchables. Here is a break not just from prior artistic traditions, but a rupture from the singular civilizational claims of the dominant majority and the overweening nation, spelling an exclusive yet hierarchical spatial and temporal core. On offer are endeavors that have brought into being a new language and idioms, a novel iconography and imaginaries, other intimations of the time-space of the everyday, including distinct emphases on issues of gender foregrounding also a Dalit feminist practice.[19]

Coda

At the close, I turn to a single modern subject whose work and life not only articulate the two tendencies outlined above, but clarify some of the wider claims of *Subjects of Modernity*. This subject is Savindra "Savi" Sawarkar, an expressionist and Dalit artist of extraordinary imagination and prowess, whose representations track the interplay between meaning and power within hierarchical regimes of religion, caste, gender, and politics, while drawing upon distinctive artistic and ideological influences (see Figures 1–6 in the middle of this book). Elsewhere, I have explored three overlapping themes in Savi's work: first, the creation of a set of unsettling aesthetic/political agendas in the realm of a critical and contemporary Dalit art; second, the elaboration of such agendas through an entwinement of Ambedkarite ideology, existential attributes of being Dalit, and diverse representational resources, including varieties of expressionism ranging across its early twentieth-century developments in Germany through to its 1960s manifestations in North America and Europe; and finally, the challenges posed to established procedures of art criticism by these distinct modalities of Dalit and expressionist artistic production.[20] Here, I turn to what such considerations can suggest about Savi as a modernist creator, a modern subject, and a subject of modernity, but first a brief introduction to our protagonist is in order.

Savindra Sawarkar was born in 1961 into a family of the Mahar caste in Nagpur, central India. As part of Dr. B. R. Ambedkar's wider initiative, in 1956 his family converted to Buddhism. Savi first studied art at the University of Nagpur. Here, the constraining premises of an institution that continued to cherish the ideals of Victorian art and colonial aesthetics meant that it was in the ceaseless sketching of peoples and places, subjects and objects that Savi honed his own artistic abilities. These capacities were later developed through his other formal and informal studies and apprenticeships in a range of institutions and places. Indeed, Savi's paintings, graphics, and drawings combine influences that range across expressionist art, the poet Rabindranath Tagore's critical drawings of the 1920s and 1930s, the "narrative movement" of the 1970s and the 1980s, the delicate brushwork of Zen masters, and a wider disposition toward Buddhist aesthetics. Yet, far from being derivative, Savi's art conjoins acute apprehensions of an unjust murky world with a vibrant use of color, conjuring figures and forms that are at once intense and haunting, forceful and haunted. The result is a radical expressionist imagination and a critical Dalit iconography.

Central to this iconography and imagination are specific representations of the past and the present, particular productions of time and space. The sources are overlapping and distinct: moving recitals of untouchable pasts by Savi's unlettered paternal grandmother, whom he describes as his "first teacher"; liturgical lists drawn up within the political movement led by Dr. B. R. Ambedkar concerning the disempowerment faced by untouchables; and Savi's own experiences as an artist, an activist, and a *Dalit* in distinct locales, from statist spaces in New

Delhi to remote places of gender and caste oppression in village India. Unlike those tacit projections of the modernist artist fabricating forms through the creative force of a pure imagination, Savi seizes upon these discursive and experiential resources, filtering them through while construing an expressionist art.

Here, the past is not separated from the present to temporally and spatially split apart prior caste hierarchies from contemporary intimations of equality. Rather, in Savi's art, the untouchable figures and upper-caste forms, each inescapably gendered, are at once densely palpable and formidably spectral, stalking the past and the present, construing times and spaces of longing and loss, which beget each other. Now the silence and sigh of the androgynous untouchables bursts forth into a scream, "We were there, then, we are here, now," and now the gaze and grasp of the sexually predatory Brahman is unraveled through the terms of its own haunting.

Far exceeding a mere documentation of history through images of oppression, Savi's art "articulate[s] the past [and the present] … [by seizing] hold of a memory as it flashes up at a moment of danger."[21] Here the unsettling realism of subterranean imaginings restlessly labors with the haunting terms of a forceful expressionism: the sun is eclipsed, the light is dark, the world is in shadows, giving the lie to the phantasms of progress that haunt modern regimes of an exclusive temporality and its spatial segregations. Yet, the critical querying is accompanied by careful affirmation. For in this mode of artistic production, the past and the present bring each other to crisis, compelling other intimations, remappings as it were, of space and time.

There is more to the picture. Behind these portrayals are particular modes of reasoning and a distinct order of subjectivity, which spell a rather specific modern subject. Careful, critical conversations and meandering, joyful exchanges with Savi – as well as revising and rewriting his MA dissertation (for submission to Academia San Carlos in Mexico City) – have clarified that, in both speech and writing, Savi reasons by analogy. This analogical reasoning is imbued with a surplus of faith, a productive literalism, regarding Dr. Ambedkar's life and words, read and heard, and neo-Buddhist verities and veracities, rehearsed and performed. Militating against logics and analyses of a modern provenance, Savi's embodied, expressionist reason sets the analogical and the literal to seize upon and sift through textual traces, oral liturgies, experiential entanglements, and graphic imaginaries. On offer is a visual hermeneutics that renders details with a twist. Here, haunting images resonate with oracular expression, prior certainties echo limiting doubts, and the force of the past sounds out the fleeting, the fragmentary, and the transitory.

All this is shored up by a vulnerable subjectivity. As a modern subject, Savi's presentation of the avant-garde artistic self, consumed by cutting-edge creativity and unconstrained by conventional norms, has to yet bear the immense burden of injuries of caste, hidden and obvious, which haunt his verve and vocation. We are in the face of a self-fashioning subject whose despair and vulnerability, loss and longing – alongside his reasoning and literalism, expression and imagination – register that there are different ways of being modern. Ahead of us is a subject of modernity whose existence calls attention to the inflection of alterity by authority; whose creativity points to the shaping of power by difference; and whose work attests to the presence of hetero-temporal terrains and socio-spatial subjects as probing and producing each other.[22]

Notes

1 This is also true of scholarship on modernism in South Asia, which appears intimately tied to modernist practices on the subcontinent. See, for example, how modernization and modernity are uneasily folded into understandings of modernism in Kapur, *When was Modernism*; and Supriya Chaudhuri, "Modernisms in India," in Peter Brooker et al. (eds.), *Oxford Handbook of Modernisms* (Oxford: Oxford University Press, 2010), pp. 942–60. See also Partha Mitter, *The Triumph of Modernism: India's Artists and the Avant-Garde, 1922–1947* (New Delhi: Oxford University Press, 2007). Needless to say, these works have all been crucial to my understandings of modernisms in India.
2 Adorno, *Minima Moralia*, p. 208.

3 Sanjukta Sunderason, "Making art modern: re-visiting artistic modernism in South Asia," in Dube (ed.), *Modern Makeovers*, p. 246.
4 Chaudhuri, "Modernisms in India," pp. 943–4.
5 See Tapati Guha-Thakurta, *The Making of a New "Indian" Art: Artists, Aesthetics and Nationalism in Bengal, c.1850–1920* (Cambridge: Cambridge University Press, 1992).
6 Chaudhuri, "Modernism in India," pp. 944–5; Mitter, *Triumph of Modernism*, pp. 18–27.
7 See Ishita Banerjee-Dube, *A History of Modern India* (New York: Cambridge University Press, 2015).
8 The two paragraphs that follow draw upon Mitter, *Triumph of Modernism*; and Chaudhuri, "Indian modernisms."
9 See also Kapur, *When was Modernism*, pp. 3–13.
10 Sunderason, "Modernism in India," p. 252.
11 Quoted in Banerjee-Dube, *Modern India*, p. 437. The place and presence of Nehru's writings, politics, and persona in expressions of modernism on the subcontinent require greater understanding.
12 Cited in Sunderason, "Making art modern," p. 254.
13 There could be frontal artistic engagements with the Partition, too, as in the writings of Sadaat Hasan Manto (in Urdu) and of Khushwant Singh (in English).
14 Edwin Mullins, *Souza* (London: Anthony Blond, 1962), p. 40.
15 Chaudhuri, "Modernism in India," p. 956.
16 Nor was Muktibodh an exception. In the sphere of Marathi literary modernisms, for instance, the simultaneous articulations of indigenous idioms and other, often Western, traditions are evident. The self-reflexive poetics of B. S. Mardhekar were acutely influenced at once by Western modernism and by the early modern saint poets of the Maharashtra region. Similarly Dilip Chitre, who wrote in both Marathi and English, began "to create a remarkable new modernist oeuvre, densely allusive, rooted in the experiences of urban loneliness, the body, and sexuality," yet simultaneously translated the early modern devotional poets Tukaram and Jnanadeva into English (as he did Baudelaire, Rimbaud, and Mallarmé into Marathi), his work profoundly shaped by such conjoint endeavors. *Ibid.*, pp. 956, 957.
17 The mainly monumental designs of architectural modernism in India – in the wake of Lutyen's New Delhi and the presence of Le

Corbusier's city of Chandigarh, the latter built with the blessings of Nehru – tell a rather different story, for which there is little space here.

18 See Kapur, *When was Modernism*; and Sheikh, *Contemporary Art in Baroda*.

19 See, for example, Toral Jathin Garawala, *Untouchable Fictions: Literary Realism and the Crisis of Caste* (New York: Fordham University Press, 2013); and Gary Michael Tartakov (ed.), *Dalit Art and Visual Imagery* (New Delhi: Indian Institute for Dalit Studies and Oxford University Press, 2012).

20 Saurabh Dube, "A Dalit iconography of an expressionist imagination," in Tartakov, *Dalit Art and Visual Imagery*, pp. 251–67; and Saurabh Dube, "Unsettling art: caste, gender, and Dalit expression," openDemocracy, August 1, 2013, www.opendemocracy.net/saurabh-dube/unsettling-art-caste-gender-and-dalit-expression (accessed on 11 July 2016).

21 Walter Benjamin, "Theses on the philosophy of history," in Walter Benjamin, *Illuminations: Essays and Reflections*, trans. Harry Zohn, ed. Hannah Arendt (New York: Schocken Books, 1969), p. 253.

22 To be sure, the force of Savi's art rests on the opposition between religious (and statist) power and the untouchable (and gendered) subaltern. At the same time, precisely this opposition makes possible decentered portrayals of power and difference. For, rather than occupying a singular locus or constituting an exclusive terrain, power appears here as decisively plural, forged within authoritative grids – of caste and gender, nation and state, and modernity and history – that interlock and yet remain out of joint, the one extending and exceeding the other. This is to say that Savi's art traces the expressions and modalities of power as coordinated portraits yet fractured profiles, effects and affects bearing the burden of the spectral subaltern and palpable difference. It follows that these representations do not announce the romance of resistant identities and the seductions of the autonomous subject, split apart from power. Rather, figures of critical difference and subaltern community appear here as inhabiting the interstices of power, intimating its terms and insinuating its limits – already inherent, always emergent – as the spanner of discrepancy inside the work of domination.

Bibliography

Abdel-Malek, Anouar, "Orientalism in crisis," *Diogenes*, 44 (1963): 104–12.

Abrams, Philip, *Historical Sociology* (Shepton Mallet: Open Books, 1982).

Adorno, Theodor, *Minima Moralia: Reflections from Damaged Life*, trans. E. F. N. Jephcott (London: Verso, 2005).

Agnani, Sunil, *Hating Empire Properly: The Two Indies and the Limits of Enlightenment Anticolonialism* (New York: Fordham University Press, 2013).

Alonso, Ana María, "The politics of space, time, and substance: state formation, nationalism, and ethnicity," *Annual Review of Anthropology*, 23 (1994): 379–400.

——, "Territorializing the nation and 'integrating the Indian': 'Mestizage' in Mexican official discourses and public culture," in Thomas Blom Hansen and Finn Stepputat (eds.), *Sovereign Bodies: Citizens, Migrants, and States in the Postcolonial World* (Princeton, NJ: Princeton University Press, 2005), pp. 39–60.

Amin, Shahid, *Event, Metaphor, Memory: Chauri Chaura 1922–1992* (Berkeley: University of California Press, 1995).

Amin, Shahid, and Dipesh Chakrabarty (eds.), *Subaltern Studies IX: Writings on South Asian History and Society* (Delhi: Oxford University Press, 1996).

Anderson, Benedict, *Imagined Communities: Reflections on the Origin and Spread of Nationalism* (London: Verso, 1983).

Appadurai, Arjun, *Worship and Conflict under Colonial Rule: A South Indian Case* (Cambridge: Cambridge University Press, 1982).

——, *Modernity at Large: Cultural Dimensions of Globalization* (Minneapolis: University of Minnesota Press, 1996).

Appadurai, Arjun, and Carol Breckenridge, "The South Indian temple: authority, honour, and redistribution," *Contributions to Indian Sociology* [n.s.], 10 (1976): 187–211.

Appleby, Joyce, Lynn Hunt, and Margaret Jacob, *Telling the Truth About History* (New York: W. W. Norton, 1995).

Apter, David E., *The Politics of Modernization* (Chicago, IL: University of Chicago Press, 1965).

Arnold, David, *Colonizing the Body: State Medicine and Epidemic Disease in Nineteenth-Century India* (Berkeley: University of California Press, 1993).

Arnold, David, and David Hardiman (eds.), *Subaltern Studies VIII: Essays in Honor of Ranajit Guha* (Delhi: Oxford University Press, 1994).

Asad, Talal, "Anthropological conceptions of religion: reflections on Geertz," *Man* [n.s.], 18 (1983): 237–59.
——, *Genealogies of Religion: Discipline and Reasons of Power in Christianity and Islam* (Baltimore, MD: John Hopkins University Press, 1993).
Asad, Talal (ed.), *Anthropology and the Colonial Encounter* (London: Ithaca Press, 1973).
Axel, Brian K., *The Nation's Tortured Body: Violence, Representation, and the Formation of a Sikh "Diaspora"* (Durham, NC: Duke University Press, 2001).
——, "Introduction: historical anthropology and its vicissitudes," in Brian K. Axel (ed.), *From the Margins: Historical Anthropology and its Futures* (Durham, NC: Duke University Press, 2002), pp. 1–44.
Bailey, F. G., *Caste and the Economic Frontier: A Village in Highland Orissa* (Manchester: Manchester University Press, 1957).
——, *Stratagems and Spoils: A Social Anthropology of Politics* (Oxford: Basil Blackwell, 1969).
Banerjee-Dube, Ishita, "Taming traditions: legalities and histories in eastern India," in Gautam Bhadra, Gyan Prakash, and Susie Tharu (eds.), *Subaltern Studies X: Writings on South Asian History and Society* (New Delhi: Oxford University Press, 1999), pp. 98–125.
——, *Religion, Law and Power: Tales of Time in Eastern India, 1860–2000* (London: Anthem Press, 2007).
——, *A History of Modern India* (New York: Cambridge University Press, 2015).
Barth, Fredrik, *Political Leadership among Swat Pathans* (London: Athlone Press, 1959).
Bartra, Roger, *El salvaje en el espejo* (Mexico: UNAM, 1992).
Baucom, Ian, *Specters of the Atlantic: Finance Capital, Slavery, and the Philosophy of History* (Durham, NC: Duke University Press, 2005).
Bauman, Zygmunt, *Intimations of Postmodernity* (London: Routledge, 1992).
Baxi, Upendra, "'The state's emissary': the place of law in subaltern studies," in Partha Chatterjee and Gyanendra Pandey (eds.), *Subaltern Studies VII: Writings on South Asian History and Society* (Delhi: Oxford University Press, 1993), pp. 257–64.
Bayly, C. A., *Indian Society and the Making of the British Empire* (Cambridge: Cambridge University Press, 1987).
Bayly, Susan, *Saints, Goddesses and Kings: Muslims and Christians in South Indian Society 1700–1900* (Cambridge: Cambridge University Press, 1989).
Bear, Laura, *Lines of the Nation: Indian Railway Workers, Bureaucracy, and the Intimate Historical Self* (New York: Columbia University Press, 2007).

Becker, Carl L., *The Heavenly City of the Eighteenth-Century Philosophers* (New Haven, CT: Yale University Press, 1932).
Bénéï, Véronique, *Schooling Passions: Nation, History, and Language in Contemporary Western India* (Stanford, CA: Stanford University Press, 2008).
Benjamin, Walter, "Theses on the philosophy of history," in Walter Benjamin, *Illuminations: Essays and Reflections*, trans. Harry Zohn, ed. Hannah Arendt (New York: Schocken Books, 1969), pp. 155–65.
Bennett, Tony, *The Birth of the Museum: History, Theory, Politics* (London: Routledge, 1995).
——, *Pasts Beyond Memory: Evolution, Museums, Colonialism* (London: Routledge, 2004).
Berlin, Isaiah, *Against the Current: Essays in the History of Ideas* (Princeton, NJ: Princeton University Press, 2001).
Berman, Russel A., *Enlightenment or Empire: Colonial Discourse in German Culture* (Lincoln: University of Nebraska Press, 2004).
Beverley, John, *Subalternity and Representation: Arguments in Cultural Theory* (Durham, NC: Duke University Press, 1999).
Bhabha, Homi K., *Location of Culture* (London and New York: Routledge, 1994).
Bhabha, Homi K. (ed.), *Nation and Narration* (London: Routledge, 1990).
Bhadra, Gautam, Gyan Prakash, and Susie Tharu (eds.), *Subaltern Studies X: Writings on South Asian History and Society* (New Delhi: Oxford University Press, 1999).
Bhambra, Gurminder, *Rethinking Modernity: Postcolonialism and the Sociological Imagination* (New York: Palgrave Macmillan, 2007).
——, *Connected Sociologies* (London: Bloomsbury, 2014).
Birla, Ritu, *Stages of Capital: Law, Culture, and Market Governance in Late Colonial India* (Durham, NC: Duke University Press, 2009).
Bloch, Marc, *The Historian's Craft*, trans. Peter Putnam (Manchester: Manchester University Press, 1954).
Boas, Franz, *Anthropology and Modern Life* (New York: W. W. Norton, 1928).
——, "The history of anthropology," in George Stocking, Jr. (ed.), *The Shaping of American Anthropology, 1883–1911: A Franz Boas Reader* (New York: Basic Books, 1974), pp. 23–35.
Bourdieu, Pierre, *Outline of a Theory of Practice*, trans. Richard Nice (Cambridge: Cambridge University Press, 1977).
——, *Algeria 1960*, trans. Richard Nice (Cambridge: Cambridge University Press, 1979).

Braudel, Fernand, *The Mediterranean and the Mediterranean World in the Age of Philip II: Vols. I and II*, trans. S. Reynolds (London: Fontana/Collins, 1973).

Breckenridge, Carol, and Peter van der Veer (eds.), *Orientalism and the Postcolonial Predicament: Perspectives on South Asia* (Philadelphia: University of Pennsylvania Press, 1993).

Burghart, Richard, *The Conditions of Listening: Essays on Religion, History, and Politics in India*, ed. C. J. Fuller and Jonathan Spencer (Delhi: Oxford University Press, 1996).

Burton, Antoinette M., *At the Heart of the Empire: Indians and the Colonial Encounter in Late-Victorian Britain* (Berkeley: University of California Press, 1998).

Butalia, Urvashi, *The Other Side of Silence: Voices from the Partition of India* (New Delhi: Viking Penguin, 1998).

Cabrujas, José Ignacio, "El estado del disímulo," in José Ignacio Cabrujas, *Heterodoxia y estado: 5 respuestas* (Caracas: COPRA, 1987), pp. 7–35.

de Certeau, Michel, *The Practice of Everyday Life*, trans. Steven F. Rendall (Berkeley: University of California Press, 1984).

Chakrabarty, Dipesh, *Rethinking Working-Class History: Bengal 1890–1940* (Princeton, NJ: Princeton University Press, 1989).

——, "Postcoloniality and the artifice of history: who speaks for 'Indian' pasts?," *Representations*, 37 (1992): 1–26.

——, "The difference-deferral of a colonial modernity: public debates on domesticity in British Bengal," in David Arnold and David Hardiman (eds.), *Subaltern Studies VIII: Essays in Honour of Ranajit Guha* (Delhi: Oxford University Press, 1994), pp. 50–88.

——, *Provincializing Europe: Postcolonial Thought and Historical Difference* (Princeton, NJ: Princeton University Press, 2000).

——, *Habitations of Modernity: Essays in the Wake of Subaltern Studies* (Chicago, IL: University of Chicago Press, 2002).

——, *The Calling of History: Sir Jadunath Sarkar and His Empire of Truth* (Chicago, IL, and London: University of Chicago Press, 2015).

Chakrabarty, Dipesh, and Saurabh Dube, "Presence of Europe: an interview with Dipesh Chakrabarty," in Saurabh Dube (ed.), *Postcolonial Passages: Contemporary History-Writing on India* (New Delhi: Oxford University Press, 2004), pp. 254–62.

Chartier, Roger, *Cultural History: Between Practices and Representations*, trans. Lydia G. Cochrane (Ithaca, NY: Cornell University Press, 1993).

Chatterjee, Indrani, *Gender, Slavery and Law in Colonial India* (New Delhi: Oxford University Press, 1999).

Chatterjee, Partha, *The Nation and its Fragments: Colonial and Postcolonial Histories* (Princeton, NJ: Princeton University Press, 1993).
——, "Introduction: history and the present," in Partha Chatterjee and Anjan Ghosh (eds.), *History and the Present* (New Delhi: Permanent Black, 2002), pp. 1–23.
——, *The Politics of the Governed: Reflections on Popular Politics in Most of the World* (New York: Columbia University Press, 2004).
Chatterjee, Partha, and Gyanendra Pandey (eds.), *Subaltern Studies VII: Writings on South Asian History and Society* (Delhi: Oxford University Press, 1993).
Chatterjee, Piya, *A Time for Tea: Women, Labor, and Post/Colonial Politics on an Indian Plantation* (Durham, NC: Duke University Press, 2001).
Chaturvedi, Vinayak, *Peasant Pasts: History and Memory in Western India* (Berkeley: University of California Press, 2007).
Chaudhuri, Supriya, "Modernisms in India," in Peter Brooker et al. (eds.), *Oxford Handbook of Modernisms* (Oxford: Oxford University Press, 2010), pp. 942–60.
Childs, Peter, *Modernism: The New Cultural Idiom* (New York: Routledge, 2000).
Clifford, James, "On *Orientalism*," in James Clifford, *The Predicament of Culture: Twentieth-Century Ethnography, Literature, and Art* (Cambridge, MA: Harvard University Press, 1988), pp. 255–76.
Cohen, David William, *The Combing of History* (Chicago, IL: University of Chicago Press, 1994).
Cohen, David William, and E. S. Atieno Odhiambo, *Siaya: Historical Anthropology* (Cleveland: Ohio University Press, 1989).
Cohn, Bernard, *India: The Social Anthropology of a Civilization* (Englewood Cliffs, NJ: Prentice-Hall, 1971).
——, "History and anthropology: the state of play," *Comparative Studies in Society and History*, 22 (1980): 198–221.
——, "Anthropology and history in the 1980s: towards a rapprochement," *The Journal of Interdisciplinary History*, 12 (1981): 227–52.
——, "The command of language and the language of command," in Ranajit Guha (ed.), *Subaltern Studies IV: Writings on South Asian History and Society* (Delhi: Oxford University Press, 1985), pp. 276–329.
——, *An Anthropologist among the Historians and Other Essays* (Delhi: Oxford University Press, 1987).
——, *Colonialism and its Forms of Knowledge: The British in India* (Princeton, NJ: Princeton University Press, 1996).

Collingham, E. M., *Imperial Bodies: The Physical Experience of the Raj, c.1800–1947* (Cambridge: Polity Press, 2001).
Comaroff, Jean, *Body of Power, Spirit of Resistance: The Culture and History of a South African People* (Chicago, IL: University of Chicago Press, 1985).
Comaroff, Jean, and John Comaroff, *Of Revelation and Revolution: Christianity, Colonialism, and Consciousness in South Africa*, vol. 1 (Chicago, IL: Chicago University Press, 1991).
Comaroff, Jean, and John Comaroff (eds.), *Millennial Capitalism and the Culture of Neoliberalism* (Durham, NC: Duke University Press, 2001).
Comaroff, John, "Images of empire, contests of conscience: models of colonial domination in South Africa," *American Ethnologist*, 16 (1989): 661–85.
Comaroff, John, and Jean Comaroff, *Ethnography and the Historical Imagination* (Boulder, CO: Westview, 1992).
——, *Of Revelation and Revolution: The Dialectics of Modernity on the South African Frontier*, vol. 2 (Chicago, IL: Chicago University Press, 1997).
——, *Ethnicity, Inc.* (Chicago, IL: University of Chicago Press, 2009).
Comaroff, John, and Jean Comaroff (eds.), *Modernity and its Malcontents: Ritual and Power in Postcolonial Africa* (Chicago, IL: University of Chicago Press, 1993).
Comaroff, John, and Simon Roberts, *Rules and Processes: The Cultural Logic of Dispute in an African Context* (Chicago, IL: University of Chicago Press, 1981).
Conlon, Frank F., *A Caste in the Changing World: The Chitrapur Saraswat Brahmans, 1700–1935* (Berkeley: University of California Press, 1977).
Connolly, William E., *Identity/difference: Democratic Negotiations of Political Paradox* (Ithaca, NY: Cornell University Press, 1991).
——, *The Ethos of Pluralization* (Minneapolis: University of Minnesota Press, 1995).
Coombes, Annie E., *Reinventing Africa: Museums, Material Culture and Popular Imagination in Late Victorian and Edwardian England* (New Haven, CT: Yale University Press, 1994).
Cooper, Frederick, "Conflict and connection: rethinking colonial African history," *American Historical Review*, 99 (1994): 1519–26.
——, *Decolonization and African Society: The Labour Question in French and British Africa* (Cambridge: Cambridge University Press, 1996).
Cooper, Frederick, and Ann Laura Stoler (eds.), *Tensions of Empire: Colonial Cultures in a Bourgeois World* (Berkeley: University of California Press, 1997).

Coronil, Fernando, "Beyond Occidentalism: toward nonimperial geohistorical categories," *Cultural Anthropology*, 11 (1996): 51–87.

——, *The Magical State: Nature, Money, and Modernity in Venezuela* (Chicago, IL: University of Chicago Press, 1997).

Crapanzano, Vincent, *Serving the Word: Literalism in America from the Pulpit to the Bench* (New York: New Press, 2000).

Darnton, Robert, *The Great Cat Massacre and Other Episodes in French Cultural History* (New York: Vintage, 1985).

Das, Veena, "Subaltern as perspective," in Ranajit Guha (ed.), *Subaltern Studies VI: Writings on South Asian History and Society* (Delhi: Oxford University Press, 1989), pp. 310–24.

——, *Critical Events: An Anthropological Perspective on Contemporary India* (Delhi: Oxford University Press, 1995).

Davin, Anna, "Imperialism and motherhood," *History Workshop*, 5 (1978): 9–65.

Davis, Natalie Z., *Society and Culture in Early Modern France: Eight Essays by Natalie Zemon Davis* (Stanford, CA: Stanford University Press, 1977).

Deshpande, Prachi, *Creative Pasts: Historical Memory and Identity in Western India, 1700–1960* (New York: Columbia University Press, 2007).

Dhanagre, D. N., *Peasant Movements in India, 1920–1950* (Delhi: Oxford University Press, 1983).

Dirks, Nicholas, *The Hollow Crown: Ethnohistory of an Indian Kingdom* (Cambridge: Cambridge University Press, 1987).

——, "Foreword," in Bernard Cohn, *Colonialism and its Forms of Knowledge: The British in India* (Princeton, NJ: Princeton University Press, 1996), pp. ix–xvii.

——, *Castes of Mind: Colonialism and the Making of Modern India* (Princeton, NJ: Princeton University Press, 2001).

Donham, Donald, *Marxist Modern: An Ethnographic History of the Ethiopian Revolution* (Berkeley: University of California Press, 1999).

Dube, Saurabh, "Social history of Satnamis of Chhattisgarh," unpublished MPhil dissertation (University of Delhi, 1988).

——, "Religion, identity and authority among the Satnamis in colonial central India," unpublished PhD dissertation (University of Cambridge, 1992).

——, "Myths, symbols, and community: Satnampanth of Chhattisgarh," in Partha Chatterjee and Gyanendra Pandey (eds.), *Subaltern Studies VII: Writings on South Asian History and Society* (Delhi: Oxford University Press, 1992), pp. 121–56.

——, "Telling tales and trying truths: transgressions, entitlements and legalities in village disputes, late colonial central India," *Studies in History*, 13 (1996): 171–201.

——, *Untouchable Pasts: Religion, Identity, and Power among a Central Indian Community, 1780–1950* (Albany, NY: State University of New York Press, 1998).

——, *Sujetos subalternos: capítulos de una historia antropológica*, trans. Germán Franco and Ari Bartra (Mexico City: El Colegio de México, 2001).

——, "Historical identity and cultural difference: a critical note," *Economic and Political Weekly*, 36 (2002): 77–81.

——, *Genealogías del presente: conversión, colonialismo, cultura*, trans. Ari Bartra and Gilberto Conde (Mexico City: El Colegio de México, 2003).

——, *Stitches on Time: Colonial Textures and Postcolonial Tangles* (Durham, NC, and London: Duke University Press, 2004).

——, "Terms that bind: colony, nation, modernity," in Saurabh Dube (ed.), *Postcolonial Passages: Contemporary History-Writing on India* (New Delhi: Oxford University Press, 2004), pp. 1–37.

——, "Anthropology, history, historical anthropology: an introduction," in Saurabh Dube (ed.), *Historical Anthropology: Oxford in India Readings in Sociology and Social Anthropology* (New Delhi: Oxford University Press, 2007), pp. 1–73.

——, *Historias esparcidas*, trans. Gabriela Uranga Grijalva (Mexico City: El Colegio de México, 2007).

——, "Ties that bind: tribe, village, nation, and S. C. Dube," in Patricia Uberoi, Satish Deshpande, and Nandini Sundar (eds.), *Anthropology in the East: Founders of Indian Sociology and Anthropology* (New Delhi: Permanent Black, 2007), pp. 444–95.

——, *After Conversion: Cultural Histories of Modern India* (New Delhi: Yoda Press, 2010).

——, *Modernidad e historia*, trans. Adrián Muñoz (Mexico City: El Colegio de México, 2011).

——, "A Dalit iconography of an expressionist imagination," in Gary Michael Tartakov (ed.), *Dalit Art and Visual Imagery* (New Delhi: Indian Institute for Dalit Studies and Oxford University Press, 2012), pp. 251–67.

——, "Unsettling art: caste, gender, and Dalit expression," openDemocracy, August 1, 2013, www.opendemocracy.net/saurabh-dube/unsettling-art-caste-gender-and-dalit-expression (accessed on 11 July 2016).

——, *Formaciones de lo contemporáneo*, trans. Lucía Cirianni (Mexico City: El Colegio de de México, forthcoming 2017).

——, *Formations of an evangelical modernity: Christianity, conversion, colonialism 1860–2005* (manuscript of book in progress).

——, *Native witness: colonial writings of a vernacular Christianity* (manuscript of book in progress).

Dube, Saurabh (ed), *Pasados poscoloniales: colección de ensayos sobre la nueva historia y etnografía de la India*, trans. Germán Franco (Mexico City: El Colegio de México, 1999).

——, *Enduring Enchantments*, special issue of *South Atlantic Quarterly*, 101 (2002): 729–1044.

——, *Enchantments of Modernity: Empire, Nation, Globalization* (London: Routledge, 2009).

——, *Modern Makeovers: Handbook of Modernity in South Asia* (New York: Oxford University Press, 2011).

Dube, Saurabh, and Ishita Banerjee-Dube (eds.), *Unbecoming Modern: Colonialism, Modernity, Colonial Modernities* (New Delhi: Social Science Press, 2006).

Dube, Saurabh, Ishita Banerjee-Dube, and Edgardo Lander (eds.), *Critical Conjunctions: Foundations of Colony and Formations of Modernity*, special issue of *Nepantla: Views from South*, 3 (2002): 193–431.

Dube, Saurabh, Ishita Banerjee-Dube, and Walter Mignolo (eds.), *Modernidades coloniales: otros pasados, historias presentes* (Mexico City: El Colegio de México, 2004).

Dube, S. C., *The Kamar* (Lucknow: Universal, 1951).

During, Simon, *Modern Enchantments: The Cultural Power of Secular Magic* (Cambridge, MA: Harvard University Press, 2004).

Dussel, Enrique, "Europe, eurocentrism and modernity (introduction to the Frankfurt lectures)," *Boundary 2*, 20 (1993): 65–76.

——, *The Invention of the Americas: Eclipse of "the Other" and the Myth of Modernity* (New York: Continuum, 1995).

——, *Etica de la liberación en la edad de la globalización y de la exclusión* (Madrid: Trotta, 1998).

——, "Transmodernity," in Saurabh Dube, Ishita Banerjee-Dube, and Edgardo Lander (eds.), *Critical Conjunctions: Foundations of Colony and Formations of Modernity*, special issue of *Nepantla: Views from South*, 3 (2002): 221–44.

Echeverría, Bolivar, *La modernidad de lo barroco* (Mexico: UAM, 1998).

Echevarría, Roberto González, *Mito y archivo: una teoría de la narrativa latinoamericana* (Mexico: Fondo de Cultura Económica, 1998).

Eisenstadt, S. N., "Functionalist analysis in anthropology and sociology: an interpretive essay," *Annual Review of Anthropology*, 19 (1990): 243–60.

Errington, Shelly, *The Death of Authentic Primitive Art and Other Tales of Progress* (Berkeley: University of California Press, 1998).
Escobar, Arturo, *Encountering Development: The Making and Unmaking of the Third World* (Princeton, NJ: Princeton University Press, 1993).
Evans-Pritchard, E. E., "Nuer time reckoning," *Africa*, 12 (1939): 189–216.
——, *The Nuer: A Description of the Modes of Livelihood and Political Institutions of a Nilotic People* (Oxford: Clarendon Press, 1940).
——, *Anthropology and History* (Manchester: Manchester University Press, 1961).
——, "Social anthropology," in E. E. Evans-Pritchard, *Social Anthropology and Other Essays* (New York: The Free Press of Glencoe, 1962), pp. 1–134.
——, "Social anthropology: past and present," in E. E. Evans-Pritchard, *Social Anthropology and Other Essays* (New York: The Free Press of Glencoe, 1962), pp. 139–57.
——, *Theories of Primitive Religion* (Oxford: Clarendon Press, 1965).
Fabian, Johannes, *Time and the Other: How Anthropology Makes its Object* (New York: Columbia University Press, 1983).
——, *Language and Colonial Power: The Appropriation of Swahili in the Former Belgian Congo* (Cambridge: Cambridge University Press, 1986).
——, *Out of Our Minds: Reason and Madness in the Exploration of Central Africa* (Berkeley: University of California Press, 2000).
Faubion, James D., "History in anthropology," *Annual Review of Anthropology*, 22 (1993): 35–54.
Febvre, Lucien, *New Kind of History: From the Writings of Febvre*, trans. K Folca (London: Routledge, 1973).
Ferguson, James, *Expectations of Modernity: Myths and Meanings of Urban Life on the Zambian Copperbelt* (Berkeley: University of California Press, 1999).
Fischer, Sibylle, *Modernity Disavowed: Haiti and the Cultures of Slavery in the Age of Revolution* (Durham, NC: Duke University Press, 2004).
Florida, Nancy, *Writing the Past, Inscribing the Future: History as Prophecy in Colonial Java* (Durham, NC: Duke University Press, 1995).
Fox, Richard G., *Kin, Clan, Raja and Rule* (Berkeley: University of California Press, 1971).
——, *Lions of the Punjab: Culture in the Making* (Berkeley: University of California Press, 1985).
Fox, Richard G. (ed.), *Realm and Region in Traditional India* (Durham, NC: Duke University Press, 1977).
Franco, Jean, *Plotting Women* (New York: Columbia University Press, 1989).

——, *Critical Passions: Selected Essays* (Durham, NC: Duke University Press, 1999).
——, *The Decline and Fall of the Lettered City: Latin America in the Cold War* (Cambridge, MA: Harvard University Press, 2002).
Fraser, Valerie, *Building the New World: Modern Architecture in Latin America* (London: Verso, 2001).
Freitag, Sandra B., *Collective Action and Community: Public Arenas and the Emergence of Communalism in North India* (Berkeley: University of California Press, 1989).
Fuller, C. J., and Véronique Bénéï (eds.), *The Everyday State and Society in Modern India* (New Delhi: Social Science Press, 2000).
Gandhi, Leela, *Postcolonial Theory: A Critical Introduction* (New York: Columbia University Press, 1998).
Ganeri, Jonardon, *The Lost Age of Reason: Philosophy in Early Modern India* (Oxford: Oxford University Press, 2011).
Garawala, Toral Jathin, *Untouchable Fictions: Literary Realism and the Crisis of Caste* (New York: Fordham University Press, 2013).
García Canclini, Néstor, *Culturas híbridas: estrategias para entrar y salir de la modernidad* (Mexico: Grijalbo, 1989).
Gautam Bhadra, Gyan Prakash, and Susie Tharu (eds.), *Subaltern Studies X: Writings on South Asian History and Society* (New Delhi: Oxford University Press, 1999).
Genovese, Eugene, *Roll, Jordan, Roll: The World the Slaves Made* (New York: Pantheon, 1974).
Giddens, Anthony, *Central Problems in Social Theory: Action, Structure, and Contradiction in Social Analysis* (Berkeley: University of California Press, 1979).
——, *Consequences of Modernity* (Stanford, CA: Stanford University Press, 1990).
Gikandi, Simon, *Maps of Englishness: Writing Identity in the Culture of Colonialism* (New York: Columbia University Press, 1996).
Gilroy, Paul, *The Black Atlantic: Modernity and Double Consciousness* (Cambridge, MA: Harvard University Press, 1993).
Ginzburg, Carlo, *The Cheese and the Worms: The Cosmos of a Sixteenth Century Miller*, trans. John and Ann Tedeschi (Baltimore, MD: Johns Hopkins University Press, 1980).
Glassman, Jonathon, *War of Words, War of Stones: Racial Thought and Violence in Colonial Zanzibar* (Bloomington: Indiana University Press, 2011).

Gluckham, Max, *Order and Rebellion in Tribal Africa* (London: Cohen and West, 1963).
Gold, Ann, and Bhoju Ram Gujar, *In the Time of Trees and Sorrows: Nature, Power, and Memory in Rajasthan* (Durham, NC: Duke University Press, 2002).
Goswami, Manu, *Producing India: From Colonial Economy to National Space* (Chicago, IL: University of Chicago Press, 2004).
Gough, Kathleen, *Rural Society in Southeast India* (Cambridge: Cambridge University Press, 1981).
Greenough, Paul, *Prosperity and Misery in Modern Bengal* (New York: Oxford University Press, 1982).
Gregory, Derek, *The Colonial Present* (Oxford: Blackwell, 2007).
Grewal, Inderpal, *Home and Harem: Nation, Gender, Empire, and the Cultures of Travel* (Durham, NC: Duke University Press, 1996).
Grosfoguel, Ramon, "Decolonizing post-colonial studies and paradigms of political economy: transmodernity, decolonial thinking, and global coloniality," *Transmodernity: Journal of Peripheral Cultural Production of the Luso-Hispanic World*, 1, 1 (2011): 1–37.
Grosrichard, Alain, *The Sultan's Court: European Fantasies of the East*, trans. Liz Heron, (London: Verso, 1998).
Gruzinski, Serge, *Images at War: Mexico from Columbus to Blade Runner (1492–2019)* (Durham, NC: Duke University Press, 2001).
Guha, Ranajit, "On some aspects of the historiography of colonial India," in Ranajit Guha (ed.), *Subaltern Studies I: Writings on South Asian History and Society* (Delhi: Oxford University Press, 1982), pp. 1–7.
——, "Preface," in Ranajit Guha (ed.), *Subaltern Studies I: Writings on South Asian History and Society* (Delhi: Oxford University Press, 1982), pp. viii–ix.
——, *Elementary Aspects of Peasant Insurgency in Colonial India* (Delhi: Oxford University Press, 1983).
——, "The prose of counter-insurgency," in Ranajit Guha (ed.), *Subaltern Studies II: Writings on South Asian History and Society* (Delhi: Oxford University Press, 1983), pp. 1–42.
——, "Introduction," in Bernard Cohn, *An Anthropologist among the Historians* (Delhi: Oxford University Press, 1987), pp. vii–xxvi.
——, *Dominance without Hegemony: History and Power in Colonial India* (Cambridge, MA: Harvard University Press, 1997).
——, "Not at home in empire," in Saurabh Dube (ed.), *Postcolonial Passages: Contemporary History-Writing on India* (New Delhi: Oxford University Press, 2004), pp. 38–46.

Guha, Ranajit (ed.), *Subaltern Studies I–VI: Writings on South Asian History and Society* (Delhi: Oxford University Press, 1982–89).

Guha, Ranajit, and Gayatri Chakravorty Spivak (eds.), *Selected Subaltern Studies* (New York: Oxford University Press, 1988).

Guha-Thakurta, Tapati, *The Making of a New "Indian" Art: Artists, Aesthetics and Nationalism in Bengal, c.1850–1920* (Cambridge: Cambridge University Press, 1992).

——, *Monuments, Objects, Histories: Art in Colonial and Post-Colonial India* (New York: Columbia University Press, 2004).

Gumbrecht, Hans Ulrich, "A history of the concept 'modern,'" in Hans Ulrich Gumbrecht, *Making Sense in Life and Literature*, trans. Glen Burns (Minneapolis: University of Minnesota Press, 1992), pp. 79–110.

Gupta, Akhil, *Postcolonial Developments: Agriculture in the Making of Modern India* (Durham, NC: Duke University Press, 1998).

——, *Red Tape: Bureaucracy, Structural Violence, and Poverty in India* (Durham, NC: Duke University Press, 2012).

Gupta, Charu, *Sexuality, Obscenity, and Community: Women, Muslims, and the Hindu Public in Colonial India* (New Delhi: Permanent Black, 2002).

Habermas, Jürgen, *The Philosophical Discourse of Modernity: Twelve Lectures*, trans. Frederick G. Lawrence (Cambridge, MA: MIT Press, 1987).

Hansen, Thomas Blom, *The Saffron Wave: Democracy and Hindu Nationalism in Modern India* (Princeton, NJ: Princeton University Press, 1999).

——, *Wages of Violence: Naming and Identity in Postcolonial Bombay* (Princeton, NJ: Princeton University Press, 2001).

Hansen, Thomas Blom, and Finn Stepputat, "Introduction: states of imagination," in Thomas Blom Hansen and Finn Stepputat (eds.), *States of Imagination: Ethnographic Explorations of the Postcolonial State* (Durham, NC: Duke University Press, 2001), pp. 1–38.

Hardiman, David, *Peasant Nationalists of Gujarat: Kheda District, 1917–1934* (Delhi: Oxford University Press, 1981).

——, *The Coming of the Devi: Adivasi Assertion in Western India* (Delhi: Oxford University Press, 1987).

Harootunian, Harry, *Overcome by Modernity: History, Culture, and Community in Interwar Japan* (Princeton, NJ: Princeton University Press, 2000).

Hartman, Saidiya H., *Scenes of Subjection: Terror, Slavery, and Self-Making in Nineteenth-Century America* (New York: Oxford University Press, 1997).

——, *Lose Your Mother: A Journey Along the Atlantic Slave Route* (New York: Farrar, Straus and Giroux, 2007).

Hedrick, Tracey, *Mestizo Modernism: Race, Nation, and Identity in Latin American Culture, 1900–1940* (New Brunswick, NJ: Rutgers University Press, 2003).
Henare, Amiria, *Museums, Anthropology and Imperial Exchange* (Cambridge: Cambridge University Press, 2009).
Hill, Christopher, *The World Turned Upside Down: Radical Ideas during the English Revolution* (New York: Penguin Books, 1973).
Hobsbawm, Eric, *Nations and Nationalism since 1780: Programme, Myth, Reality* (Cambridge: Cambridge University Press, 1993).
Hunt, Nancy Rose, *A Colonial Lexicon of Birth Ritual, Medicalization, and Mobility in the Congo* (Durham, NC: Duke University Press, 1999).
Inden, Ronald B., *Marriage and Rank in Bengali Culture: A History of Caste and Clan in Middle Period Bengal* (Berkeley: University of California Press, 1976).
——, *Imagining India* (Cambridge, MA: Basil Blackwell, 1990).
Jain, Ravindra K., *Between History and Legend: Status and Power in Bundelkhand* (Hyderabad: Orient Longman, 2002).
JanMohamed, Abdul R., *Manichean Aesthetics: The Politics of Literature in Colonial Africa* (Amherst: University of Massachusetts Press, 1983).
JanMohamed, Abdul R., and David Lloyd (eds.), *The Nature and Context of Minority Discourse* (New York and Oxford: Oxford University Press, 1990).
Jha, Hetukar, *Social Structures of Indian Villages: A Study of Rural Bihar* (New Delhi: Sage, 1991).
Kapur, Geeta, *When was Modernism: Essays on Contemporary Cultural Practice in India* (New Delhi: Tulika, 2000).
Kasturi, Malavika, *Embattled Identities: Rajput Lineages and the Colonial State in Nineteenth-Century North India* (New Delhi: Oxford University Press, 2002).
Keane, Webb, *Christian Moderns: Freedom and Fetish in the Mission Encounter* (Berkeley: University of California Press, 2007).
Kelley, Donald R., *Faces of History: Historical Inquiry from Herodotus to Herder* (New Haven, CT: Yale University Press, 1998).
Kelly, John, and Martha Kaplan, "History, structure, and ritual," *Annual Review of Anthropology*, 19 (1990): 119–50.
Kessinger, Tom G., *Vilyatpur, 1848–1968: Social and Economic Change in a North Indian Village* (Berkeley: University of California Press, 1974).
Klein, Kerwin Lee, *Frontiers of Historical Imagination: Narrating the European Conquest of Native America, 1890–1990* (Berkeley: University of California Press, 1999).

Knauft, Bruce, "Critically modern: an introduction," in Bruce Knauft (ed.), *Critically Modern: Alternatives, Alterities, Anthropologies* (Bloomington: Indiana University Press, 2002), pp. 1–54.

Kolff, D. H. A., *Naukar, Rajput, and Sepoy: The Ethnohistory of the Military Labour Market of Hindustan, 1450–1850* (Cambridge: Cambridge University Press, 1990).

Koselleck, Reinhart, *Futures Past: On the Semantics of Historical Time*, trans. Keith Tribe (Cambridge, MA: MIT Press, 1985).

——, *The Practice of Conceptual History: Timing History, Spacing Concepts*, trans. Todd Samuel Presner (Stanford, CA: Stanford University Press, 2002).

Kraniauskas, John, and Guillermo Zermeño (eds.), "Historia y subalternidad," special issue of *Historia y Grafía*, 12 (1999): 7–176.

Krech III, Shepard, "The state of ethnohistory," *Annual Review of Anthropology*, 20 (1991): 345–75.

Kumar, Nita, *The Artisans of Banaras: Popular Culture and Identity, 1880–1986* (Princeton, NJ: Princeton University Press, 1988).

Kumar, Ravinder (ed.), *Essays on Gandhian Politics: The Rowlatt Satyagraha of 1919* (Oxford: Clarendon Press, 1971).

Kuper, Adam, *Anthropologists and Anthropology: The British School, 1922–1972* (London: Allen Lane, 1973), pp. 92–109.

Ladurie, Emmanuel Le Roy, *Montaillou: The Promised Land of Error*, trans. Barbara Bray (New York: Vintage Books, 1979).

Lal, Vinay, *The History of History: Politics and Scholarship in Modern India* (New Delhi: Oxford University Press, 2003).

Lander, Edgardo (ed.), *La colonialidad del saber: eurocentrismo y ciencias sociales. Perspectivas latinoamericanas* (Buenos Aires: UNESCO/CLACSO, 2000).

Lazarus, Neil (ed.), *The Cambridge Companion to Postcolonial Literary Studies* (New York: Cambridge University Press, 2004).

Leach, Edmund, *Political System of Highland Burma: A Study of Kachin Social Structure* (London: G. Bell and Sons, 1954).

Lefebvre, Henri, *The Production of Space*, trans. Donald Nicholson-Smith (Oxford: Blackwell, 1991).

Lejeune, Jean-François, *Cruelty and Utopia: Cities and Landscapes of Latin America* (Princeton, NJ: Princeton Architectural Press, 2005).

Lelyveld, David, *Aligarh's First Generation: Muslim Solidarity in British India* (Princeton, NJ: Princeton University Press, 1978).

Lester, Rebecca J., *Jesus in Our Wombs: Embodying Modernity in a Mexican Convent* (Berkeley: University of California Press, 2005).

Levinas, Emmanuel, *Time and the Other*, trans. Richard A. Cohen (Pittsburgh, PA: Duquesne University Press, 1987).
——, *Totality and Infinity: An Essay on Exteriority*, trans. Alphonso Lingis (Pittsburgh, PA: Duquesne University Press, 1987).
Levine, Lawrence, *Black Culture and Consciousness: Afro-American Folk Thought from Slavery to Freedom* (Oxford: Oxford University Press, 1977).
Lewis, Martin W., and Wigen, Kären, *The Myth of Continents: A Critique of Metageography* (Berkeley: University of California Press, 1997).
LiPuma, Edward, *Encompassing Others: The Magic of Modernity in Melanesia* (Ann Arbor: University of Michigan Press, 2001).
Lomnitz-Adler, Claudio, *Exits from the Labyrinth: Culture and Ideology in the Mexican National Space* (Berkeley: University of California Press, 1993).
——, *Modernidad indiana: nueve ensayos sobre nación y mediación en México* (Mexico: Planeta, 1999).
Loomba, Ania, *Colonialism/postcolonialism* (London and New York: Routledge, 1998).
Lowe, Lisa, and David Lloyd (eds.), *The Politics of Culture in the Shadow of Capital* (Durham, NC: Duke University Press, 1997).
Lüdtke, Alf (ed.), *The History of Everyday Life: Reconstructing Historical Experiences and Ways of Life*, trans. William Templer (Princeton, NJ: Princeton University Press, 1995).
McClintock, Anne, *Imperial Leather: Race, Gender, and Sexuality in the Colonial Contest* (New York: Routledge, 1995).
McCutcheon, Russell, *Manufacturing Religion: The Discourse on Sui Generis Religion and the Politics of Nostalgia* (New York: Oxford University Press, 1997).
McGowan, John, *Postmodernism and its Critics* (Ithaca, NY: Cornell University Press, 1991).
MacIntyre, Alasdair, *After Virtue* (Notre Dame, IN: University of Notre Dame Press, 1983).
McKee, Robert Irwin, and Szurmuk, Mónica (eds.), *Dictionary of Latin American Cultural Studies* (Gainesville: University Press of Florida, 2012).
MacKenzie, John M., *Museums and Empire: Natural History, Human Cultures and Colonial Identities* (Manchester: Manchester University Press, 2010).
McLeod, John, *Beginning Postcolonialism* (Manchester: Manchester University Press, 2000).
McMahon, Darrin M., *Enemies of the Enlightenment: The French Counter-Enlightenment and the Making of Modernity* (New York: Oxford University Press, 2002).

Maldonado-Torres, Nelson, *Against War: Views from the Underside of Modernity* (Durham, NC: Duke University Press, 2008).

Malinowski, Bronislaw, *Argonauts of the Western Pacific: An Account of Native Adventures in the Archipelagoes of Melanesian New Guinea* (London: Routledge, 1922).

Mallon, Florencia E., "The promise and dilemma of subaltern studies: perspectives from Latin American histories," *American Historical Review*, 99 (1994): 1491–515.

——, *Courage Tastes of Blood: The Mapuche Community of Nicolás Ailío and the Chilean State, 1906–2001* (Durham, NC: Duke University Press, 2005).

Manderson, Lenore, and Margaret Jolly (eds.), *Sites of Desire, Economies of Pleasure: Sexualities in Asia and the Pacific* (Chicago, IL: University of Chicago Press, 1997).

Mani, Lata, *Contentious Traditions: The Debate on Sati in Colonial India* (Berkeley: University of California Press, 1998).

Marriott, Mckim, "Village structure and the Punjab government: a restatement," *American Anthropologist*, 55 (1953): 137–43.

Mathur, Saloni, "History and anthropology in South Asia: rethinking the archive," *Annual Review of Anthropology*, 29 (2000): 89–106.

——, *India by Design: Colonial History and Cultural Display* (Berkeley: University of California Press, 2007).

Mayaram, Shail, *Resisting Regimes: Myth, Memory and the Shaping of a Muslim Identity* (Delhi: Oxford University Press, 1997).

——, *Against History, Against State: Counterperspectives from the Margins* (New Delhi: Permanent Black, 2004).

Mazzarella, William, *Shoveling Smoke: Advertising and Globalization in Contemporary India* (Durham, NC: Duke University Press, 2003).

Mbembe, Achille, *On the Postcolony* (Berkeley: University of California Press, 2001).

Medick, Hans, "Plebian culture in the transition to capitalism," in Raphael Samuel and Gareth Stedman Jones (eds.), *Culture, Ideology and Politics* (London: Routledge and Kegan Paul, 1983), pp. 84–113.

——, "'Missionaries in the rowboat'? Ethnological ways of knowing as a challenge to social history," in Alf Lüdtke (ed.), *The History of Everyday Life: Reconstructing Historical Experiences and Ways of Life*, trans. William Templer (Princeton, NJ: Princeton University Press, 1995), pp. 41–71.

Mehta, Uday Singh, *Liberalism and Empire: A Study in Nineteenth Century British Liberal Thought* (Chicago, IL: University of Chicago Press, 1999).

Menon, Ritu, and Kamla Bhasin, *Borders and Boundaries: Women in India's Partition* (New Delhi: Kali for Women, 1998).
Meyer, Birgit, and Peter Pels (eds.), *Magic and Modernity: Interfaces of Revelation and Concealment* (Stanford, CA: Stanford University Press, 2003).
Middleton, Townsend, *The Demands of Recognition: State Anthropology and Ethnopolitics in Darjeeling* (Stanford, CA: Stanford University Press, 2015).
Mignolo, Walter, *The Darker Side of the Renaissance: Literacy, Territoriality, and Colonization* (Ann Arbor: University of Michigan Press, 1995).
——, *Local Histories/Global Designs: Coloniality, Subaltern Knowledges and Border Thinking* (Princeton, NJ: Princeton University Press, 2000).
——, "*The* enduring enchantment (or the epistemic privilege of modernity and where to go from here)," in Saurabh Dube (ed.), *Enduring Enchantments*, special issue of *South Atlantic Quarterly*, 101 (2002): 927–54.
——, "Coloniality at large," in Saurabh Dube (ed.), *Enchantments of Modernity: Empire, Nation, Globalization* (London: Routledge, 2009), pp. 67–95.
——, *The Darker Side of Western Modernity: Global Futures, Decolonial Options* (Durham, NC: Duke University Press, 2011).
Mitchell, Timothy, *Colonizing Egypt* (Berkeley: University of California Press, 1988).
——, "The stage of modernity," in Timothy Mitchell (ed.), *Questions of Modernity* (Minneapolis: University of Minnesota Press, 2000), pp. 1–34.
Mitter, Partha, *The Triumph of Modernism: India's Artists and the Avant-Garde, 1922-1947* (New Delhi: Oxford University Press, 2007).
Mohanty, Chandra Talpade, *Feminism without Borders: Decolonizing Theory, Practicing Solidarity* (Durham, NC: Duke University Press, 2003).
Mongia, Padmini (ed.), *Contemporary Postcolonial Theory: A Reader* (London: Hodder Arnold, 1996).
Moore, R. Laurence, *Touchdown Jesus: The Mixing of Sacred and Secular in American History* (Louisville, KY: Westminster John Know Press, 2003).
Moore-Gilbert, Bart, *Postcolonial Theory: Contexts, Practices, Politics* (London: Verso, 1997).
Morris, Meaghan, "Metamorphoses at Sydney Tower," *New Formations*, 11 (1990): 5–18.
Mudimbe, Valentin Yves, *The Invention of Africa: Gnosis, Philosophy, and the Order of Knowledge* (Bloomington: Indiana University Press, 1988).
——, *The Idea of Africa* (Bloomington and London: Indiana University Press, 1994).

Muir, Edward, and Guido Ruggiero (eds.), *Microhistory and the Lost Peoples of Europe*, trans. Eren Branch (Baltimore, MD: Johns Hopkins University Press, 1991).
Mullins, Edwin, *Souza* (London: Anthony Blond, 1962).
Munn, Nancy, "The cultural anthropology of time: a critical essay," *Annual Review of Anthropology* (1992): 93–123.
——, *The Fame of Gawa: A Symbolic Study of Value Transformation in a Massim (Papua New Guinea) Society* (Durham, NC: Duke University Press, 1992).
Muthu, Sankar, *Enlightenment against Empire* (Princeton, NJ: Princeton University Press, 2003).
Nandy, Ashis, *The Intimate Enemy: Loss and Recovery of Self under Colonialism* (Delhi: Oxford University Press, 1982).
——, *Traditions, Tyranny, and Utopias: Essays in the Politics of Awareness* (Delhi: Oxford University Press, 1992).
——, *The Savage Freud and Other Essays on Possible and Retrievable Selves* (Princeton, NJ: Princeton University Press, 1995).
——, "History's forgotten doubles," *History and Theory*, 34 (1995): 44–66.
——, *An Ambiguous Journey to the City: The Village and Other Odd Remains of the Self in the Indian Imagination* (New Delhi: Oxford University Press, 2001).
Nash, June, *We Eat the Mines and the Mines Eat Us: Dependency and Exploitation in Bolivian Tin Mines* (New York: Columbia University Press, 1979).
O'Hanlon, Rosalind, "Recovering the subject: subaltern studies and histories of resistance in colonial South Asia," *Modern Asian Studies*, 22 (1988): 189–224.
Ortner, Sherry, "Theory in anthropology since the sixties," *Comparative Studies in Society and History*, 26 (1984): 126–66.
——, "Resistance and the problem of ethnographic refusal," *Comparative Studies in Society and History*, 37 (1995): pp. 173–93.
Overmyer-Velázquez, Mark, *Visions of the Emerald City: Modernity, Tradition, and the Formation of Porfirian Oaxaca, Mexico* (Durham, NC: Duke University Press, 2006).
Owen, Alex, *The Place of Enchantment: British Occultism and the Culture of the Modern* (Chicago, IL: University of Chicago Press, 2004).
Palmié, Stephan, *Wizards and Scientists: Explorations in Afro-Cuban Modernity and Tradition* (Durham, NC: Duke University Press, 2002).
Pandey, Gyanendra, *The Ascendancy of the Congress in Uttar Pradesh, 1926–1934: A Study in Imperfect Mobilization* (Oxford: Clarendon Press, 1978).
——, *The Construction of Communalism in Colonial North India* (New Delhi: Oxford University Press, 1990).

——, "In defense of the fragment: writing about Hindu–Muslim riots in India today," *Representations*, 37 (1992): 27–55.

——, "The prose of otherness," in David Arnold and David Hardiman (eds.), *Subaltern Studies VIII: Essays in Honour of Ranajit Guha* (Delhi: Oxford University Press, 1994), pp. 188–221.

——, *Remembering Partition: Violence, Nationalism and History in India* (Cambridge: Cambridge University Press, 2001).

——, *Routine Violence: Nations, Fragments, Histories* (Stanford, CA: Stanford University Press, 2006).

Pandian, Anand, *Crooked Stalks: Cultivating Virtue in South India* (Durham, NC: Duke University Press, 2009).

Paz, Octavio, *El ogro filantrópico: historia y política, 1971–1978* (Mexico: Joaquín Mortiz 1979).

——, *Vislumbres de la India* (Barcelona: Seix Barral, 1995).

Pels, Peter, "The anthropology of colonialism: culture, history, and the emergence of Western governmentality," *Annual Review of Anthropology*, 26 (1997): 163–83.

Pinney, Christopher, *Camera Indica: The Social Life of Indian Photographs* (Chicago, IL: University of Chicago Press, 1998).

——, *Photos of the Gods: The Printed Image and Political Struggle in India* (London: Reaktion Books, 2004).

Piot, Charles, *Remotely Global: Village Modernity in West Africa* (Chicago, IL: University of Chicago Press, 1999).

Pocock, J. G. A., *Barbarism and Religion, Volume Two: Narratives of Civil Government* (Cambridge: Cambridge University Press, 1999).

Pocock, David F., *Social Anthropology* (London: Sheed and Ward, 1961).

Porter, Roy, *The Creation of the Modern World: The Untold Story of the British Enlightenment* (New York: Norton, 2001).

Prakash, Gyan, "Subaltern studies as postcolonial criticism," *American Historical Review*, 99 (1994): 1475–94.

——, *Another Reason: Science and the Imagination of Modern India* (Princeton, NJ: Princeton University Press, 1999).

Pratt, Mary Louise, *Imperial Eyes: Travel Writing and Transculturation* (London: Routledge, 1992).

Price, Richard, *First-Time: The Historical Vision of an Afro-American People* (Baltimore, MD: Johns Hopkins University Press, 1983).

——, *Alabi's World* (Baltimore, MD: Johns Hopkins University Press, 1990).

——, *The Convict and the Colonel: A Story of Colonialism and Resistance in the Caribbean* (Boston, MA: Beacon Press, 1998).

Quijano, Aníbal, "Colonialidad y modernidad/racionalidad," *Perú Indígena*, 29 (1991): 11–21.

——, "La colonialidad del poder y la experiencia cultural latinoamericana," in Roberto Briceño-León and Heinz R. Sonntag (eds.), *Pueblo, época y desarrollo: la sociología de América Latina* (Caracas: Nueva Sociedad, 1998), pp. 139–55.

——, "Coloniality of power, ethnocentrism, and Latin America," *Nepantla*, 1 (2000): 533–80.

Rabasa, José, *Inventing America: Spanish Historiography and the Formation of Eurocentrism* (Oklahoma: University of Oklahoma Press, 1993).

——, *Writing Violence on the Northern Frontier: The Historiography of Sixteenth-Century New Mexico and Florida and the Legacy of Conquest* (Durham, NC: Duke University Press, 2000).

——, *Tell Me the Story of How I Conquered You: Elsewheres and Ethnosuicide in the Colonial Mesoamerican World* (Austin: University of Texas Press, 2011).

Rabasa, José, Javier Sanjines, and Robert Carr (eds.), *Subaltern Studies in the Americas*, special issue of *dispositio/n: American Journal of Cultural Histories and Theories*, 46 (1994 [published 1996]).

Rabinovich, Silvana, "Alterity," in Robert McKee Irwin and Mónica Szurmuk (eds.), *Dictionary of Latin American Cultural Studies* (Gainesville: University Press of Florida, 2012), pp. 17–22.

Radcliffe, Sarah A., "Imagining the state as a space: territoriality and the formation of the state in Ecuador," in Thomas Blom Hansen and Finn Stepputat (eds.), *States of Imagination: Ethnographic Explorations of the Postcolonial State* (Durham, NC: Duke University Press, 2001), pp. 123–45.

Radcliffe-Brown, A. R., *Structure and Function in Primitive Society* (Glencoe, IL: The Free Press of Glencoe, 1952).

Rafael, Vicente, *Contracting Colonialism: Translation and Christian Conversion in Tagalog Society under Early Spanish Rule* (Ithaca, NY: Cornell University Press, 1988).

Rama, Ángel, *La ciudad letrada* (Hanover, NH: Ediciones del Norte, 1984).

Ramos, Julio, *Desencuentros de la modernidad en América Latina: literatura y política en el siglo XIX* (Mexico: Fondo de Cultura Económica, 1989).

Rancière, Jacques, *The Names of History: On the Poetics of Knowledge*, trans. Hassan Melehy (Minneapolis: University of Minnesota Press, 1994).

——, *The Philosopher and His Poor*, trans. Andrew Parker, Corrine Oster, and John Drury (Durham, NC: Duke University Press, 2004).

Rao, Anupama, *The Caste Question: Dalits and the Politics of Modern India* (Berkeley: University of California Press, 2009).

Rappaport, Joanne, *Cumbe Reborn: An Andean Ethnography of History* (Chicago, IL: University of Chicago Press, 1994).

——, *Intercultural Utopias: Public Intellectuals, Cultural Experimentation, and Ethnic Pluralism in Colombia* (Durham, NC: Duke University Press, 2005).

Rebel, Herman, "Cultural hegemony and class experience: a critical reading of recent ethnological-historical approaches (parts one and two)," *American Ethnologist*, 16 (1989): 117–36, 350–65.

Redfield, Peter, *Space in the Tropics: From Convicts to Rockets in French Guiana* (Berkeley: University of California Press, 2000).

Redfield, Robert, *Peasant, Society, and Culture* (Chicago, IL: University of Chicago Press, 1956).

Rivera Cusicanqui, Silvia, and Rossana Barragan (eds.), *Debates post coloniales: una introducción a los estudios de la subalternidad* (La Paz: Sierpe, 1997).

Rodríguez, Ileana (ed.), *A Latin American Subaltern Studies Reader* (Durham, NC: Duke University Press, 2001).

Rofel, Lisa, *Other Modernities: Gendered Yearnings in China after Socialism* (Berkeley: University of California Press, 1999).

Rorty, Richard, *Contingency, Irony, and Solidarity* (New York: Cambridge University Press, 1989).

Rosaldo, Renato, *Ilongot Headhunting, 1883–1974: A Study in Society and History* (Stanford, CA: Stanford University Press, 1980).

Rostow, W. W., *The Stages of Economic Growth: A Non-Communist Manifesto* (Cambridge: Cambridge University Press, 1960).

Roy, Anupama, *Gendered Citizenship: Historical and Conceptual Explorations* (Hyderabad: Orient Longman, 2005).

Sabean, David Warren, *Power in the Blood: Popular Culture and Village Discourse in Early Modern Germany* (Cambridge: Cambridge University Press, 1984).

Sahlins, Marshall, *Islands of History* (Chicago, IL: University of Chicago Press, 1985).

——, *Culture in Practice: Selected Essays* (New York: Zone Books, 2000).

Said, Edward W., *Orientalism* (New York: Pantheon, 1978).

——, *Culture and Imperialism* (New York: Vintage, 1994).

Saldaña-Portillo, María Josefina, *The Revolutionary Imagination in the Americas and the Age of Development* (Durham, NC: Duke University Press, 2003).

Saler, Michael, "Modernity and enchantment: a historiographic review," *American Historical Review*, 111 (2006): 692–716.

——, *As If: Modern Enchantment and the Literary Prehistory of Virtual Reality* (New York: Oxford University Press, 2012).

Sarkar, Sumit, *Modern India: 1885–1947* (New Delhi: Macmillan, 1983).
——, *Writing Social History* (Delhi: Oxford University Press, 1997).
Sarkar, Tanika, *Hindu Wife, Hindu Nation: Community, Religion, and Cultural Nationalism* (New Delhi: Permanent Black, 2001).
Scott, David, *Formations of Ritual: Colonial and Anthropological Discourses on the Sinhala Yaktovil* (Minneapolis: University of Minnesota Press, 1994).
——, *Refashioning Futures: Criticism after Postcoloniality* (Princeton, NJ: Princeton University Press, 1999).
——, *Conscripts of Modernity: The Tragedy of Colonial Enlightenment* (Durham, NC: Duke University Press, 2005).
Sears, Laurie J., *Shadows of Empire: Colonial Discourse and Javanese Tales* (Durham, NC: Duke University Press, 1996).
Seth, Sanjay, *Subject Lessons: The Western Education of Colonial India* (Durham, NC: Duke University Press, 2007).
Sewell, Jr., William H., *Work and Revolution in France: The Language of Labor from the Old Regime to 1848* (New York: Cambridge University Press, 1980).
Shah, A. M., *Exploring India's Rural Past: A Gujarat Village in the Early Nineteenth Century* (New Delhi: Oxford University Press, 2002).
Shah, A. M., and R. G. Shroff, "The Vahivancha Barots of Gujarat: a caste of genealogists and mythographers," in Milton Singer (ed.), *Traditional India: Structure and Change* (Philadelphia, PA: American Folklore Society, 1959), pp. 40–70.
Sheikh, Gulammohammed (ed.), *Contemporary Art in Baroda* (New Delhi: Tulika, 1997).
Shohat, Ella, "Notes on the post-colonial," in Padmini Mongia (ed.), *Contemporary Postcolonial Theory: A Reader* (London: Arnold, 1996), pp. 321–34.
Siddiqi, Majid, *Agrarian Unrest in North India: The United Provinces, 1918–22* (New Delhi: Vikas, 1978).
Sider, Gerald M., "The ties that bind: culture and agriculture, property and propriety in the New foundland village fishery," *Social History*, 5 (1980): 1–39.
——, *Culture and Class: A Newfoundland Illustration* (Cambridge: Cambridge University Press, 1986).
Simpson, Audra, *Mohawk Interruptus: Political Life across the Border of Settler States* (Durham, NC: Duke University Press, 2014).
Singer, Milton B., *When a Great Tradition Modernizes: An Anthropological Approach to Indian Civilization* (New York: Praeger, 1972).
Singer, Milton B., and Bernard Cohn (eds.), *Structure and Change in Indian Society* (Chicago, IL: Aldine, 1968).

Singh, K. S. (ed.), *Tribal Situation in India* (Shimla: Indian Institute of Advanced Study, 1972).
Sinha, Mrinalini, *Colonial Masculinity: The "Manly Englishman" and the "Effeminate Bengali" in the Late Nineteenth Century* (Manchester: Manchester University Press, 1995).
——, *Specters of Mother India: The Global Restructuring of an Empire* (Durham, NC: Duke University Press, 2006).
Sinha, Surajit, "State formation and Rajput myth in tribal central India," *Man in India*, 42 (1962): 25–80.
Sivaramakrishnan, K., *Modern Forests: Statemaking and Environmental Change in Colonial Eastern India* (New Delhi: Oxford University Press, 1999).
Skaria, Ajay, *Hybrid Histories: Forests, Frontiers and Wildness in Western India* (New Delhi: Oxford University Press, 1999).
——, *Unconditional Equality: Gandhi's Religion of Resistance* (Minneapolis, University of Minnesota Press, 2016).
Soja, Edward, *Postmodern Geographies: The Reassertion of Space in Critical Social Theory* (London: Verso, 1989).
Sommer, Doris, *Foundational Fictions: The National Romances of Latin America* (Berkeley: University of California Press, 1991).
Spivak, Gayatri Chakravorty, "Subaltern studies: deconstructing historiography," in Ranajit Guha (ed.), *Subaltern Studies IV: Writings on South Asian History and Society* (Delhi: Oxford University Press, 1985), pp. 330–63.
——, *In Other Worlds: Essays in Cultural Politics* (London: Methuen, 1987).
——, "Can the subaltern speak?," in Cary Nelson and Lawrence Grossberg (eds.), *Marxism and the Interpretation of Culture* (Urbana/Chicago: University of Illinois Press, 1988), pp. 271–313.
——, *A Critique of Postcolonial Reason: Toward a History of the Vanishing Present* (Cambridge, MA: Harvard University Press, 1999).
Steinmetz, George, *The Devil's Handwriting: Precoloniality and the German Colonial State in Qingdao, Samoa, and Southwest Africa* (Chicago, IL: University of Chicago Press, 2007).
Steinmetz, George (ed.), *Sociology and Empire: The Imperial Entanglements of a Discipline* (Durham, NC: Duke University Press, 2013).
Stern, Steve, *Battling for Hearts and Minds: Memory Struggles in Pinochet's Chile, 1973–1988* (Durham, NC: Duke University Press, 2006).
——, *Remembering Pinochet's Chile: On the Eve of London 1998* (Durham, NC: Duke University Press, 2006).
Stocking, Jr., George, *The Ethnographer's Magic and Other Essays in the History of Anthropology* (Madison: University of Wisconsin Press, 1992).

——, *After Tylor: British Social Anthropology, 1888–1951* (Madison: University of Wisconsin Press, 1995).
Stoler, Ann Laura, "Rethinking colonial categories: European communities and the boundaries of rule," *Comparative Studies in Society and History*, 13 (1989): 134–61.
——, *Race and the Education of Desire: Foucault's History of Sexuality and the Colonial Order of Things* (Durham, NC: Duke University Press, 1995).
——, *Carnal Knowledge and Imperial Power: Race and the Intimate in Colonial Rule* (Berkeley: University of California Press, 2002).
——, *Along the Archival Grain: Epistemic Anxieties and Colonial Common Sense* (Princeton, NJ: Princeton University Press, 2008).
Stoler, Ann Laura, and Frederick Cooper, "Between metropole and colony: rethinking a research agenda," in Frederick Cooper and Ann Laura Stoler (eds.), *Tensions of Empire: Colonial Cultures in a Bourgeois World* (Berkeley: University of California Press, 1997), pp. 1–56.
Subramanian, Ajantha, *Shorelines: Spaces and Rights in South Asia* (Stanford, CA: Stanford University Press, 2009).
Sunder Rajan, Rajeswari, *Scandal of the State: Women, Law, and Citizenship in Postcolonial India* (Durham, NC: Duke University Press, 2003).
Sunderason, Sanjukta, "Making art modern: re-visiting artistic modernism in South Asia," in Saurabh Dube (ed.), *Modern Makeovers: Handbook of Modernity in South Asia* (New York: Oxford University Press, 2011), pp. 245–61.
Tarlo, Emma, *Clothing Matters: Dress and Identity in India* (Chicago, IL: University of Chicago Press, 1996).
——, *Unsettling Memories: Narratives of India's "Emergency"* (New Delhi: Permanent Black, 2003).
Tartakov, Gary Michael (ed.), *Dalit Art and Visual Imagery* (New Delhi: Indian Institute for Dalit Studies and Oxford University Press, 2012).
Taussig, Michael, *The Devil and Commodity Fetishism in South America* (Chapel Hill: University of North Carolina Press, 1980).
——, *Shamanism, Colonialism, and the Wild Man: A Study in Terror and Healing* (Chicago, IL: University of Chicago Press, 1987).
——, *The Magic of the State* (New York and London: Routledge, 1997).
——, *Defacement: Public Secrecy and the Labor of the Negative* (Stanford, CA: Stanford University Press, 1999).
——, *My Cocaine Museum* (Chicago, IL: University of Chicago Press, 2004).
Taylor, Charles, *Modern Social Imaginaries* (Durham, NC: Duke University Press, 2005).

———, *A Secular Age* (Cambridge, MA: Harvard University Press, 2007).

Tenorio-Trillo, Mauricio, *Artilugio de la nación moderna: México en las exposiciones universales, 1880–1930* (Mexico: Fondo de Cultura Económica, 1998).

Thomas, Nicholas, *Out of Time: History and Evolution in Anthropological Discourse* (Cambridge: Cambridge University Press, 1989).

———, *Colonialism's Culture: Anthropology, Travel and Government* (Princeton, NJ: Princeton University Press, 1994).

Thompson, E. P., "Time, work-discipline and industrial capitalism," *Past and Present*, 38 (1967): 56–97.

———, "The moral economy of the English crowd in the eighteenth century," *Past and Present*, 50 (1971): 76–136.

———, "Patrician society, plebian culture," *Journal of Social History*, 7 (1974): 382–405.

———, "Eighteenth century English society: class struggle without class," *Social History*, 3 (1978): 133–65.

———, *The Poverty of Theory and other Essays* (New York: Monthly Review Press, 1978).

———, *Customs in Common: Studies in Traditional Popular Culture* (New York: The New Press, 1993).

Thurner, Mark, *From Two Republics to One Divided: Contradictions of Postcolonial Nationmaking in Andean Peru* (Durham, NC: Duke University Press, 1997).

———, *History's Peru: The Poetics of Colonial and Postcolonial Historiography* (Gainesville: University Press of Florida, 2011).

Thurner, Mark, and Andrés Guerrero (eds.), *After Spanish Rule: Postcolonial Predicaments of the Americas* (Durham, NC: Duke University Press, 2003).

Trautmann, Thomas, *Dravidian Kinship* (Cambridge: Cambridge University Press, 1982).

Trouillot, Michel-Rolph, "Anthropology and the savage slot: the poetics and politics of the otherness," in Richard Fox (ed.), *Recapturing Anthropology: Working in the Present* (Santa Fe, NM: School of American Research Press, 1991), pp. 17–44.

———, *Silencing the Past: Power and the Production of History* (Boston, MA: Beacon Press, 1995).

———, "North Atlantic universals: analytical fictions, 1492–1945," in Saurabh Dube (ed.), *Enchantments of Modernity: Empire, Nation, Globalization* (New Delhi: Routledge, 2009), pp. 45–66.

Turner, Victor, *Schism and Continuity in an African Society* (Manchester: Manchester University Press, 1957).
Uberoi, J. P. S., *The Politics of the Kula Ring: An Analysis of the Findings of Bronislaw Malinowski* (Manchester: Manchester University Press, 1962).
van der Veer, Peter, *Gods on Earth: The Management of Religious Experience and Identity in a North Indian Pilgrimage Centre* (Delhi: Oxford University Press, 1988).
——, *Religious Nationalism: Hindus and Muslims in India* (Berkeley: University of California Press, 1994).
——, *Imperial Encounters: Religion and Modernity in India and Britain* (Princeton, NJ: Princeton University Press, 2001).
van der Veer, Peter, and Hartmut Lehmann (eds.), *Nation and Religion: Perspectives on Europe and Asia* (Princeton, NJ: Princeton University Press, 1999).
Vaughan, Megan, *Curing their Ills: Colonial Power and African Illness* (Stanford, CA: Stanford University Press, 1991).
Vincent, Joan, *Anthropology and Politics: Visions, Traditions, and Trends* (Tuscon: University of Arizona Press, 1990).
Voekel, Pamela, *Alone Before God: The Religious Origins of Modernity in Mexico* (Durham, NC: Duke University Press, 2002).
Watson, Stephen, *Tradition(s): Refiguring Community and Virtue in Classical German Thought* (Bloomington: Indiana University Press, 1997).
Weidman, Amanda J., *Singing the Classical, Voicing the Modern: The Postcolonial Politics of Music in South India* (Durham, NC: Duke University Press, 2006).
White, Hayden, "Foreword: Rancière's revisionism," in Jacques Rancière, *The Names of History: On the Poetics of Knowledge*, trans. Hassan Melehy (Minneapolis: University of Minnesota Press, 1994), pp vii–xx.
White, Luise, *Speaking with Vampires: Rumour and History in Colonial Africa* (Berkeley: University of California Press, 2000).
White, Stephen K., *Sustaining Affirmation: The Strengths of Weak Ontology in Political Theory* (Princeton, NJ: Princeton University Press, 2000).
Williams, Gareth, *The Other Side of the Popular: Neoliberalism and Subalternity in Latin America* (Durham, NC: Duke University Press, 2002).
Wolfe, Patrick, "History and imperialism: a century of theory, from Marx to postcolonialism," *American Historical Review*, 102 (1997): 380–420.
——, *Settler Colonialism and the Transformation of Anthropology: The Politics and Poetics of an Ethnographic Event* (London: Cassell, 1999).

Yegenoglu, Meyda, *Colonial Fantasies: Towards a Feminist Reading of Orientalism* (Cambridge: Cambridge University Press, 1998).
Young, Robert, *White Mythologies: Writing History and the West* (London: Routledge, 1990).
——, *Postcolonialism: An Historical Introduction* (Cambridge, MA: Wiley-Blackwell, 2001).
——, *Postcolonialism: A Very Short Introduction* (Oxford: Oxford University Press, 2003).
Yúdice, George, *The Expediency of Culture: Uses of Culture in the Global Era* (Durham, NC: Duke University Press, 2004).
Zammito, John H., *Kant, Herder, and the Birth of Anthropology* (Chicago, IL: University of Chicago Press, 2002).

Index

Note: page numbers underlined refer to illustrations.

Abbas, Khwaja Ahmad 182
Abrams, Philip 32
adivasi 34, 177
Adorno, Theodor 74
aesthetics 18–19, 42, 74–5, 84, 95n.53, 112, 172, 172–85 *passim*
Afghanistan 79
Africa 23n.8, 27n.31, 33, 41, 69, 77, 122, 181
African-American 32, 69, 126, 130
agency 12, 32, 122, 130, 162n.3
Ajneya (S. H. Vatsyayan) 181
Algeria 116
alienation 66, 112, 179
Al-Qaeda 67, 72
Altagsgeschichte (history of everyday life) 126
alterity 6, 9, 36–7, 40, 43, 48, 50–1, 62n.69, 93n.49, 131, 147, 158–9, 161, 183, 186
Ambedkar, B. R. 183–5
ambivalence 1, 5, 10, 17, 19, 45, 82–3, 91n.30, 93n.51, 105–6, 109–10, 116–17, 126
America 27n.31, 43, 181, 184
  see also Latin America; United States
Americas, the 23n.8, 33, 69, 77
Amin, Shahid 154
analysis 1–2, 5, 8–9, 16–17, 39, 46, 50–1, 60n.57, 65–6, 73, 80, 89n.19, 90–1n.30, 105–10 *passim*, 114–16, 119, 122, 126, 132n.1, 133n.9, 136n.39, 139n.58, 148, 151, 159–60, 163n.4, 175
Anderson, Benedict 157
Annales School, the 126, 128
anthropology 27n.30, 66, 132nn.1–2, 133n.6, 134n.15, 137n.46, 137n.48, 138n.57, 139n.58
  and time 105–18 *passim*, 135n.36, 137n.48
  see also history: and anthropology
anticolonial thought 10, 13, 81, 93n.45, 93n.49, 158, 173, 176–8
antinomies 5, 77, 161
  see also oppositions
Appleby, Joyce 90n.25
Asad, Talal 73
Asia 41
autonomy 12, 32, 78, 121–2, 175, 177, 179–80
  see also agency
Axel, Brian 14

Baij, Ramkinkar 177
Banerjee-Dube, Ishita 154, 156
Bangladesh 182
Baroque 42, 85
Baudelaire, Charles 75
Bauhaus 174–5
Bayly, C. A. 57n.35
Bear, Laura 169n.60

Berlin, Isaiah 133n.9
Bhabha, Homi 10
Boas, Franz 17, 110–13, 134n.15
Bose, Nandalal 176–7
Bourdieu, Pierre 17, 32, 110, 115–16
Brahman 31, 185
Braudel, Fernand 128, 140n.67
Britain 38–40, 68, 150
British Communist Group of Historians 126
Buddhism 79

Cabral, Amílcar 13
Cambridge 16, 36, 57n.35
capitalism 66, 85, 123–5, 128–9
Césaire, Aimé 13
Chakrabarty, Dipesh 36, 47–9, 51, 52n.2, 83, 155
Chatterjee, Partha 40, 54n.11, 62n.69
Chhattisgarh region 32, 117, 156
Childs, Peter 75
China 69
Chitre, Dilip 187n.16
Christianity 38–9, 68–9, 131, 180–1
citizen 38, 46–7, 82, 144, 158–9, 178
class 10–12, 33–4, 36–7, 46–7, 81–2, 146–7, 152, 158–9, 176
coeval 1, 4, 31, 39, 44, 49, 72, 77, 81, 86n.2, 107, 117, 131, 161, 177
coevality *see* coeval
coevalness *see* coeval
Cohn, Bernard S. 34–5, 55n.21, 55n.25, 56n.26, 106–7
colonialism 13, 30–1, 39–42, 44, 58n.40, 62n.69, 81–2, 124–5, 148–9
coloniality 41–4, 50–1, 58n.44
Comaroff, Jean 149
Comaroff, John 149
communism 126, 178
community 31, 36–8, 40–1, 46, 48–50, 57n.34, 79, 83, 93n.45, 144, 155–6, 176–7
Connolly, William 160
contingency 83–4

contradictions 5, 7, 38, 59n.47, 66, 75–7, 85, 91n.30, 105–6, 110, 123, 126, 144, 148–50
conversion 38–9
convert *see* conversion
cosmopolitan 29, 177
Counter-Enlightenment 68, 119, 133n.9
Crapanzano, Vincent 92n.42
Cuesta, Jorge 84
culture 2–4, 36, 90–1n.30, 106, 109, 111–13, 117–20, 124–6, 128, 134n.15, 138n.57, 139n.58, 144–5, 148, 150–2, 162n.4

Dalit 18–19, 182–5
decoloniality *see* coloniality
Delhi 16, 29–30
democracy 83, 160
Derrida, Jacques 162n.4
Devi, Sunayani 175
diachrony 106, 111, 122, 134n.15
diaspora 23n.8, 77, 139n.58, 159
discipline *see* power
discourse 10–11, 47, 58n.40, 74–5, 84, 91n.32, 93n.45, 93n.51, 108, 145, 149–50, 176–7
disenchantment 63, 72, 82, 86n.1
domination 10, 37, 39, 42, 47, 107, 124, 131, 138n.53, 147, 188n.22
  see also hegemony; power
Dube, S. C. 116–18, 135n.37
Durkheim, Émile 114, 128
Dussel, Enrique 43, 58n.44, 59n.47
Dutt, Guru 182
dystopia 42–3, 50–1

East 2, 4, 64, 84, 151, 154
elite 23n.8, 32, 46, 77, 176
emotion 38, 64, 68
empire 9, 41–2, 46, 148–52
  see also identity; power; subaltern studies; West
enchantment 41, 70, 86
enchantments 76, 86n.1, 90n.25
  see also oppositions

England 11, 32, 128
Enlightenment, the 41–2, 68–9, 82, 90n.25, 91n.30, 108–10, 119, 133n.9, 158
entitlement xiv, xvi-xvii
epic 179–83
epistemic 42–6, 48–51, 61n.64, 105–6
Euro-American *see* Europe
Europe 2, 7, 19n.2, 33, 39, 42–3, 45, 47, 71–2, 74, 77, 82, 84, 87n.9, 113, 118–19, 126, 149, 152, 158, 172, 175
evangelism 38, 131, 148–9, 156, 174
Evans-Pritchard, E. E. 17, 35, 110, 113–15, 135n.32, 137n.51
evolutionism 33, 106, 109, 110–11, 117, 172

Fabian, Johannes 107, 132–3n.4
Fanon, Frantz 13
Febvre, Lucien 128
fetish 66, 83, 85, 139n.58, 162n.4
Foucault, Michel 50, 131, 162n.4
France 68, 128
Freitag, Sandra 57n.34
functionalism 106–7, 113–14, 121–2, 132nn.1–2, 137n.48

Gandhi, M. K. (Mahatma) 82, 176
gender xvi, 11–12, 18, 32, 38, 46, 125, 144, 146, 151–9 *passim*, 174, 183, 185, 188n.22
genocide 76, 144, 178
Genovese, Eugene 130
geopolitical 11, 43–4, 153
Ghatak, Ritwik 182
Giddens, Anthony 32, 88n.10
Global North 42
globalization 23n.8, 64–5, 81, 146–7, 155
Gramsci, Antonio 12
Guha, Ranajit 11, 31, 39, 52n.2, 58n.39, 58n.40
Gumbrecht, Hans Ulrich 87n.9, 88n.10

Habermas, Jürgen 70, 88n.10, 90n.25, 90n.28
Hamas 72
Hansen, Thomas 82, 92n.45, 159
hegemony 36, 39, 43, 147, 162n.3
Heidegger, Martin 47, 63, 162n.4
hierarchy xvi-xvii, 1–2, 6, 36–7, 45, 50, 63–74 *passim*, 81, 87–8, 91n.30, 106, 109, 118, 171, 183, 185
see also space
Hill, Christopher 129
Hindu Right 82–3, 93n.51
Hinduism 30, 79, 93n.51, 156, 178
historical anthropology 14–15, 27n.31, 28n.32, 28n.35, 47, 55n.25, 60n.57, 61n.64, 162n.4
see also history: and anthropology; identity
historicism 47–8, 110, 133n.9
history
  and anthropology 3–6, 17, 27n.31, 28n.32, 28n.34, 29, 32–8, 54n.12, 55n.25, 60n.57, 121–5, 130–1, 134n.15, 137nn.51–2, 143, 148, 155–6, 160–1, 162n.4, 169n.60
  and modernity 45–50, 63–4, 66–8, 71–4, 84, 86n.1, 87n.9, 90n.25, 91n.30, 93n.51
  monumental 79–80, 92–3n.45
  universal 2, 67–70, 89n.19, 156, 172
  writing of 11, 29–31, 36, 54n.11, 118–20, 125–30, 133n.9, 136n.39, 144–5, 149–50, 153–5
  see also anthropology: and time; oppositions
humanities 16, 151
Hunt, Lynn 90n.25
Hussain, M. F. 180

identity 5–6, 143–8, 150–1, 155, 159, 161, 169n.60
ideology 66–7, 75, 86, 91n.30, 146, 176–7, 184
Imperial Assemblage (1877) 35
Inden, Ronald 35

India 11–12, 18, 29–30, 33–40 *passim*, 47–8, 53n.10, 69, 79, 81–3, 95n.53, 110, 119–20, 136n.37, 149–50, 154, 156, 171–4, 176–9, 181–2, 184–5, 186n.1, 187n.17
Indian National Congress 176
Indian People's Theatre Association (IPTA) 178–9
indigenous 23n.8, 34, 69, 77, 145, 174, 177, 187n.16
ISIS 67, 72
Islam 79

Jacob, Margaret 90n.25

Kahlo, Frida 84, 177
Kamar, the 116–18, 135–6n.37
Kandinsky, Wassily 175
Kant, Immanuel 69
Klee, Paul 175
Knauft, Bruce 65
Koselleck, Reinhart 70

language 35–6, 92n.45, 110–11, 133n.9, 151–2, 159
Latin America 3, 26n.26, 41–3, 45, 58n.44, 84–5
law 32, 34–5, 37, 92n.42, 93n.45, 154–6
Levinas, Emmanuel 43, 59n.47
Levine, Lawrence 130

Maldonado-Torres, Nelson 59n.47
Malinowski, Bronislaw 113–14
Mardhekar, B. S. 187n.16
margin xvi-xvii, 3, 11, 19n.2, 23n.8, 40, 42, 44, 46, 49–50, 58n.40, 71, 76–7, 85, 124–5, 129, 150–2, 163n.4
Marriott, McKim 35
Marx, Karl 66
Marxism 13, 33–4, 36, 116, 123, 131, 139n.58
Medieval period 4, 54n.12, 63–4, 67, 72, 74, 171, 181
Mehta, Uday 150

memory 173, 180, 185
messianism 42, 69
Mexico 16, 47, 79, 84
Mexico City 41, 58n.43
Michelet, Jules 127
micro-history 126
middle-class 37, 81–2, 93n.49, 158, 176
Mignolo, Walter 58n.44, 60n.52
minority 48, 130, 144, 152, 160
missionary 39, 107
modernism 4, 16, 18–19, 64, 73–6, 84, 91n.38, 95n.53, 171–3, 178–9, 182–3, 186n.1, 187n.11
  in architecture 187n.17
  in art 174–8, 180–1, 183–6
  in cinema 181–2
  in literature 181, 187n.16
  in theater 179–80
modernist 127
  see also modernism
modernization 73–6, 88n.10, 91n.32, 128, 171–2
Modi, Narendra 93n.51
Muktibodh, G. M. 181, 187n.16
multiculturalism 12, 160
Munn, Nancy 115, 135n.26
myth 31–2, 37, 53n.10, 64–6, 106–8, 148–9, 154–5, 173, 179–83

Nandy, Ashis 61n.65, 83
narrative 16, 29, 39, 41, 45, 63, 78, 92n.40, 107, 120, 128, 136n.37, 158, 175, 182–4
nation 13, 40–2, 81–3, 117–20, 129–31, 144, 153–5, 176, 178–83
  and state 49–50, 79–80, 93n.45, 157–61
nationalism 62n.69, 81–3, 93n.49, 154–6, 157–9, 175–7, 178–80, 182
Nehru 178
New World 42, 88n.14
Novo, Salvador 84
Nuer people 114–15

oecological time 114–15
ontology 16, 43–4, 51, 65–7, 86n.1, 158, 168n.57
oppositions 1–5, 16, 32, 63–8, 71–3, 78–81, 88n.10, 90n.30, 91n.32, 106, 109, 116, 118–19, 123, 129, 145, 154–6
Orient *see* Orientalism
Orientalism 9–10, 84, 174–5
otherness 41, 69, 108, 110–11, 120, 144–5

pain 119–20, 180, 182–3
Pakistan 120, 178, 182
Pandey, Gyanendra 36, 119–20, 155
particulars 8, 48, 50–1, 62n.72, 161
Partition 18, 119–20, 136n.43, 178–81, 187n.13
patriarchy 50
peasant 13, 23n.8, 30–1, 33–4, 39, 54n.13, 76–7, 81–2, 85, 176
personhood 18, 48, 143, 146
philosophy 43–4, 69, 71, 90n.25, 111, 131
pollution 37
Portugal 42
postcolonialism 3–4, 10–13, 17–18, 19n.2, 44–7, 60n.57, 131, 148–50, 155–7, 161, 162n.4
postmodernism 65
Pound, Ezra 75
power 2–3, 6, 9, 11, 30, 35–44, 48–51, 62n.69, 66, 73, 83, 85, 121–5, 131, 150–61 *passim*, 162n.4, 176, 183, 186, 188n.22
practice 6, 13, 15–17, 33, 44, 47, 50–1, 61n.64, 78–9, 83, 116, 121–5, 131, 146–7, 149–50, 154, 157–9, 162n.4, 169n.60, 173, 175, 177, 179–80
Prakash, Gyan 62n.69
primitivism 84, 172–7
private sphere 76, 78, 80
process 1, 92n.39, 114
see also practice

progress 2–3, 5, 17, 69, 73, 78, 105, 111–13, 119–21, 125, 144, 153, 172, 181–2, 185
Progressive Artists' Group 180
property 156, 174
prophecy 70, 72
public sphere 48, 57n.34, 80–1, 128–30, 145–6
purity 37, 83

Quijano, Aníbal 58n.44

race 6, 11–12, 38, 41, 46–7, 69–70, 76, 112, 125, 144, 146–7, 151–2, 156, 169n.60
racism 13, 121
Radcliffe-Brown, A. R. 27n.31, 113
Rancière, Jacques 127
rationalism 68, 91n.30, 110
rationality 2, 109, 113, 145
Ray, Satyajit 182
reason 2, 6, 38, 41, 46–7, 63–4, 68–9, 71, 75–6, 86, 106, 119–20, 133n.9, 144–5, 152, 172, 186
religion 30, 38, 46–7, 78–9, 85, 92n.42, 113–14, 150–1
see also Buddhism; Christianity; Hinduism; Islam
resistance xvi, 30
Rhodes Livingstone Institute 122, 137n.49
ritual xiv, 2, 4, 35, 37, 64, 68, 70, 73, 93n.45, 106, 125, 146, 156
Rivera, Diego 84
Romanticism 75, 82, 87n.9, 91n.30, 108, 110–13, 126–7, 133n.9
romanticist *see* Romanticism
Roy, Jamini 175, 177

Said, Edward 9–10, 24n.14, 162n.4
St. Stephen's College 30
Sarkar, Sumit 54n.11
Satnamis 30–1, 36–7
Sawarkar, Savindra "Savi" 19, 183–6, 188n.22
illustrations by <u>99–104</u>

secular 42, 47, 70, 131, 146, 151
secularization 68–9, 71, 76, 78–80, 89n.20, 90n.26, 92n.40, 92n.42
Senapur 34
sexuality 11, 18, 46, 130, 146, 151–2, 169n.60, 183, 187n.16
Sher-Gill, Amrita 177
Shimla 29
Sivaramakrishnan, K. 149–50
Skaria, Ajay 57n.35, 154, 156
socialism 178, 182
sociology 19n.2, 27n.30, 37, 71, 106, 123, 126, 129
South Africa 149
South Asia 3, 11–12, 18–19, 23n.8, 28n.35, 34–5, 38–9, 41, 55n.21, 76, 171–4, 177, 179, 182, 186n.1
Souza, F. N. 180
space 52n.8, 178–9
 production/representation of 1, 3–8, 11, 16–19, 22n.6, 28n.35, 41, 48–51, 55n.25, 61n.64, 62n.69, 63–4, 67–78 *passim*, 81, 86nn.1–2, 88n.10, 89n.19, 91n.30, 91n.32, 127–9, 132–3n.4, 135n.32, 184–6
 see also anthropology: and time; coloniality; community; culture; empire; history; modernism; nation; subaltern studies
Spain 42
spatial/spatialization *see* space
Spivak, Gayatri C. 12
Sri Lanka 182
state 31, 36–41, 46–50, 53n.10, 57n.34, 60n.57, 66, 76, 79–80, 83, 92n.45
 see also nation: and state
Stepputat, Finn 92n.45, 159
Stocking, George Jr. 108, 111, 134n.15
structuralism 121–2, 137n.48
structure xvi, 32, 35, 50, 53n.10, 68, 106–7, 120–3, 137n.48, 148, 162n.4
subaltern 3, 11, 23n.8, 29, 76–7, 81, 93n.49, 126, 147, 154, 159, 162n.3, 163n.4, 176–8, 182, 188n.22

see also coloniality; subaltern studies
subaltern studies 3–4, 11–13, 17–18, 26n.26, 30–2, 36–41 *passim*, 44–51 *passim*, 60n.57, 62n.69, 130–1, 143, 147–50, 153, 155–8, 161, 162n.4
subject 1–2, 5–7, 10, 12, 16–19, 23n.8, 27n.31, 29, 31–2, 39, 46–7, 64, 68, 73, 76–8, 81–4, 92nn.38–9, 105, 108, 117–18, 122, 124–32 *passim*, 143–6, 150–1, 158–60, 162, 162n.4, 169n.60, 171–2, 177–8, 181, 183–6, 188n.22
subjects *see* subject
subordination 12, 147, 174
Subramanyan, K. G. 177
Swadeshi 175–6
synchrony 34
 see also diachrony

Tagore, Gaganendranath 175
Tagore, Rabindranath 174–7, 184
Taliban 67, 72
Taylor, Charles 90n.24, 92n.40
telos 69, 74, 78, 120–1
temporal/temporalization *see* time
theory xviii, 1, 6, 10, 15–17, 30, 34, 38, 58n.44, 66, 68, 88n.10, 113, 123, 130–1, 150
Thompson, E. P. 128–9
time 135n.26, 135n.32, 178–9
 see also anthropology: and time; coloniality; community; culture; empire; history; modernism; nation; space: production/ representation of; subaltern studies
tradition 63–4, 67–70, 72–4, 79, 81–3, 88n.10, 90–1n.30, 91n.32, 92n.43, 107, 109, 116, 118–20, 124, 126, 128–9, 144–5, 155, 171–7
trans-modernity 3, 43
Trevor-Roper, Hugh 27n.31

United Kingdom 78
United States 32, 34, 38, 78, 92n.42, 126, 130, 137n.52
universals 47–8, 75, 112, 161
  see also history: universal
untouchables 30, 156, 183–5, 188n.22
  illustrations of <u>99–100</u>
US *see* United States

van der Veer, Peter 150
vernaculars 29–30, 38–9, 54n.11, 85, 161, 181
Vico, Giambattista 69
Victoria, Queen 35

violence 42–3, 48, 93n.45, 105–6, 119–20, 154–5, 178–82
Voltaire 69
von Herder, Johann Gottfried 69, 127
von Ranke, Leopold 127

West 2–4, 9–10, 20n.2, 32, 39–42, 46–7, 64, 67, 69, 71–2, 74, 78–9, 82–4, 91n.30, 92n.39, 106, 109, 111–13, 115, 119, 123–4, 128, 144, 151–5, 160, 172, 175
White, Stephen 160
working classes 34, 36
world system 13, 44, 123–4, 151

Lightning Source UK Ltd.
Milton Keynes UK
UKHW010901190519
342878UK00005B/391/P